The Evolution of Strategic Foresight

For Julius and Linnea

The Evolution of Strategic Foresight

Navigating Public Policy Making

TUOMO KUOSA
AlternativeFutures, Finland

Routledge
Taylor & Francis Group

LONDON AND NEW YORK

First published 2012 by Gower Publishing

2 Park Square, Milton Park, Abingdon, Oxon OX14 4RN
711 Third Avenue, New York, NY 10017, USA

Routledge is an imprint of the Taylor & Francis Group, an informa business

First issued in paperback 2016

Gower Applied Business Research
Our programme provides leaders, practitioners, scholars and researchers with thought provoking, cutting edge books that combine conceptual insights, interdisciplinary rigour and practical relevance in key areas of business and management.

British Library Cataloguing in Publication Data
Kuosa, Tuomo.
  The evolution of strategic foresight : navigating public
  policy making.
  1. Strategic planning. 2. Political planning. 3. Political
  planning--European Union countries. 4. Forecasting.
  I. Title
  320.6-dc23

Library of Congress Cataloging-in-Publication Data
The evolution of strategic foresight : navigating public policy making /
by Tuomo Kuosa.
    p. cm.
  Includes bibliographical references and index.
  ISBN 978-1-4094-2986-9 (hbk)
  1. Political planning. 2. Public administration. 3. Forecasting.
  4. Strategic planning. I. Title.
  JF1525.P6K86 2011
  320.6--dc23

                                                                        2011052070

    ISBN 978-1-4094-2986-9 (hbk)
    ISBN 978-1-138-27078-7 (pbk)

Contents

List of Figures

List of Tables

Preface

If you know the enemy and yourself, you need not to fear the result of a hundred battles. If you know yourself but not the enemy, for every victory gained you will also suffer a defeat. If you know neither the enemy nor yourself, you will lose in every battle.

Sun Tzu

Strategic foresight is a branch of strategic thinking, which has been practiced in politics, military and business management for as long as the disciplines have existed. It is about situational awareness and understanding your viable options based on your resources and preferences, and your opponents' probable actions and counter strategies in each situation. Alongside strategic thinking, strategic foresight is a branch of foresight in its own right. It is a process of visioning alternative futures through a combination of hindsight, insight and forecasting. It attempts to say something about the probabilities and diverse options for action not just from immediate perspectives, but from future perspectives too. When these two branches are merged we get strategic foresight, which focuses on generating analyses of possible futures and alternative strategies, based on available intelligence, visioning, what-if-questions and foreknowledge. It is about understanding the whole landscape of a particular situation and the options that a decision maker has within it. And it does not matter if we talk about decision makers in military, economic or political situations, as the principles for each are the same. So far strategic foresight has not been considered as an independent discipline, but it can be said to be steadily evolving towards that direction. This book discusses the practical and theoretical foundations from which that emergence is steadily taking place.

Echoing the philosophy of Sun Tzu, it is essential to have a good foreknowledge and understanding of yourself and your enemy and the timing and terrain of where you fight before you select your options and set your strategy, no matter what your field of business. As when you have a good foreknowledge and a winning strategy you can win without fighting. This is fundamental to strategic foresight for those who are in power. Hence, foresight that is done by those who are not in a position to make big decisions is different, and should be called by a different name. Such foresight needs to involve as many stakeholders as possible in order to launch a change from grass-root level. Should we call that 'participatory foresight'? Nevertheless, foresight, whether it is strategic or participatory by its nature, is necessary for steering the future. Without any foresight we are like logs adrift in a river.

Acknowledgements

There are many people who have greatly contributed to this book project and who, therefore, deserve my sincere gratitude. First I owe special thanks to Dr John P. Geis, Colonel and Director of the US Air Force's Center for Strategy and Technology who has made a big contribution to the book by commenting on the content and suggesting many supplementary ideas for its development. The other special thanks go to Henry Kwok who is a Singaporean long-term business developer, global partner of Haines Centre for Strategic Management and founder of Spaces@work consultancy. Henry wrote a large and valuable discussion chapter for the end of the book from his viewpoint. I also want to give my warmest thanks to all of the nine expert interviewees, who represent very versatile domains of strategic foresight. Without you the book would lack much of its substance. Thank you, Patrick Nathan, Ilan Mizrahi, Jyrki Kasvi, Helene Lavoix, Riitta Kirjavainen, Markku Wilenius, Rauno Kuusisto, Devadas Krishnadas and Osmo Kuusi. Thanks also goes to Finland Futures Research Centre where I have practiced many of this book's methods in various types of projects in past years, together with great colleagues. I want to thank both Singapore's Prime Minister's Office's National Security Coordination Centre (NSCC) and the S. Rajaratnam School of International Studies (RAHS) of Nanyang Technological University in Singapore, for honouring me with their shared post-doctoral fellowship of the year 2010, and believing and kindly supporting my data gathering and interview project, alongside my other official assignments. Finally, I want to thank my agent Francesca White and the editors of Gower for all their support and faith in the value of the proposed book project.

Tuomo Kuosa

Kerava, Finland

Reviews for *The Evolution of Strategic Foresight*

Drawing on the wisdom of the past, The Evolution of Strategic Foresight *by Tuoso Kuosa guides the reader through strategic thought to the present and guides to the future.*

Jerome C. Glenn, CEO, The Millennium Project

According to my professional experience Dr Tuomo Kuosa is one of leading experts in the foresight field. His new book will be a key reference in the field of strategic foresight. His new book is really a value adding product with high intellectual capital input. It is also insightful, innovative and professional.

Jari Kaivo-oja Adviser in Foresight R&D, Crisis Management Initiative, New York & Helsinki Offices, Expert and researcher, Finland Futures Research Centre and the Academy of Finland, University of Turku

A superior guide to futures methodologies, their history and contemporary use, especially in European public sectors.

Dr John P. Geis, Professor; Colonel, retired; Author of the Air Force 2025 and Blue Horizons Studies

This book by Tuomo Kuosa sheds new light in the growing field of strategic foresight. Through theoretical considerations and practical examples, he emphasizes the usefulness of strategic foresight, with applications from the military to business to academia. The book is well presented and serves as an excellent reference for futures studies in a professional environment.

José Cordeiro, Director, Venezuela Node, The Millennium Project and Energy Advisor/Faculty, Singularity University, NASA Ames, California, USA

PART I
Knowledge

He will win who knows when to fight and when not to fight.

Sun Tzu

Introduction

The objective of this book is to introduce the extension and boundaries of contemporary strategic foresight and discuss the long evolution and foundations of its theory and practice. The analysis method used attempts to go beyond the surface level of just listing the definitions, parts and used practices. That is why I use many chapters to discuss our contemporary understanding of the 'game situation' and the inferring methods that the strategic foresight is dealing with. In the time of Sun Tzu, the 'game situation' of a battle was understood as something very dynamical, all the time changing and contextual, and the available methods were considered highly flexible. The systemic understanding of the 'game situation' of a battle or transformation was changed towards mechanical view in the seventeenth century, and it was not until the 1970s when the dynamical systemic view, and understanding of co-evolution and complexity, started to re-emerge. Yet both the management and foresight of the 1970s were still very linear and control oriented in comparison to the contemporary approaches that are beginning to focus on paradoxes, interpretations and social glue instead of dilemmas, categories and structure.

Because the world has changed, and is much more knowledge intensive, broader in many senses, technological, better educated and more hectic, in comparison to Sun Tzu's times, the available methods and inferring principles have evolved too. That is why I devote numerous chapters to discussing the usability of scientific method and different epistemological and methodological approaches in present foresight and strategy work. Hence, contemporary strategic foresight should simultaneously utilize many tools and principles to deal with the co-evolutive 'game situations' where there may be no dominating centres and where knowledge ages very fast.

1

Introduction

*After studying these seven conditions I can forecast which side wins and
which loses.*

Sun Tzu

This book is organized into four parts. The first three parts 'Knowledge',
'Structure', and 'Process' echo Aristotle's three 'domains of the world'. The
final part is 'Discussion', which summarizes the conclusions and synthesizes
the themes discussed into new observations.

The first part of the book, 'Knowledge', focuses on strategic foresight theory,
including its concepts, methodologies, research strategies and philosophy
of science. It defines the concepts of future domains, strategic thinking and
intelligence, and the logic behind evolutionary, complexity and systems
thinking, together with the logic and practices of scientific and informal
reasoning. Finally it aggregates existing foresight methods, methodological
principles and research strategies into a new set of futures domain's which itself
is divided into ten major methodologies and their subsets. This presentation is
meant to help readers understand the usability and fundamental nature behind
the domain's different method types and to help plan an integrated strategic
foresight process.

The second part, 'Structure', presents the public strategic foresight system
of 23 countries, regions, federations, or other transnational thematic areas
of the world. These cases are mainly from the European Union as some of
the agents of its member states, such as France's General du Plan, and some
individual European researchers, have been willing to map the European
Union's old and new member states foresight systems for public policy making.
Outside Europe, Singapore and the United States (US) are given as examples,
as these two countries have put considerable effort into strengthening their
national security through various intelligence practices. This part concludes
with discussion of the strategic foresight systems of three transnational
organizations, the Organisation for Economic Co-operation and Development

(OECD), the United Nations Industrial Development Organization (UNIDO) and the International Institute for Applied Systems Analysis (IIASA).

The third part, 'Process', presents the views and suggestions of selected 'strategic foresight knowledge producers' and 'strategic foresight knowledge users such as policy makers and high government officials'. These experts have been selected based on their specific experience and knowledge of the different sides of strategic foresight. This part of the book describes the practice and practical suggestions for public strategic foresight. It begins with questions such as, 'how could strategic foresight better facilitate national decision making', 'how would you measure the success of foresight work', and 'how could we improve our public strategic foresight systems'. The 'Process' part is based on my work and the book[1] that I wrote at the S. Rajaratnam School of International Studies of Nanyang Technological University, Singapore when I worked there as a post-doctoral fellow in 2010.

The final part, 'Discussion', concludes the book. It contains two autonomous parts. The first is written by Henry Kwok, a long-term strategic management consultant from Singapore, who I asked to write about his understanding of the themes from a strategic management point of view. This chapter can stand alone as a solid article in answer to the question, 'how can we produce better strategic understanding for strategic decision making?' It is also an important summarizing part of the book, which merges its three focal themes, systems and evolutionary thinking, foresight thinking, and strategic management into a new type of management approach.

The other discussion chapter is my summary of the 23 international country cases and the views of the nine interviewed strategic foresight experts. This chapter also presents a new type of centrally steered public strategic foresight system, and a practical table that aggregates the book's systemic themes, inferring and methodology themes, and foresight themes, into a list, which summarizes the suitability of different futures domain methods in the seven most common types of systems logics. This list[2] can be used in planning different types of strategic foresight processes for different research contexts or purposes.

---

1   Kuosa, Tuomo (2011a): Practicing strategic foresight in government: The cases of Finland, Singapore and European Union. RSIS Monograph No. 19. S. Rajaratnam School of International Studies of Nanyang Technological University, Singapore, Booksmith.
2   This book's copyright figures and tables can be freely borrowed by anyone in their original form, or be further modified, as long as the valid citing to this book is attached inside the figure or in the title line.

2

Foresight Concepts

Foreknowledge enables the wise general to achieve things beyond the reach of ordinary men.

Sun Tzu

What is Foresight?

The term *foresight* was used for the first time in a BBC broadcast in 1932 by visionary author H.G. Wells, who called for the establishment of 'Departments and Professors of Foresight'. Here it refers to a process of visioning alternative futures through a combination of hindsight, insight and forecasting. That kind of foresight attempts to say something about future probabilities and options for actions. (Hind)sight is about systematically understanding the past, (In)sight is about systematically understanding the true nature of the present,[1] and (Fore)sight is about systematically understanding the future.

Foresight and futures studies are intertwined in many ways. The guiding principle in both is that in almost all cases the future cannot be predicted, as it is not here yet. At best, alternative scenarios and some probabilities can be given to social phenomena, as they are too complex to be foreseen. Yet, the future can be created through the actions of today – and therefore can be partly known too. And much of the future is here already in today's values, objectives, drivers and trends, and that can be studied systematically. Two things are of particular concern in both foresight and futures studies:[2]

---

1   Insight, as defined by Clive Simmonds, is the ability to perceive the true nature of a thing, especially through intuitive understanding (in this context, what and how something is happening, who is making it happen and why). Insight is also the ability to look beyond, behind, and through the actions of others to the new principles that they are consciously or unconsciously disclosing. 'Insight requires perceptiveness and leads on to the search for the emergent, and therefore for ways to detect it – because you are now looking for something the seeds for which are already being sown' (c.f. Simmonds, W.W. Clive (1993): Monograph. *Insight Analysis*, 2–3, September 1993; c.f. Glenn (2009b): Genius forecasting, intuition, and vision).

2   See definition in Wikipedia. Available at: http://en.wikipedia.org/wiki/Foresight_(futures_studies)

- Concern of the longer-term futures that are at least 10 years away (though there are some exceptions to this in foresight, especially in its use in private business – see business intelligence).

- Concern of the alternative futures. It is helpful to examine alternative paths of development, not just what is currently believed to be most likely or usual. Often futures work will construct multiple scenarios. These may be an interim step on the way to creating what may be known as positive visions, success scenarios, or aspirational futures. Sometimes alternative scenarios will be a major part of the output of futures work.

On the other hand, foresight and futures studies have several things in contrast too. For example, the origins of the two are different. The roots of futures studies can be traced back to the humanistic orientation of Futurology[3] (1972), which will be discussed in the next sub-chapter, the history of foresight/technocratic orientation of futures studies, can be traced back to military strategies and military technology foresight particularly in US military's research units and think tanks, such as RAND (Research and Development – a mutual project of US Army Air Corps and Douglas Aircraft Company) in 1940s and 1950s.[4] Today, much of the technology in foresight work, that is systematic and which involves various technology fields' experts, is called *technological assessment*, but it can also be called technological foresight. Nowadays, the biggest differences between these two concepts are, i) time range, as foresight pursues to longer time range meaning at least 10 years away, and ii) the creation of alternatives, as foresight emphasizes the creation of alternatives, but technological assessment favours systematic planning, for example, *roadmapping* and a large group of experts in Delphi.

The word foresight has earlier origins than concept futures studies or futurology, but it was not until the late 1980s that it began to be increasingly used. By then it started to gain specific reference to approaches to informing decision-making, by improving inputs concerning the longer-term future and by drawing on wider social networks than had been the case in most 'futures studies' or *long-range planning*.[5] To specify the approach of foresight, we can say that it attempts to become more systematic, logical, participatory and planning or management oriented, but it has less rational value in comparison to futures studies.

---

3   Ossip Flechtheim in 1943. Futurologie (1972).
4   Bell (2005).
5   Miles, Ian, Keenan, Michael and Kaivo-oja, Jari (eds) (2002, 20). Available at: http://foresight.jrc.ec.europa.eu/documents/eur20128en.pdf

The strategic foresight group defines foresight simply as a combination of forecasting with insight. According to the group, foresight is developed by applying forecasting methodology to the insight. And while *forecasting* requires methodologies, generated by computers or otherwise, insight requires a deep understanding of the subject concerned. However, despite the strategic foresight group's definition being quite clear, it is too narrow to cover the whole idea of foresight and particularly strategic foresight.

Another way to define foresight has been presented by Richard Slaughter,[6] who defined it as a process that attempts to broaden the boundaries of perception in four ways:

- By assessing the implications of present actions, decisions, etc. (consequent assessment).

- By detecting and avoiding problems before they occur (early warning and guidance).

- By considering the present implications of possible future events (pro-active strategy formulation).

- By envisioning aspects of desired futures (preparing scenarios).

On the other hand, Averil Horton[7] has defined the entire foresight process[8] in the following way, which starts to encompass the dynamics of foresight approach much better.

> It has three distinctive phases which are: 'input', 'foresight' and 'output' (.) each phase creates a greater value than the previous one, as the outputs move up the information value chain from information through knowledge to understanding, and finally to wisdom. However, this value is only realized at the very end of the process and even then often with a significant time lag. Each phase is also more difficult and time consuming, more abstract, and less easy to measure than the preceding one. In a successful foresight process, these three phases will result in taking decisions and actions which will be different to those which would have been carried out in the absence of the process.

---

6   Slaughter (1995, 48).
7   Horton (1999, 6–8).
8   See the description of strategic foresight process in Figure 3.1, in Chapter 3.

Horton's first phase of the foresight process, the input phase, is comprised of the following parts: collection, collation and summarization of available information. Its first part, collection of information is comprised of: information collected on futures themes, trends,[9] ideas, early signs and wild cards from a wide range of sources such as experts, universities, business networks, personal networks, customers, suppliers, the 'literature', government, other foresight reports, research and surveys. There are many methodologies and processes, which can be employed, such as horizons or environmental scanning,[10] Delphi,[11] surveys, systematic reading, brainstorming sessions, abstracting, and simply talking to people. The major characteristic of this type of information gathering is its sheer volume; it is broad in scope, overlapping and often contradictory.

The second and third parts of the input phase are comprised of the collation and summarization of the collected information. The information is given a structure and form, its volume is reduced, and the irrelevant parts are eliminated. The knowledge gained is then summarized in order to present it in a manageable form. Again, there are general methodologies and processes available, such as scenario building, list writing and prioritizing, graphical comparisons, matrix production, and cross impact analysis.[12]

Horton's second phase of the foresight process, the actual foresight phase, is comprised of the translation and interpretation of this knowledge to produce an understanding of its implications for the future from the specific point of view of a particular organization.[13] It involves activities, tools, skills and people to translate and interpret the work. The foresight phase should answer the following questions:

- What does all this mean for my organization?

---

9   The idea of trend analysis in strategic foresight process has been explained in Liebl, Franz and Schwarz, Jan Oliver (2010): Normality of the future: Trend diagnosis for strategic foresight. *Futures*, 42, 313–27.
10 See Slaughter, Richard A. (1999): A new framework for environmental scanning. *Foresight*, 1 (5), 441–51; Reinhardt, W.A. (1984): An early warning system for strategic planning. *Long Range Planning*, 17 (5), 25–34; Schultz, Wendy L. (2006): The cultural contradictions of managing change: Using horizon scanning in an evidence-based policy context. *Foresight*, 8 (4), 3–12; and Voros, Joseph (2001): Re-Framing environmental scanning: An integral approach. *Foresight*, 3 (6), 533–51.
11 The modern Delphi method was created by RAND in the 1950s. Some more recent applications can be found, for example, from Kuusi (1999).
12 Voros (2003) and I have added many methods and principles to Horton's phases of foresight – see Figure 3.1 in Chapter 3.
13 For example Kuusisto (2008).

- What are the implications for us?

- What can we do about it today?

According to Horton, the second phase, especially the interpretation step, is what foresight is all about; it is critical to the process. It is where most of the value is added, generating an understanding of what can (or cannot) be done for the future. Interpretation, the most crucial step in the whole process, is poorly understood, and has few theoretical techniques.

Horton's third phase of the foresight project, the output phase, is comprised of the assimilation, and evaluation of this understanding to produce a commitment to action in a particular organization.

However, there is one aspect that has received little attention in Horton, or indeed in Slaughter, the Strategic Foresight Group, and many other foresight definitions, and this is the participatory element. The interactive, dialogic, involving and networking part, that commits all stakeholders to the process and to shared views and visions. Many foresight experts, such as Erik Terk, Riitta Kirjavainen, Ian Miles, Michael Keenan and Jari Kaivo-oja have emphasized the participatory part of foresight as one of its most important elements. This is particularly clear in *A Practical Guide to Regional Foresight (FOREN)* which many foresight practitioners consider to be the 'official' definition of foresight by the European Union.

The FOREN report[14] defines foresight as follows:

> *Foresight is a systematic, participatory, future-intelligence-gathering and medium-to-long-term vision-building process aimed at present-day decisions and mobilizing joint actions. Foresight arises from a convergence of trends underlying recent developments in the fields of 'policy analysis', 'strategic planning' and 'future studies'. It brings together key agents of change and various sources of knowledge in order to develop strategic visions and anticipatory intelligence'. FOREN working group highlighted the value of the participatory element in foresight by saying, 'The difference between Foresight*

---

14 European Commission Research Directorate General (2001): A Practical Guide to Regional Foresight (FOREN). European Commission – Joint Research Centre – Institute for Prospective Technological Studies (IPTS) (eds). European Communities, STRATA Programme, v–viii. Available at: http://foresight.jrc.ec.europa.eu/documents/eur20128en.pdf

and other planning activities relates to the participative dimension of Foresight (.) Common features of Foresight include: a long-term orientation, the examination of a wide range of factors, the drawing on widely-distributed knowledge, the institutionalization and creation of networks and the use of formal techniques/methods. Formal methods provide more operational results, assess the consistency of different aspects of the vision, help to identify where more knowledge is needed and legitimize the exercise (.) Foresight is a very evocative label for the rise to prominence of participative methods and long-term strategic futures techniques, in the wake of more traditional ways of informing policy planning.

According the FOREN group,[15] there are different types of foresight that arise from three specific distinctions, these are namely: bottom-up vs. top-down approaches; product vs. process-orientations; and the examination of experts' views vs. consequences. Foresight approaches are usually a mix of several of these types.

- The first type, top-down exercises, place less stress on interaction and involve highly formal methods such as the Delphi method.

- The second, bottom-up exercises, are more interactive – they take into account a greater number of views, increase legitimacy and yield more process benefits but are more time consuming and more difficult to organize.

- The third, product orientation, is necessary if there is a need to inform specific decisions (a report, list of priorities).

- The fourth, process orientation, is more suitable when there is a lack of networking between key actors.

- The fifth, involves examining and articulating the views of experts.

- The sixth, involves investigating the consequences of future assumptions.

15 European Commission Research Directorate General (2001): A Practical Guide to Regional Foresight (FOREN). European Commission – Joint Research Centre – Institute for Prospective Technological Studies (IPTS) (eds). European Communities, STRATA Programme, v–viii. Available at: http://foresight.jrc.ec.europa.eu/documents/eur20128en.pdf

Furthermore, in *The Practical Guide to Regional Foresight (FOREN)*[16] the following five elements are given as essential parts of 'real' foresight:

- Structured anticipation and projections of long-term social, economic and technological developments and needs.

- Interactive and participative methods of exploratory debate, analysis and study, involving a wide variety of stakeholders, are also characteristic of foresight (as opposed to many traditional futures studies that tend to be the preserve of experts).

- These interactive approaches involve forging new social networks. Emphasis on the networking role varies across foresight programmes. It is often taken to be as equal to, if not more important than the more formal products such as reports and lists of action points.

- The formal products of foresight go beyond the presentation of scenarios (however stimulating these may be), and beyond the preparation of plans. What is crucial is the elaboration of a guiding strategic vision, to which there can be a shared sense of commitment (achieved, in part, through networking processes).

- The shared vision shall not be a utopia. There has to be explicit recognition and explication of the implications for present day decisions and actions.

What is Fully-fledged and Participatory Foresight?

> *Those who become Princes only due to their good luck get their power with little effort, but they will have to put in lots of effort to stay in power*
> *– and vice versa.*
>
> Niccolo Machiavelli, 1532

The *Handbook of Knowledge Society Foresight*,[17] is another of the European Union's more or less 'official' foresight defining documents, which highlights the fact

---

16 European Commission Research Directorate General (2001, 4).
17 Miles, Ian, Keenan, Michael and Kaivo-oja, Jari (eds) (2002). *Handbook of Knowledge Society Foresight*. Prepared by PREST and FFCR for the European Foundation for the improvement of living and working conditions, 20–24. Available at: http://www.eurofound.europa.eu/pubdocs/2003/50/en/1/ef0350en.pdf

that, since the late 1980s there has been much re-branding of technology, environmental scanning, forecasting and all sorts of similar activities as foresight, as the term has been linked to many successful exercises. However, all such narrow futures methods are not foresight even if they are called that. In practice, foresight exercises may be limited, but only at a cost. Hence, the authors of the *Handbook of Knowledge Society Foresight* recommend the use of the term 'fully-fledged foresight' to describe those approaches that go beyond the narrower futures methods. Fully-fledged foresight places emphasis on policy networking as well as on longer-term analyses to inform present-day decisions, and it incorporates the following features:

- It is based on the need to inform decision making with knowledge, for policies and strategies need to be based on sound evidence and expert opinion.

- It recognizes that this knowledge is widely dispersed, and needs to be accessed through social networks.

- It recognizes that change is a constant, and that it is important to be aware of the long-term context within which present decisions are being made and will have an effect.

Figure 2.1 refers to 'fully-fledged foresight' as 'participatory foresight' to distinguish it from other futures approaches, and especially to separate it from 'strategic foresight' which is a far less 'bottom-up' and far less 'participatory' approach. Actually both participatory foresight and strategic foresight operate in the same scenario level that is the intermediating level between pre-active empirical research and value rational pro-activity. The purpose of this scenario level is to produce alternative policy options, visions, and ways to see and tackle the hard evidence data and sense-made environmental change. The 'political' decisions are made closer to the U-curve's two top ends, the part to which I have located futurology, visionary management and la prospective.

Participatory foresight produces policy alternatives for bottom-up approaches affecting citizens, activists, NGOs etc., and encouraging them to tackle identified problems and promoting preferred visions from a grass-root level perspective. Strategic foresight, in contrast, produces strategically viable policy alternatives for public or private decision makers in power, who want to stay in power, and who want to win political, military or economic battles.

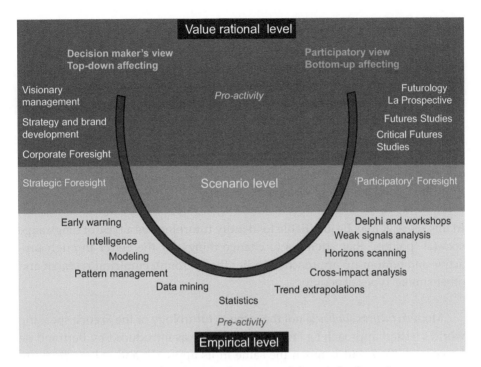

Figure 2.1   U-curve of actions in futures and foresight domain

What are Futures Studies and Futurology?

> *Unless we invent a better future, we won't have one of any kind.*
>   *Arthur C. Clarke*

The roots of futures studies or research can be traced back to the humanistic orientation of *futurology*, which was introduced by Ossip Flechtheim in 1943. Flechtheim's book[18] (1972) can be seen as the key player in launching the idea of modern 'soft, visionary or idealistic' futures research, echoing much of the United Nation's great objectives. In his book Flechtheim stated, that futurology should attempt to solve the following great problems of all human kind:

1.   preventing wars and guaranteeing peace;

2.   preventing famine and poverty;

---

18   Flechtheim's book (1972). Flechtheim org. in 1943.

3.   preventing oppression;

4.   enhancing democracy;

5.   ending the extortion of nature and enhancing the conservation of nature;

6.   fighting against alienation;

7.   creating the new Homo Humanus.[19]

In this sense, it may be justifiable to identify futurology as a type of long-range societal 'politics' that attempts to change things for the better through pro-active and bottom-up approaches, rather than through empirical research and other similar types of activity.

Modern *futures studies* is not the same as futurology or the French speaking world's 'sister' approach *La Prospective*, which was introduced by Bertrand de Jouvenel in 1967, but is much the same in its approach and values. Both are highly visionary and pro-active approaches. However, in contrast to futurology, and also to most forecasting exercises, futures studies has adopted a vast range of methods and principles from various traditional disciplines, where they have been steadily combined and modified into quite unique holistic and more or less systematic approaches to uncertain futures knowledge. In other words, futures studies seek to connect together various change factors such as driving forces, trends, emerging issues and conditioning factors in order to envisage alternative futures (rather than predict the future). As discussed in the *Handbook of Foresight*, 'futures studies has waxed and waned in terms of fashions in methods and popularity, and has been strongly influenced by the rise of issues such as environmental problems and new technologies. They have often found influential proponents in the military and large corporations, both of whom have interests in strategic analysis across a wide spectrum of problems, as well as in government and academia'.[20]

To specify the approach of futures studies, Pentti Malaska[21] has identified it as a value-rational field of knowledge, putting it in contrast with all normal

19 Bell (2005, 29).
20 Miles, Ian, Keenan, Michael and Kaivo-oja, Jari (eds) (2002, 20): *Handbook of Knowledge Society Foresight*.
21 Malaska (2003a, 13).

sciences, which aim to value neutralism. Futures studies takes its stance on different alternatives and describes pro-actively its own desired futures images. It attempts to explicate the possible prospects and consequences of different decisions in order to question or promote certain values or procedures. It claims that even values can be rationally discussed and studied. Malaska stresses that futures studies[22] is a scientific field of knowledge. It just has a broader scope of research than the normal sciences, as its research objective does not exist in an empirical sense, because it is contingent and undefined by nature. Yet, this does not mean that we could not get relevant futures knowledge from our present environment, in the same way as we can get, for example, history or marketing knowledge. Hence, this unusual research objective has led the research field into a unique epistemology which differentiates it from the principles and methodologies of all normal sciences.

To conclude the discussion on foresight and futures studies, we should go back to Henry Mintzberg's[23] distinct strategic work approaches: strategic planning and strategic thinking, that were introduced in the strategic chapter. The first refers to strongly analytical, logical, deductive and pragmatic thinking, in order to ensure that things stay on track. The second refers to thinking, which involves intuitive, experimental, disruptive, creative attempts that go beyond what purely logical thinking can inform, to integrated perspectives or visions of where an organization should be heading.

In regard to Mintzberg's strategic work approaches, Joseph Voros[24] argued that, as information about potential futures is always incomplete, the thinking required for success in foresight needs to be synthetical and inductive, rather than analytical or deductive. Hence according to Voros, a good 'foresight is an aspect of strategic thinking, as it is meant to open up an expanded range of perceptions of the strategic options available, so that strategy making is potentially wiser. Foresight (as strategic thinking) is concerned with exploration (based on limited and patchy information) and options, not with the steps needed for the implementation of actions, which is the realm of strategic planning. The former is intuitive, disruptive and "what if?" in nature, the latter is goal-oriented, pragmatic, deductive and "make it happen/can do" in nature'. However, based on the discussion and divisions presented above and in the previous chapter, I would argue that futures studies is merely an aspect of

---

22 Pentti Malaska and Eleonora Masini have defined futures research as the field which focuses on research of futures knowledge, and futures studies as the field which combines both research and education of futures knowledge.

23 Mintzberg (1994).

24 Voros (2003, 12).

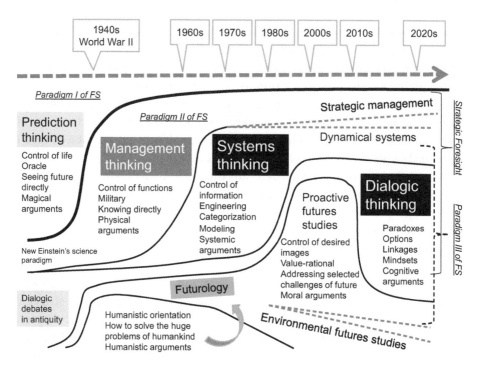

Figure 2.2   Evolution of futures and foresight domain

strategic thinking (the former a combination of visionary, pro-active and value rational approaches), when both participatory foresight and strategic foresight combine both aspects equally strongly, strategic planning and strategic thinking. Both forms of foresight contain much less value rational emphasis, but much more pragmatic and short-term strategic emphasis in comparison to futures studies.

If we take a view of futures studies from which we try purely to map the evolution of the field of futures interests, the change in the field's objectives and its methodological understanding, we can draw the following figure.

The evolution of futures domain in Figure 2.2[25] attempts to describe the paradigms of futures studies, the interests of futures knowledge, and to anticipate the forthcoming direction of futures studies, but it can also be used to describe the difference between (strategic) foresight and futures studies. If we think that futures studies is heading towards value rational, visionary, dialogic thinking, including critical futures studies, we may say that (strategic)

---

25 Figure is from Kuosa (2011c).

foresight is heading towards a combination of strategic management and thinking, dynamical systems thinking, and partly dialogic thinking.[26] The fully-fledged participatory foresight is located somewhere between the two.

To conclude, in terms of time ranges and interests of knowledge, we may say that (strategic) foresight focuses on helping strategic decisions. It aims to know more directly, and to help establish more robust strategies in the area of strategic management. It operates mostly in mid-long-range futures (3–15 years). In terms of time ranges, the fully-fledged participatory foresight operates similarly to the strategic foresight but, as already discussed, it pursues grass-root level value changes or changes of mutual understanding instead. In contrast to both forms of foresight, the futures studies operate only on long-term futures (10–50 years)[27] where it focuses on visionary decisions, which means that it attempts to go deeper and more critically, to the un-predetermined and uncertain foundations of futures emergence, and to define visions and novel actions for survival and good future.[28]

What are the Objectives of Foresight and Futures Domain?

The concept 'futures domain' refers to the combination of foresight, futures studies and everything else, which work for the sake of obtaining better futures knowledge. The futures domain concept is meant to solve the question, which is the macro concept and which is only a part of the other, foresight or futures studies, or is it futures research, or la prospective, or maybe futurology that is the top concept etc? Hence, it names the territory, which contains a lot of different functions, principles, methodologies, paradigms, and disciplinary approaches.

The three levels of future domain, the value rational level, scenario level, and empirical level, and the two major views of the domain, top-down affecting view and bottom-up affecting view, alongside the 'schools' principles

---

26 See the discussion around six pillars methodology and integrated foresight.
27 We may say that the time range which goes over 50 years is out of the domain of futures research as it is almost entirely unpredictable. Hence, we could call the time range that goes over 50 years as the domain of science fiction.
28 Malaska and Holstius (1999, 355) define the domain of opportunistic management to range 1–3 years in the future, strategic management to 3–5 years in the future, and the visionary management to +5 years in the future in their Figure 2. Kaivo-oja et al. (2004, 543) have modified the idea to their Figure 7, where they say that, operational management operates in time range 0–1 years in the future, strategic management operates in time range 1–10 years in the future, and visionary management in time range 10–50 years in the future.

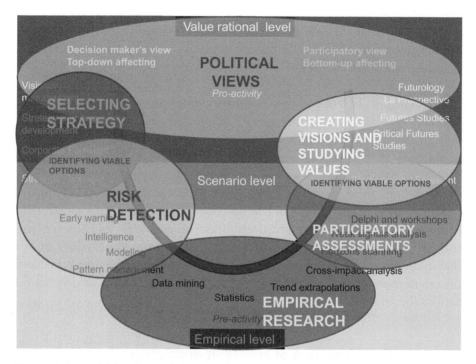

Figure 2.3   Objectives of the futures and foresight domain

and methods were presented in Figure 2.1. Figure 2.3 continues that theme by showing the objectives that are central to each part of the domain.

If we start looking from the value rational level, we can name the most pro-active elements, including top-down affecting view, bottom-up affecting view, futurology, la prospective and visionary management, as politically driven views and objectives. Here an agent wants to start a visionary oriented change either in civil society, the policies of a company, the politics of a particular country, or at a global level. A part of futures studies follows this objective.

Selecting the best strategy is the objective of the corporation's strategy and brand development, corporate foresight and is partly an objective of visionary management too. Identifying viable options for decision makers is the obvious objective of strategic foresight, and of course identifying viable options for bottom-up affecting is the objective of participatory foresight in the same way.

Risk detection is the natural objective of the early warning and intelligence types of functions, and empirical research is the objective of all scanning and statistical functions. Participatory assessment is the first primary objective of all workshops and expert panel based methods. Finally, creating visions and studying values can be said to be the main objective of all futures research related approaches. This is a particular focal point in critical futures studies, but actually all research that operates with intangible futures knowledge has this as its main objective.

What is Anticipation?

> *I think there is a world market for maybe five computers.*
> *Thomas Watson senior, Director of IBM, 1943*

The *Oxford Dictionary* defines the word anticipation as a noun that originates from the Latin *anticipat-* 'acted in advance', from the verb *anticipare*, based on *ante-* 'before' + *capere* 'take'. In mid-sixteenth century English, the word anticipation was used, e.g., for purposes such as 'to take something into consideration', 'mention something before the proper time'. Today the noun anticipation refers to intuition of something that one wishes, hopes or prefers with a confidence of fulfilment. Its 'sister' concept verb, anticipate, refers to the act of obtaining prognosis knowledge of the future by reasoning from divine sources, or by projecting or extrapolating from past observations. As the *Oxford Dictionary* suggests 'it was anticipated that the rains would slow the military campaign'.

According to the *Audio English Dictionary* there are three general types of anticipation: suspense (excited anticipation of an approaching climax); fever (intense nervous anticipation); and hope (a specific instance of feeling hopeful). Dictionary.com links foretaste, intuition, foreknowledge, a sense of realization in advance and prescience to it as well.[29]

Anticipation means that one is intuitively expecting that something is going to happen, and it should be differentiated from the other more formal futures concepts that involve specific methods such as forecast, foresight or prognosis. Anticipation is a more informal and automatic brain function that is related to forms of informal inferring which are discussed in Chapter 5. It should not be confused with prediction or prophecy either, as anticipation is not meant to be a statement of the distant future for other people. Anticipation

---

29 See http://www.audioenglish.net/dictionary/anticipation.htm; and http://dictionary.reference.com/browse/anticipation

is quite immediate and a personal intuition based on belief. For example, when a person is planning a journey by car they anticipate the traffic jams before selecting a road.

What are Prediction and Fortune-telling?

Aircraft heavier than the air are impossible.

Lord Kelvin, 1895

The human endeavour to be better prepared for the challenges of the future is ages old. It may even be thought of as a natural part of human nature. This almost eternal endeavour of human kind has changed and taken many forms in the past. We may say that during this evolution, the first predecessors of futures work consisted of representatives of the early *animism*, the belief that all artefacts and objects around us have spirits; *magic*, the use of supernatural and ritual methods such as witchcraft to manipulate natural forces; *herbalism*, the belief that eating, for example a leaf reminds the heart that it can heal its problems; and *shamanism*, the beliefs regarding communication with the spiritual world.[30] These lines continued in classical antiquity in many forms of *predicting*, *foretelling*, *prophesy* or *foreseeing* the future; classified into inductive prediction (by detecting and interpreting signs of the future) and intuitive fortune-telling orientation (by internally 'perceiving' the future). The inductive fortune-telling was especially dominant in the Pre-Roman Etruscan culture of Northern Italy. The seeds of the tradition of utopia/dystopia imagination have been sown ever since Plato and they have become inherent in futures thinking as well. These prediction traditions of classical antiquity contained more than 100 documented methods which are described or represented in texts by Cicero, Seneca, Aristotle, St Augustine, and in prophecies by the oracles of Delphi.[31]

The deterministic prediction orientation, where the postulate of the possibility of receiving 'knowledge' of the future either inductively or intuitively is valid, has not vanished from our operational landscape. According to some sources, it may even be strengthening in certain areas.[32] Magical thinking is still common especially among people who have low tolerance for uncertainty.[33] Once a person believes in supernatural or paranormal phenomena, it is

---

30 Kuosa (2009).
31 See Heinonen (1990, 1999).
32 For example Dawkins (2006).
33 Lindeman-Viitasalo (1995, 18).

extremely easy to find signals from the environment, which seem to verify the fixed beliefs of the person in question. Supernatural belief systems help people to get the complex and unpredictable world in order.[34] A structured and predictable world helps certain types of people to make their plans for the future, to make everyday decisions, and to stop worrying about unpredictable incidents. It also helps such a person to save energy as he/she does not have to constantly reason complex phenomena and many sources of confusing information. In many cases, it is too big a burden for an individual to carry all the responsibility of every decision they have made during their lifetime. Furthermore, if the phenomena, which the person has to deal with are becoming more hectic and complex, it is even more tempting to give up rational science-based reasoning and select some form of fixed external explanation. *Astrology* is a good example here. If the past, present, future, and all the personalities are written in the stars, it is no longer worthwhile to worry about your actions or decisions. Following this line of thought, you are no longer responsible.[35]

Astrology is not the only form of fortune-telling and foretelling in modern times. The deterministic *fortune-telling* orientation lives strongly, for example in *Tarot card reading*, Nostradamus predictions interpretations, graphology, psychic seeing, automatic writing, Ouija board playing, past-lives-telling, soul map reading, hand or crystal ball reading, and even in animal organs reading for weather prediction purposes (Ibid.). For example, the so called 'frog-men' give annual weather predictions through the Finnish Broadcasting Company YLE, and this is certainly not the only case in the western world. Furthermore, even esteemed publishers seem to be publishing books in these fields, which tells us something about the overall consumer demand in the market.

Playing with the supernatural basic instincts of people is a big business in Hollywood too. Hollywood movies and TV series are constantly pushing supernatural schemes. Sometimes the ghosts and spirits depicted in the shows are real, sometimes the wizards or witches are casting real spells and only fools do not believe in them, UFOs are here or some undercover people are visiting other planets, sometimes there are deterministic predictions or curses, which will happen unless a hero prevents the future by a magical intervention. Sometimes psychics are solving present or forthcoming crimes for the police, sometimes people are using time-machines to visit the past in order to change the present or they are visiting the future to know what to do in the present time, and so forth. As presented, these may be entertaining shows and they

---

34 See Durkheim (1912).
35 Lindeman-Viitasalo (1995, 18, 23, 34, 54–94); Kuosa (2009).

may bring some meaning into people's lives, but there is a flip side. When people constantly see supernatural things happening and solving otherwise tricky problems, some people may get used to such easy explanations. Even if they know that movies are one thing and the real world is another, such shows may be feeding their basic supernatural instincts and needs in a harmful way. It may lead people to look for answers in the wrong places, to waste their money, to make wrong assumptions and decisions,[36] but it can be especially devastating for seriously conducted modern futures studies and foresight.

It is not to say that, before modern futures studies emerged, the inductive or intuitive prediction paradigm would always have been the dominant and unquestioned way of producing future knowledge. For instance in ancient Greece, the peripatetic school, and cynics such as Cicero and Epicureans, were determined opponents of foretellers and *oracles*. Aristophanes, Demosthenes and Lucian even attempted to reveal the ridiculousness of the entire Delfoi's pythias oracle institution.[37] Nevertheless, it did not help. Predictions became even more popular and the countries' leaders supported them into a new renaissance.

Alongside supernatural prediction, there are many scientific prediction practices too. A big part of modern macro and micro economics is based on attempts to predict market changes – to remove ambiguity from economic fluctuations and to make wiser decisions and investments. Usually that prediction follows the principle of *ceteris paribus* where only one constrained statistical set or time series is a trend extrapolated in certain time frames, and all other effecting factors are closed off from the calculation. Alongside economics many forms of modelling and simulations, such as climate and weather forecasts, pursue to such predictability of dynamical or social systems or at least of forecasting, that they are evolving with a very high rate of accuracy.

As discussed in the chapter *Causality and Correlations,* there are some systemic functions that are mechanically predictable, some are probable based on statistics and quantitative analysis which produces trends and correlations between things, but most of the behaviours that are related to dynamical economy and complex adaptive system's behaviour are unpredictable in a long-run. Through such a system, dynamic processes contain no real causalities, which is the foundation of any scientifically valid predictions. Weak correlations are not the same as causality. In other words, it doesn't

---

36 Ibid.
37 Heinonen (1990, 22).

matter how good scientists work is within the field of economics, or by how much computer models improve, they are still unable to achieve the ultimate goal, which is to make accurate long-term predictions of the behaviour in the economy's dynamical level. As mathematician John L. Casti[38] put it, prediction requires computability and mathematically only a small subset of all possible functions is computable. It is therefore plausible that mathematical descriptions of many natural or human phenomena are inherently incomputable. The more a system is susceptible to human influence, the lower its predictability becomes.

The situation with a big part of modern economics and many other disciplines, which aim to make predictions of social or dynamical systems' future, or at least to forecast their future with high accuracy, share many similarities with the situation of alchemy a few centuries ago. The possible rewards for discovering a way to cheaply produce large quantities of gold was so high, and there was so much invested money available for such attempts, that ordinary people, investors, alchemists and decision makers didn't want to believe the contrary argument, that it was most likely impossible to make gold. In the same way, the ultimate goal of predicting dynamical system in the long-term can never be achieved as gold cannot be made cheaply, but other good discoveries, a deeper understanding, and better informed decisions and initiatives can be made while trying to reach such goals.

What is Forecasting?

By the end of the century we will live in a paper-free society.
Roger Smith, President of General Motors, 1986

In futures domain terminology, forecasting is not exactly the same as predicting which could refer, for example. to the precise number of times floods will occur over a long period of time in a certain area. Forecasting, however, is about making more or less linear systematic estimations, statements, extrapolations,

---

38 Casti (2004). However, it should be noticed, as meteorologist Dr John Geis has argued, that computational power and modelling fidelity are no longer the real show-stoppers to good modelling. The problem with keeping the weather forecasts stable isn't anymore our ability of observing the initial conditions at the level of fidelity commensurate. Instead of math, the biggest problem with meteorology is related on the initial boundary conditions of the model. That problem is due to the fact that meteorologists can now model at a level so small, that they need to develop an observation network to observe on the smaller scale, which changes the conditions of the model.

projections or predictions of future events, rate or value of change whose actual outcomes have not yet been observed and of which are not fully sure. When a prediction does not usually give estimations of probabilities or ways to prevent the 'prophesy', a forecast is always a probabilistic statement in futures domain.[39]

Two characteristics that are linked to forecasting are accuracy and precision. Forecasts can be very precise, but quite inaccurate. Forecasts can be self-fulfilling or self-defeating too. Forecasting the possible existence of a condition or technology may make that condition or technology become more likely – this is what is referred to as a self-fulfilling forecast, according to Glenn.[40]

The mechanism for that is clear: others, hearing and reading about the possibility, work to bring it about. A forecast of famine may make the famine less likely if it triggers action – this is what is referred as a self-defeating forecast. Thus, forecasting itself can have political implications. Furthermore, if a self-defeating forecast triggers action to avoid the forecasted problem, then the forecast may have been highly inaccurate; nevertheless, the forecast may have been extremely useful.

There is a wide range of methodological approaches that are linked to forecasting. The general division can be made between formal statistical methods that often employ ICT software, and more human centric judgemental methods. Some formal statistical methods, such as regression analysis, which belong to causal and econometric forecasting methods, work on the assumption that it is possible to identify the underlying factors that might influence the variable that is being forecast. For example, including information about weather conditions might improve the ability of a model to predict umbrella sales. Some are much more linear by their nature such as trend estimations, extrapolations, growth curve analysis, and time series methods which all use historical data as the basis for estimating future outcomes; and rolling forecasts that give a projection of the future based on past performances, are routinely updated to incorporate data.[41] However, pursuing forecasts with such a high

---

39 However, the difference between these two concepts, forecast and prediction, is not understood exactly the same way in all disciplines. For instance, in meteorology weather forecast for tomorrow is not a probabilistic statement. It is merely a synonymous concept to weather prediction for tomorrow.

40 Glenn (2009a, 7).

41 Armstrong (2001); Coates and Glenn (2009); and Glenn (2009b). Available at: http://www.forecastingprinciples.com/index.php?option=com_content&task=view&id=17&Itemid=17

accuracy of the future in a complex dynamical system have some serious problems as discussed in a previous sub-chapter, 'What are Prediction and Fortune-telling?'. This statistical forecasting or quantitative inferring approach is described in the SIF-model in Table 6.3.

Human centric judgemental methods of forecasting, such as technology forecasting or assessment, surveys and Delphi, represent less formal but still systematic ways of giving estimations of the most probable future, or most viable ways to get to a certain objective in the future. Alongside these participatory judgemental methods, the judgemental methods can also contain much more subjective forecasting approaches. Actually many normative and critical futures studies approaches are highly subjective. The most subjective of all would, however, be the genius forecasting method, which is strongly connected to intuition, visioning, visualizing and foreseeing the future, but which is still called forecasting instead of prophesy or prediction. These human centric judgemental methods or qualitative inferring approaches of the future domain will be discussed further in SIF-model in Chapter 6.

What is Exploratory and Normative Forecasting?

> *Inventions have already reached their limits and I don't believe that there*
> *is any hope of new inventions in the future.*
> *Julius Sextus Frontinus, Roman engineer, AD 10*

The seven most common ways of describing the methodological principles and research strategies of the futures domain involve making the distinction between:

1. statistical/quantitative and human centric/qualitative approaches;

2. pre- and pro-active approaches;

3. prediction/linear and probabilistic/non-linear approaches;

4. for client and with client approaches;

5. designing/engineering/standing-outside-the-system and understanding/allowing ambiguity/standing-inside-the-system;

6.   inside-out and outside-in approaches; and

7.   analytic, synthetic and heuristic approaches, as partly discussed in Chapter 2.

The eighth alternative of describing the methodologies of the futures domain is to divide the field into top-down strategic approaches and bottom-up participatory approaches, as presented in Figure 2.1. And finally, the ninth way is to make the distinction between strategies of *normative forecasting* and approaches of *exploratory forecasting*.

Exploratory forecasting explores what is possible and probable regardless of what is desirable. It tends to rely heavily on mathematical analysis and formal, quantitative trend forecasting, as well as extensive use of probabilistic methods, meaning that it rather suggests alternative outcomes. In other words, it begins pre-actively with the present as a starting point, examines the various ways in which those forces and components may play out, and moves forward to the future.[42] Such forecasting also has an implicit assumption that the variables of interest are outside the customer's control.[43]

Normative approach is based on norms, values, aims and strategic goals. Such goal-oriented forecasting tends to take into account an organization's purpose, its mission, and most importantly, its future achievements. It starts with a view of possible and desired futures even if all variables of interest are not under the control of the customer. After defining these possible futures goals, the forecaster backs away from these futures to the present to identify the necessary steps for reaching the preferred goal. Now he asks, what trends, events and actions would take us there? Thus, the normative forecaster makes a jump from the present to the future, which does not have to be continuous with current trends. Here it relies more heavily on qualitative tools, since it involves more open-ended, uncertain, and creative elements of the futures enterprise. Normative forecasting addresses the questions: what future do we want? What do we want to become?

However, this general division of futures work into normative and exploratory can be misleading when applied to methodology. Futurists' 'tools' are usually quite flexible and adaptable to specific contexts and purposes. Many techniques can be used for both normative and exploratory forecasting,

---

42   Coates and Glenn (2009, 1–4).
43   For example Schwartz (1996, 2003); and Englebrecht, et al. (1996).

methods from both approaches can be combined into a new method, as is the case with a mixed scenario approach.[44] Basically there are no strict rules for the order or the use of different types of methods in either of the approaches, except that the use of normative tools naturally requires ability to control the key drivers. Some tend to use certain types of methods more frequently for one purpose than the other.

Furthermore, it should be noted that every statement of a goal is not a normative forecast, as every prediction with a probability is not explorative forecast. The majority of them are not. As Coates and Glenn[45] put it:

> *Chairman Mao's goal in the great leap forward was no more a normative forecast than Franklin D. Roosevelt's New Deal. Why? Because no detailed analysis backed up what was necessary to achieve those objectives. The characteristic weakness of political goals-setting is the absence of supporting analysis on feasibility or necessity for achieving the goal. Normative forecasting is not emotive political arm-waving, but a detailed process of elaborate technique usable primarily in organizational or governmental planning. Normative forecasting is surely not the tool for the timid, the unimaginative, the fearful, or the fatalistic. The mere forecasting of a future state, such as in science fiction, or the description of a range of alternative futures, such as in the familiar alternative scenarios of Herman Kahn, are not examples of normative forecasting.*

Crucial to the process of normative forecasting is the detailed analysis, which reveals the specific steps or stages that must be met and how they will be met at specific times when moving towards the goal. From a different point of view, the function of a normative forecast is to allow an organization to orchestrate its resources in a highly targeted way in order to achieve a goal. Ideally, normative forecasting, as with any other kind of forecast, should leave the user and other professionals with the sense that they understand the process and that, if they had gone through the process, they would come to similar results. Hence, normative forecasting is usually associated with large organizations, both public and private, as an important component of decision making and a factor in resource allocation.[46]

---

44 Coates and Glenn (2009, 1–4).
45 Ibid.
46 Coates and Glenn (2009).

What is Greek Triangle and La Prospective?

> *If we do not know the consequences of our choices, our freedom to choose*
> *is an illusion. Hence, no freedom exists without forecasting.*
> Bertrand de Jouvenel, in the Art of Conjecture

The concept 'Greek triangle' originates from ancient Greece. Aristotle particularly used the idea of the 'three power vectors' of a triangle. Aristotle had many triangles such as rhetoric's: writer, text and reader, and ethos, logos and pathos.[47] Figure 2.4 presents one of my modifications of a 'Greek triangle', which combines Aristotle's the 'world's three basic forms'; structure, process and knowledge, and his idea of an efficient process for influencing the future. It starts from anticipation, which refers to visioning the wished for futures and pre-actively gathering enough futures knowledge in order to intuitively understand the context. It is followed by appropriation, which refers to sense-making and setting a strategy, based on the anticipation phase. As setting a

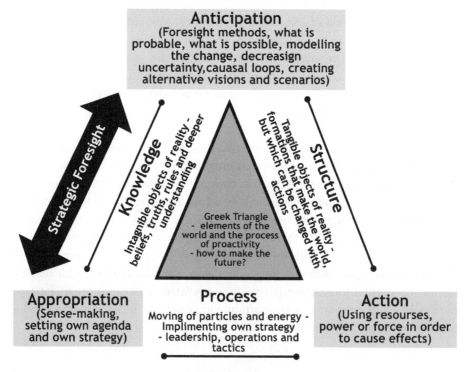

Figure 2.4   Location of strategic foresight in a Greek triangle

---

47 Aristotle (2007): *On Rhetoric.*

strategy is not sufficient for influencing the future, the strategy needs to be followed by action. Once the action has been taken, the system has been influenced, and we need to do a new round of anticipation. Hence, the 'Greek triangle' is a continuous process,[48] which must be repeated always after the functional environment has been influenced.

In the French speaking world this approach, which attempts to involve and commit all people to a mutually wished for future objective is called *La Prospective*, which was originally initiated by Gaston Berger, a philosopher in the 1950s and 1960s, and recognized and used by another French philosopher Bertrand de Jouvenel who wrote the classic *Art of Conjecture* (1967).

In terms of the English speaking world, *La Prospective* could be thought of as an anticipatory consciousness, and it can be defined as a bottom-up proactive approach, which is a combination of futurology and participatory foresight. The current editor of *Futuribles*, Hugues de Jouvenel[49] defines *La Prospective* as follows:

> *La prospective is neither prophecy or prediction, but a tool to help us create the future. Prospective rests on three basic premises: 1) the future is a realm of freedom (it is open to many possible futures, or – futuribles); 2) it is a land to be explored; 3) it is a land to be built. – One must identify an array of possible futures that is constantly changing. Some futuribles disappear as others emerge – hence, it must be monitored on a permanent basis.*

La Prospective was popularized beyond the francophone world by Michel Godet[50] who believed that it is:

> *neither forecasting nor futurology, but a mode of thinking for action and against fatalism. La Prospective recognizes that the future is the 'raison d'être of the present', that is multiple and uncertain, and that it is a way for everyone to take control of their own futures (.) Thus, the first aim of prospective thought is to illuminate the choices of the present by the light of possible futures.*

---

48 Godet (1993).
49 Jouvenel, Hugues de (2004): Invitation á La Prospective/An invitation to Foresight. *Futuribles Perspectives Series*. Paris, Futuribles, July 2004.
50 Godet (1993).

What is Critical Futures Studies?

Critical futures studies (CFS) was introduced by Richard Slaughter in his PhD thesis in 1982.[51] The ideas behind CFS come from various sources as outlined in Ramos's monograph,[52] which discusses its origins, evolution and practices. Two of the origins are however decisive. First the philosophy behind CFS is based directly on the emancipatory interests of knowledge, which refers to our deep-seated need to reveal and overcome dogmatism, compulsion, and domination. The emancipatory interests, alongside technical and practical/ hemeneutical interests of knowledge were introduced by Jürgen Habermas in 1972,[53] and these are further discussed in fifth chapter of this book.

The second decisive origin of CFS comes from the philosophy of Ken Wilber who wrote how an inner journey, inner growth, and inner dimensions of the individual – consciousness – has been neglected, ignored, repressed or looked down upon, when it is actually a vital aspect of modern life. Based on Wilber's understanding of the importance of inner dimension and of reality and futures visions, Slaughter introduced a CFS method of Four-Quadrant Model.

Due to this alliance between the emancipatory interests of knowledge and Wilber's inner dimension of reality, CFS is also known as the 'emancipatory tradition' of futures studies. It is an intellectual practice that aims to critique reified and oppressive social structures and destructive cultural traits.[54] It prefers the use of subjective methods and tools to bring future thoughts to the surface and strives to develop new tools (futures wheel, futures workshop techniques, and causal layered analysis, etc.) for stimulation of discourse about the future.

According to Eva Hideg,[55] the critical futures studies' key feature is the understanding that the future is something that already exists in the present in the thoughts and emotions of people. These future thoughts and perceptions affect present occurrences and form an organic part of our 'life world'. Future thoughts are forming and reforming in the process of discourses, so the futures

---

51 Slaughter, Richard (1982): *Critical Futures Studies and Curriculum Renewal*, PhD dissertation, University of Lancaster, Britain.
52 Ramos, José M. (2003): From critique to cultural recovery: Critical futures studies and Causal Layered Analysis. *Monograph Series*, 2003, No. 2, Australian Foresight Institute Swinburne University.
53 Habermas (1986).
54 Ramos (2003).
55 Hideg (2007).

existing in the present are open and humanly constructed. Thinking about the future and having a notion of the future can no longer be regarded as separate forms of thinking. All human perception and meaning are characterized by an original future intention, which is invariably linked to experience, and intentions rooted in the past. Furthermore, not only certain distinguished individuals (fortune-tellers, prophets, sci-fi writers, futurists) can think about the future and develop future views, every human being has such ability.

One of the most well-known methods of critical futures studies is Causal Layered Analysis (CLA), which has been moulded into its current form by Sohail Inayatullah. According to Inayatullah, CLA is not about a methodology, but about opening up spaces to alternative epistemes, cultural worldviews, and discourses, hence opening up pathways to substantively alternative futures from that which is currently offered through mainstream 'pop' and 'problem oriented' scenarios and the like. CLA has four levels: litany, social causes, cultural beliefs and myths, and the analysis moves back and forth between these.[56]

Another major contribution to the field of critical futures studies by Inayatullah[57] is his introduction of the three research dimensions of futures studies. He begins with Slaughter's emancipatory interest of knowledge in futures studies/critical tradition and adds some post-structural elements to it. He then continues to the two remaining research traditions of futures studies, that are mostly based on Haberma's interests of knowledge and, as he puts it, on Amara's,[58] Bezold's, Linstone's, Gillward's, Saldar's, and Masini's work and discussions. The outcome of Inayatullah's discussion can be summarized in Figure 2.5, on the following page, which presents the three research dimensions that all have different assumptions about the real, about truth, about the role of the subject, about the nature of the universe, and about the nature of the future.

What is Vision?

Imagination governs the world.

Napoleon

The term 'vision' has a broad range of meanings. Originally it was used to describe some religious hallucinations or images that a long-term alcoholic may

---

56 Inayatullah (2008).
57 Inayatullah (1990, 115–41).
58 Amara (1981).

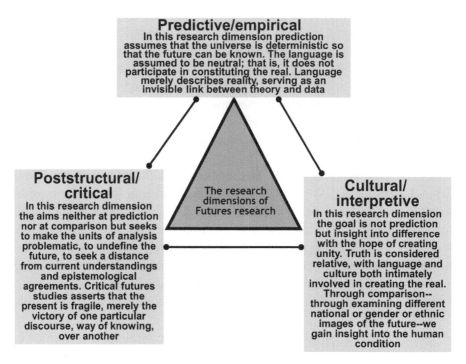

Figure 2.5   The research dimensions of futures studies

see, but according to Glenn, a popular way to talk about vision is as an ability to see what the vast majority do not. It is also the ability to think in images rather than just ideas. It is a description of some future condition rather than a whole scenario of a desired future. As an example, one could have a vision of some catastrophe for which people need to prepare, such as a vision of years of famine leading to plans to build grain storage, etc. A vision can be a mental image of some future danger seen during a dream or a ceremony to invoke such experience. It can be a view of some desirable future, like a religious or political utopia. It can be the result of people working together to create a new condition for themselvesand it can be static, like the goal of landing on the moon, or dynamic, like exploring the unknown.[59]

From a management point of view, a vision is a compelling statement of the preferred future that an organization or community wants to create. As Glenn puts it, visions move and inspire us by stating why we are working together, what higher contribution flows from our efforts, and what we are striving to

59 Glenn (2009b, 3–4).

become. Vision development is the most powerful way to clarify where you would like change to be.[60]

According to Malaska and Holstius,[61] a vision is created by using all three human faculties: the thoughts, emotions and willpower of the members of the envisioning team. It is not a result of outside expert analysis. What each person in the team wants for themselves in the company has to be disciplined so that the vision also serves as a personal success story. A vision is an entrepreneurial perception which reveals and points to something new and which sees beyond what is already being utilized to what is emerging and becoming invented. A vision is also an empowering tool, which makes people pro-active. A vision created by the management team serves as a basis for defining the concrete management tasks of a strategic nature. The company vision created as a result of teamwork also leads to the commitment of key personnel, and thereby facilitates its own realization.[62]

What is Weak Signal?

> *To make judgements on which side wins, you need reliable knowledge of the enemy and this knowledge cannot be elicited from spirits, it cannot be obtained inductively from experience, nor by any deductive calculation. It can only be obtained from other men.*
>
> *Sun Tzu*

Weak signal is an anomaly in the known transformation. It is an observation that surprises us somehow. It is something that we cannot easily link to any known trends or phenomenon. Weak signal is a completely subjective construction. One thing may be a weak signal to you, but to another it is old information or nonsense. We tend to consider things that come outside our own domain of expertise as weak signals, and new things that are emerging inside our own domain, we tend to ignore or just link to something that already exists. There is no such thing as a contemporary real weak signal, as we are unable to identify things that can be objectively agreed as a contemporary weak signal. This is explained more thoroughly in the figure showing filters of knowledge that can be found in the fifth chapter. There have been many attempts to create a system, which separates objective weak signals from subjective intuition, but it

---

60 Ibid.
61 Malaska and Holstius (1999, 354–7).
62 Ibid.

has never really helped to identify objective weak signals due to the identified difficulties. At best the software systems have been able to produce lists of issues that some informants consider highly important change factors and whilst others consider them to be nonsense.

We can say that weak signals are observations or strange ideas that someone has subjectively reasoned to have some special foresight value. They are based on subjective interpretations and the tacit knowledge of something. Weak signals help us to manage patterns of chance. Any emerging pattern of chance will certainly give out signals in many ways and one should not rely on only one signal when attempting to reason something. Use of pattern management and Future Signals Sense-making Framework (FSSF) helps one to assess and cluster signals and to make conclusions of the emerging or changing issues.

Weak signals should not be confused with strong signals, which are things that are already quite well-known, or with trends, which are big transformation processes that we cannot easily stop, for example the ageing of a population. Weak signals should not be confused with drivers or wild cards either.

Weak signals exist in many layers. There are signals of something that could possibly start affecting something else which in turn could eventually have a significant effect. Such potential signals at an early stage are particularly subjective and theoretical constructions. It is very difficult to get any collective agreement of possible causalities between intuitive observations and large future events. At the other extreme weak signals are very late tangible signals. To give an example, there is a direct observation of something which gives us a good reason to believe that there will be a direct causal effect following that observation (e.g. we see that an airplane is highjacked by a terrorist and we know that it is heading towards New York).

When we look to history, we can easily name certain things that were real tangible weak signals at the time. For instance, as we have hindsight of the year 2011 revolutions in Arab countries, we can say retrospectively that one true weak signal of the coming events was the US foreign intelligence's discovery of exponential growth of text and SMS messages in Tunis in the last 10 years. Another significant signal, which is stronger and more direct than the first signal, however, was the incident in which a young man burned himself in public in Tunis as a political protest. That was a signal of a deep mistrust of the political system, which may have evolved into a collective bifurcation point of full-scale revolution. That signal can be compared to the 1914 Sarajevo assassination of the Archduke Ferdinand of Austria, which led to World War I only one month after the incident.

To avoid confusion – weak signals do not need to be anything as special as the three examples given above. Those are examples of real tangible and direct weak signals, which are uncommon. Usually weak signals are much more modest. They are the kinds of things that are somehow anomalies to you, which may tell you about large changes, as explained above. No matter what the type of the weak signal, we can only know retrospectively if the detected signal was accurate foresight knowledge or misinterpretation. Furthermore, weak signals are not the same thing as the triggering or tipping points or the thing itself, which is changing or doing something. A terrorist carrying a bomb is not a weak signal. The weak signal is your direct observation of a man carrying an item that looks like a bomb.

The world's biggest open source database for collecting and analysing weak signals has been created by the iKnow project,[63] which was funded by the EU's Blue Sky programme. In 2008–2009, when I worked on the iKnow project there were already nearly one thousand analysed weak signals and wild cards from all fields of life. At the time of writing, the database is already much bigger.

What are Change Factors, Wild Cards, Drivers, Trends and Scenarios?

> *The purpose of theory is not to uncover fixed laws or principles, but rather to educate the mind.*
>
> Carl von Clausewitz

Change factor is a macro-level concept, which covers all types of futures knowledge such as trends, drivers, weak signals or anomalies, emerging issues, transition period, tipping points, triggering incidents, initial conditions, chain reaction, turbulence, wild cards or wild guesses, visions, values, predictions, forecasts, beliefs, imagination, strategies, roadmaps, plans and scenarios. The Governing the Future report[64] has presented a practical and useful description

---

63 Available at: www.iknowcommunity.eu
64 House of Commons Public Administration Select Committee, Governing the Future, Second Report of Session 2006–07. HC 123–I. Published on 6 March 2007 by authority of the House of Commons. London: The Stationery Office Limited.

of the relationships between some of these concepts, which can be found in Chapter 15.

Wild card is an idea of some kind of sudden and unexpected[65] event, or alternatively 'known unknown'[66] thing, which would have a strong impact on large parts of a society. Wild card is a wild guess of a radical thing that may happen, which goes beyond the current change/transition period. When a (dynamical) system is very sensitive to initial conditions, it is almost expected that one small event, or triggering or tipping points, will sooner or later start a chain reaction/turbulence in the system as discussed in Chapter 4. Wild card is a statement of such candidate triggering incidents. 'Prediction' that the Sarajevo assassination will occur and start World War I, or the burning suicide of Tunis will occur and start a chain of revolutions in Arab countries, are both political wild cards if they are presented before the actual incidents.

Driver or driving force is the agent or factor, which drives a change forward. To use the concepts from the fourth chapter, a driver is the attractor of a dynamical system. The two basic types of drivers in social systems are pulling and pushing drivers. A pulling driver refers to a broad grass-root-level demand for something. For instance the deep public mistrust of the political systems in Arab countries is a thing that pulls change forward. A pushing driver is for example, a political decision to put something forward. The most widely recognized example is the American space program. Its most crucial objective was set by President Kennedy, 'We will put a man on the moon and return him home safely within a decade'.

> *Surely, the forces at play did not make the man on the moon a likely outcome from incrementally developing military rockets. Rather, what happened was that a powerful public figure set the goal. That automatically launches a flood of studies on the steps to reach that*

---

65 There is a literature that suggests these events need not be 'unexpected' as e.g. John Geis has argued. 'A slip on the Cascadia fault along the US northwest coast would generate an earthquake measuring around 10 on the Richter scale. This is not a black swan. It's overdue. It will send a 50–100 metre tsunami across the entire Pacific Basin wiping out San Francisco, Los Angeles, Sydney, Brisbane, Singapore, Tokyo, etc. We know it is coming, but we haven't planned for it. These kind of things are wild cards too, because they also change everything – even if we know they are coming'.

66 For instance, Peter Schwartz (2003) says in his book *Inevitable Surprises*, that there are many 'known unknowns' – things we know will happen (e.g., peak oil, a Vesuvius eruption, the next great California earthquake, etc.) though we may not know exactly when. These events are inevitable. We know they will occur, yet because of the difficulty of planning for them, we act surprised when they occur (...) and they have the effect of a 'Wild Card' even though there is nothing unexpected or wild about them.

goal. Its planners had to go from the macro social goal to forecasts of what kinds of social systems would be implied in order to make that objective real.[67]

Trend is a flow of transformations that cannot be changed easily. A current trend is a push of path-dependence from history, which we believe will continue in the future. One of the most obvious social trends in the western world is the ageing population. Thus a trend is something that can be proven to exist based on statistics or collective agreement. A trend can be identified from time-series analysis or it can be said to exist by experts who are well attached to the contemporary transformation. For instance a fashion trend may be hard to identify from statistics, but it can be seen on the streets.

There are lots of ways to analyse trends. The most well-known forms are trend impact analysis, trend-extrapolation and S-curve analysis. Trend impact analysis focuses on identifying the sub-trends that a large trend carries forward and analyses the impact of each of these separately or combined. Trend-extrapolation is based on the idea of extrapolating directly the development shown in a historical or current time-series to the future – what if this development continues to the future without any barriers? The S-curve analysis is based on understanding the nature of trends and the utilizing of that knowledge through analysis. Trends are usually S-curves, which start with modest pace, but after a while start a rapid acceleration until the potential of the trend is consumed and it turns into a slow pace or stagnation. If we are making decisions based on trend knowledge, it is very important to know at which stage it is in the S-curve.

Scenario is a detailed description of the potential developments from the present to the futures. The term 'scenario' originates from outlines of plots in dramatic arts, and from movie directors illustrating sketches, which describe the action sequences in movies. The father of scenario construction for futures studies and policy analysis was Herman Kahn,[68] who introduced the term 'scenario' into planning, military and strategic studies in the 1950s. At the time he worked at the RAND Corporation (Research and Development), which had a mutual long-range-planning project between the US Army Air Corps and the Douglas Aircraft Company.

---

67 Coates and Glenn (2009, 1–4).
68 Kahn, Herman, Brown, William and Martel, Leon (1976): *The Next 200 Years: A Scenario for America and the World.* New York, Morrow; and Kahn, Herman and Wiener, Anthony J. (1967): *The Year 2000: The Framework for Speculation on the Next Thirty-three Years.* New York, Macmillan.

In any scenario process, the objective is to open up the whole spectrum of future possibilities. It is to introduce novel views that are beyond the existing linear trends and time series, and to help the current decision making and risk analysis to better understand the causes and effects of certain low probability triggering points for the future. And finally, it is to help decision makers see some perspectives, causes and effects that are related to the decisions that should be made today. As Jerome C. Glenn et al.[69] put it:

> The purpose of scenarios is to systematically explore, create, and test consistent alternative future environments that encompass the broadest set of future operating conditions that the user might possibly face. Scenarios can help generate long-term policies, strategies, and plans, which help bring desired and likely future circumstances in closer alignment. While writing the scenarios, the process can also expose ignorance; show that we do not know how to get to a specific future or that it is impossible. Furthermore, they serve to bring assumptions about the field they cover to the foreground and can serve as a tool to discuss, test and perhaps re-evaluate these assumptions, for example, about how certain trends or factors interact and shape the field. Scenarios are also used for innovation development, when scenarios describing, for example, future living conditions and specific fields of consumption are used to generate new product ideas.

Contemporary scenarios are used especially in futures studies, strategy work, military, and long-range-planning, and there are many different applications of scenarios based on the objectives, context, or nature of the user organization. Scenarios are regularly used by companies, consultants, scholars, public and non-governmental organizations, and it is therefore difficult to provide any exhaustive list of scenario methods. However, we can identify two distinctive general methodological principles or strategies of scenario work, explorative scenarios and normative scenarios, which echo the explorative forecasting and normative forecasting that are among the general approaches of futures studies.

Alongside the two general methodological strategies, Coates and Glenn[70] identified three specific applications of scenarios: The first option is to put forward a future situation and use that as the jumping-off place for further planning, thinking, or research. The next scenario is to present a completed image of some future situation, representing a full story about the future. A

---

69 Glenn, Jerome C. and The Futures Group International (2009): Scenarios.
70 Coates and Glenn (2009, 1–4): Normative forecasting.

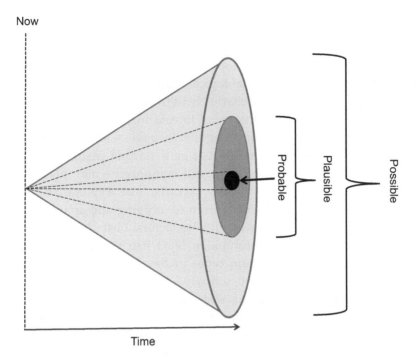

Figure 2.6   **Probable, plausible and possible futures**

third application is to present a situation radically at odds with traditional thinking. By being organized and coherent, the scenario drives home the central point that the organization had to begin thinking in new terms and considering new goals.

All three of Coates and Glenn's applications of scenario work can be applied in the production of both explorative and normative scenarios. As discussed in the explorative and normative forecasting sub-chapter, in normative scenario work, the author can first make a jump to non-linear imaginary future images, visions or objectives that have been named, and afterwards attempt to explain how it could be possible to end up with that kind of future from the state of affairs in the present time. The method allows the author to leave certain transformations in the path unexplained. When using normative scenario methods, we do not need to ground the storyline to historical and evident insight data in the same way as explorative scenario methods. Thus, it is enough to say that certain things emerged or happened in a certain year and then launched for example, a huge demand for solar panels, which again led to new situations.

Again, the explorative scenarios explore, according to the principle of explorative forecasting, what is possible and probable regardless of what is desirable. They must be grounded in empirical evidence and the method requires the identification of a logical path from the present towards possible futures. Explorative scenarios tend to rely heavily on mathematical analysis and formal, quantitative trend forecasting, as well as the extensive use of probabilistic methods, meaning that it suggests alternative outcomes. It begins pre-actively with the present as a starting point, examines the various ways in which those forces and components may play out, and moves forward to the future.[71] In other words, 'true' explorative scenario[72] works basic method usually starts from identifying and analysing all the contemporary trajectories, trends, drivers, actors, obstacles and objectives that are relevant in future transformation. Next, it explains which trajectories and drivers could lead to certain types of development, and argues how they may interact and co-evolve and why. After that, it identifies possible triggering points in development, which could turn the change away from the identified linear path. Then the method starts to explain how these new paths could evolve in the new circumstances. Finally, the method explains what type of futures there could be at the end of such paths in a certain year, if we presume that the development could continue all the way in that particular path. Hence, 'true' explorative method is going from the present to possible futures, and not knowing where the scenarios finally end, once the work is started.

Whatever methodological strategy, application or method is selected, scenario work can, in principle, be used to produce an almost infinite number of scenarios, which again can be brief, only one paragraph long, or very descriptive multi-page essays.[73] Nevertheless, a scenario should always be created systematically and should contain a logical backbone that identifies the variables in the situation under study, sets some overall themes for the scenario, and then assigns qualitative and quantitative values to the scenario variables. From there, one creates the integrated image. Not every projection or statement of future development is a scenario. What usually passes as a scenario is a discussion about a range of future possibilities with some

---

71 Ibid.
72 For example, Global Trends 2025: The National Intelligence Council's 2025 Project. C.f. Glenn, Jerome C. and The Futures Group International (2009): Scenarios. In *Futures Research Methodology – Version 3.0* (eds) Jerome C. Glenn and Theodore J. Gordon. CD-rom. World Federation of United Nations Associations.
73 Such as Global Trends 2025: The National Intelligence Council's 2025 Project.

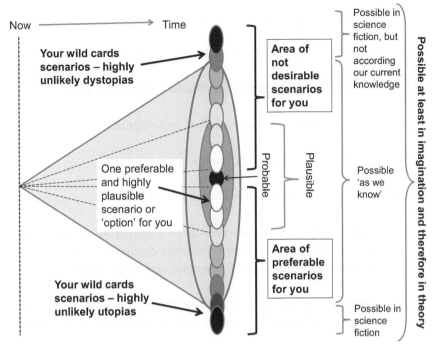

Figure 2.7   Futures cone and wild cards

kind of storyline from the present to the future, including some data and analysis.[74]

However, in practical terms, one could argue that there are usually not that many basic storylines that a scenario tends to follow. No matter what the working method is, the basic scenario's storyline quite often follows one or several of the following:

1.   Everything is fantastic.

2.   Everything goes very badly.

3.   Everything goes on as usual.

4.   One thing works well, but another works badly (e.g. good economy but low happiness, or some gain a lot but some lose a lot).

---

74   Ibid.; Godet, Michel, Monti, Régine, Meunier, Franci and Robelat, Fabrice (2000); Godet (1993).

5.   Everything starts badly at first, but then will see better days.

6.   Everything goes well at first, but then turns out badly.

7.   Society is run by technology or hard economic values.

8.   Society is run by fundamentalism and dogmas.

9.   Society is run by nationalism and protectionism.

10. Society is run by humanistic and liberal values.

11. There is a game change y because of a triggering incident (e.g. one power falls and the other rival takes dominance – or all winners become new losers and all losers become new winners).

12. There is a game change z because of a triggering incident (e.g. one suddenly takes full dominance but the other falls or is exploited).

What are Grand Challenges?

The European Union's Lund Declaration[75] stated in July 2009 that Europe must focus on tackling the *grand challenges* of our time. 'The global community is facing grand challenges. The European Knowledge Society must tackle these through the best analysis, powerful actions and increased resources. Challenges must turn into sustainable solutions in areas such as global warming, tightening supplies of energy, water and food, ageing societies, public health, pandemics and security. It must tackle the overarching challenge of turning Europe into an eco-efficient economy'. According to the Lund Declaration, identifying and responding to grand challenges should involve stakeholders from both public and private sectors, with the European Parliament, Council, and Commission in transparent processes that take into account the global dimension. Furthermore, European research must focus on the grand challenges of our time moving beyond the current rigid thematic approaches. This calls for a new deal among European institutions and Member States, in which European and national instruments are well aligned and cooperation builds on transparency and trust.

---

75 LUND Declaration. Available at: http://www.se2009.eu/polopoly_fs/1.8460!menu/standard/file/lund_declaration_final_version_9_july.pdf

Based on the Lund Declaration, the ISI Community[76] has identified the following 13 specific grand challenges that EU must tackle with the global community:

1. *Global warming*: In the current changing climate, how to better manage (prevention and recovery) the consequence of natural disasters such as flooding, forest fires, hurricanes, and dry area extension, which tend to increase in number but also in intensity?

2. *Tightening supplies of energy, water and food*: In a constrained resource environment, how to improve the efficiency of consumption and the recycling rate while further reducing waste?

3. *Ageing societies*: As the life span of people increases, this raises numerous issues regarding economics, social inclusion and accessibility.

4. *Public health*: How to provide medical care to everyone while minimizing discrimination?

5. *Pandemics*: With the global circulation of people and animals, disease can spread fast. How to improve the prevention and recovery in the case of widespread diseases that potentially have a huge impact on the economy and social stability?

6. *Security*: How to improve the security of European citizens and their goods within and outside Europe?

7. *Smart energy grids*: The aim is to optimize the overall energy consumption while minimizing the risk of congestion and black-out; accommodate renewable sources of energy; handle the charging of devices and provide better information to customers;

8. *Smart environmental information systems*: The aim is to collect real time environmental data to support the location and operation of various renewable energy production centres; the efficient management of intelligent buildings, safer road transport systems

---

76 ISI Contribution to Grand Societal Challenges, by Nicolas, Chuberre (Thales Alenia Space) and Konstantinos Liolis (Space Hellas), on 30 April, 2010. Available at: http://ec.europa.eu/invest-in-research/pdf/download_en/isi_contribution.pdf

and general information made public on environmental risks and hazards;

9.   *Smart systems for transport and mobility*: Intelligent Transport Systems (ITS) will prevent traffic jams by bringing efficiency to mobility through real time management of public and private transport resources, traveller information and decision making tools;

10.   *Smart healthcare systems*: The aim is to reduce the medical costs and improve patient comfort by increasingly providing medical treatment in a domestic environment rather than in hospitals;

11.   *Smart culture and knowledge (content) management systems*: The aim is to develop smart Internet-enabled content management systems in order to help people manage the increased volume of information and archives produced by the rich European culture and knowledge;

12.   *Broadband for all*: The right of each European citizen to access to the Information society without any geographical discrimination, particularly for the new generation networks which will provide extra-broadband capacity for enterprises and citizens, as crucial tools for the economic development and social well-being;

13.   *Smart Security systems*: The need to develop solutions to efficiently address disaster management and external security actions, border and maritime surveillance, critical infrastructure protection and transport security.

The list of the European Union's 13 grand challenges has many similarities with Futurology's, La Prospective's and Futures studies' proactive approaches of mobilizing all people on tackling the greatest challenges facing human kind. Basically one could argue that the EU has started a large scale strategic foresight process, which echoes the principles of Futurology.

3

Strategic Concepts

A skilful leader subdues the enemy's troops without any fighting, he captures their cities without laying siege to them, he overthrows their kingdom without lengthy operations in the field.

Sun Tzu

What is Strategic?

The word *strategic* originates from the military where it refers to military planning, which is concerned with the overall plan and means for achieving a long-term outcome. *It defines the terms and conditions in which the battle is fought on, and whether it should be fought at all.*[1]

'Successful strategy is based upon clearly identifying political goals, assessing one's comparative advantage relative to the enemy, calculating costs and benefits carefully, and examining the risks and rewards of alternative strategies'.[2] Where Carl von Clausewitz once said that the purpose of military strategy is to win the war[3] by destroying the enemy's army and thus compelling him to do our will, Sun Tzu recommends that the best alternative is to attack the enemy's strategy – to convince the enemy that he cannot achieve his aims. This is what he calls winning without fighting. The next best alternative is to attack his alliances and supplies. Destroying the enemy's army ranks third on Sun Tzu's list of preferred strategies for winning a war.[4]

In a hierarchical sense, the strategic level is the third level of military planning or warfare. Above it are the *political goals* or the military's grand

---

1 See Clausewitz (1989): *On War*.
2 Mahnken and Maiolo (2008).
3 The fact that war involves the use of force differentiates it from other forms of competition, such as economic, political and social competition. The fact that war is an instrument that is used to achieve political goals differentiates it from other forms of violence. Ibid. As Bismarck said, when the work of politicians ends, the work of soldiers begins.
4 Ibid., 51; Clausewitz (1989): *On War*.

strategy,[5] and under it is the second level, which is the *operational level*. Their units are organized into formations, comprising a higher level of planning known as the operational use of forces. Operational warfare is thus an intermediate level in which the aim is to convert the strategy (higher level) into *tactics* (lowest level of planning), which is concerned with the conduct of an engagement – how a battle is fought on the front line.[6]

On the one hand, the basic logic of strategy is universal, for the reason that people everywhere across time and space are very much the same is due to their basic nature. On the other hand, 'there is something missing from this style of interpretation, since to understand any war one must grasp its political as well as purely military characteristics.[7] And while the logic of strategy does transcend history and geography, politics are earthbound, the product of specific circumstances, cultures, and institutions'.[8]

Along with military planning, strategic study and planning can be considered one of the central branches of politics and political theory. The roots of strategic studies in political science go back to the work of Niccolo Machiavelli who can be considered as the first modern political strategist and scientist.[9] However, when the concepts of strategy, political power and grand goals are examined in modern political studies, the focus is usually on aspects of moral order, rhetoric, semiotic and justice, rather than on how the concepts can be refined to aid our understanding of the dynamics of political life. Lawrence Freedman argued that this is mainly due to the acknowledged dilemma – in order to go to such ultimate issues in politics, one needs to regard political life through the eyes of the practitioners, which is considered improper in the discipline of political studies.[10]

A third field where strategic planning is seriously practiced, studied and defined is business management.[11] It seems to be the field where most of

---

5   In *The Prince* (2004), Machiavelli gives the very meaning for the concepts political goals and grand strategy of the military, and explains how all other public policy, strategies and operations are subordinate to the strategic political goals of the prince.
6   For example, Kuusisto (2008), Kuosa (2011a).
7   Handel (2000).
8   Fuller (2008).
9   Edward M. Earle considers him as the first modern strategist in his book: *Makers of Modern Strategy* (1962).
10 Freedman (2008).
11 See, for example, Porter, Michael (1980): *Competitive Strategy*. New York, Free Press; Hamel, Gary (1994): The concept of core competence. In: Hamel G. and Heene, A. (eds) *Competence Based Competition*. Chichester, Wiley; Prahalad, C.K. and Hamel, Gary (1990): The core competence of the corporation. *Harvard Business Review*, May–June (1990), 79–91;

the academic writing regarding strategies is taking place with new strategy themes and views constantly emerging through discussions on business management. For instance, in recent years one of the most popular strategy themes has been to adapt Sun Tzu's teachings and war metaphors to certain branches of business, leading to book titles such as *Sun Tzu in Business*, and *Sun Tzu in Marketing* etc.

According to Henry Mintzberg et al.[12] there is a specific school in business strategy studies, which attempts to identify the ontology of strategy work – 'the cognitive school'. Through the work of this school, Mintzberg[13] has outlined the distinction between the two concepts 'strategic planning' and 'strategic thinking':

1.   *Strategic thinking* is about synthesis and it defines options. It involves intuition and creativity to formulate an integrated perspective or vision of where an organization should be heading. It is generally intuitive, experimental and disruptive, and attempts to go beyond what purely logical thinking can inform.

2.   *Strategic planning* is the process of defining a strategy, or direction, and making decisions on allocating resources to pursue this strategy. It is a process of analysis, breaking down a goal or set of intentions into steps, formalizing those steps so that they can be implemented and articulated according to the anticipated consequences or results of each step. It is clearly an activity requiring thinking which is strongly analytical, logical, deductive and pragmatic, in order to ensure that a particular course of action stays on track. It is in clear contrast with strategic thinking.

Joseph Voros[14] has emphasized the need to create a third separate concept from these two aspects of strategy work. When strategic thinking is about exploring options, and strategic planning is about implementing actions, an intermediate level between these two is *strategy development*, the actual process of decision making.

Hamel, Gary and Prahalad, C.K. (1994): *Competing for the Future*. Boston, Harvard Business School Press.

12   Mintzberg, Henry, Ahlstrand, Bruce and Lampel, Joseph (1998): *Strategy Safari: A Guided Tour Through the Wilds of Strategic Management*. New York, The Free Press.

13   Mintzberg (1994).

14   Voros (2003).

Another way to look of business strategy is to analyse its characteristics. Mintzberg et al.[15] have outlined the following five types of business strategies:

1.   plan – a vision of the future, how to get from here to there;

2.   pattern – identifying common de-nominators of historical success;

3.   position – locating successful products in particular markets;

4.   perspective – a company's way of doing things;

5.   plot – a specific operation to beat the competitor.

What is Intelligence?

> *Spies are the most important element in war, because on them depends an army's ability to move.*
>
>   *Sun Tzu*

One specific branch of national strategic foresight is the work of national intelligence agencies. Their work helps with public policy making in regard to national security issues, and in doing so, they operate in all stages of the strategic foresight process that come before the actual strategy part.

There are naturally a lot of different functions and objectives for all intelligence agencies. The key task of national intelligence agencies is usually to inform for example, the police, political decision makers, or the Interior Ministry of the plausible domestic or international risks that require pre-emptive or counter action or at least closer inspection.[16]

Most of the knowledge gained through the work of the intelligence agencies is highly classified. However, some can be freely accessed. To give just a few ideas of the tasks undertaken by the intelligence agencies, I have quoted some open access presentations, which discuss the methodologies used by the

---

15 Mintzberg (1998).
16 See Boggs, Danny J. (1985): When governments forecast. *Futures*, 17 (5), 435–9; Leigh, A. (2003): Thinking ahead: Strategic foresight and government. *Australian. Journal of Public Administration*, 62 (2), 3–10.

Central Intelligence Agency (CIA), the Federal Bureau of Investigation (FBI), and the Russian Foreign Intelligence Service (SVR).

It is well known that in the US the CIA has developed many sophisticated systems for data gathering, analysis and the outlining of potential risk.[17] The systems attempt to focus simultaneously on all forms of patterns (existing/tangible, reasoned/socially constructed and emerging/not yet formed) in the risk environment. In the systems, various types of information are assessed and clustered into patterns according to falsification and abductive reasoning methods,[18] and such patterns are managed so as to gain a broader understanding of the issue. For instance in the CIA's pursuit to identify possible central nodes or figures in terrorist networks, its systems search the subject lines of sent e-mails or internet downloads and connects this information to certain people. Alongside direct espionage and surveillance, the systems also use the information provided by anthropologists observing and interviewing local people in possible crisis hit areas, such as Iran. The stories and jokes that ordinary people tell there are especially important in this approach. In this way, the local silent knowledge (weak signals and emerging issues) at grass root level is gathered into patterns, in order to understand the early changes in public opinion. Certain patterns in common storylines are believed to reveal certain rising phenomena in the social context.[19]

The CIA observes global statistics as well. It has a special interest, for instance, in the demand and supply chains of certain chemicals and equipment which could be considered necessary for the preparation of terrorist action. It has been said that, within this kind of statistical and multi-source information collection and synthesizing, the CIA has been able to expose, for example, a large-scale cocaine poisoning process that took place in Colombia. The poisoned cocaine was intended for sale in the North American market.

Another example of the work currently undertaken by national intelligence agencies, or rather their espionage and counter espionage work, can be found in the news of the FBI's arrest of an espionage ring encompassing 11 Russian spies in the US on 27 June 2010. The espionage ring was an ambitious, long-term effort by the SVR, the successor to the Soviet KGB. The Russian agents had lived as ordinary (married) couples with children, working in ordinary

---

17 C.f. Johnson, Loch K. (2007): *Handbook of Intelligence Studies*. London, Routledge; Holm, Richard L. (2003): *The American Agent: My Life in the CIA*. London, St. Ermins Press.
18 See Peirce's abductive reasoning and Popper's fallibilism from Chapter 5.
19 Russell (2007); CIA (2000, 2006).

jobs, in US cities and suburbs from Seattle to New York for more than a decade. One of the agents was a well-known Peruvian TV reporter and US citizen, whilst another was her husband.

According to Singapore's *Today* and *CNN*,[20] the FBI's counter espionage had caught the spies by monitoring behaviour that included, swapping identical orange bags as the spies brushed past one another in a train station stairwell; sitting with a laptop in a coffee shop while waiting for a Russian agent to drive by in a minivan; and using coded language- 'excuse me, but didn't we meet in Malta in 1999?' – to identify themselves. The FBI then found coded radio messages, coded images on the internet, buried money, the use of invisible ink, and hidden video cameras in hotel rooms. One message intercepted from SVR's headquarters revealed the agents' assignment clearly: 'You were sent to USA for a long-term service trip. Your education, bank accounts, car, house – all these serve one goal: to fulfill your main mission, to search and develop ties in policy-making circles and send intelligence reports to the Centre'. The spies' assignment was particularly focused on gathering information on nuclear weapons, US policy towards Iran, CIA leadership, and congressional politics.

What are Business Intelligence and Corporate Foresight?

Never interrupt your enemy when he is making a mistake.

Napoleon

Business intelligence or corporate foresight can be considered as branches of strategic foresight in the same way as national intelligence work, yet their focus is on market information instead of security information. In that sense, business intelligence and corporate foresight are both sub-areas of strategic foresight's pragmatic foresight, 'Carrying out tomorrows' business better'[21] as can be read in the forthcoming sub-chapter on Strategic foresight.

The task of business intelligence and corporate foresight is to help a corporation's strategic management to get an insight into changes in the market and the strategies of their competitors, it also helps to identify new business fields, and it increases the innovation and self-renewal capacity of the

---

20 *Today*, June 30th 2010, *News*, 'And they thought they knew their neighbours ... '. Available at: http://www.todayonline.com/World/EDC100629-0000179/US-charges-11-with-acting-as-Russian-spies [and] http://edition.cnn.com/2010/CRIME/06/29/russian.spies.pelaez.profile/index.html?eref=igoogle_cnn&fbid=0uXL1FIsCWH)
21 Hamel and Prahalad (2004).

enterprise.[22] Basically the first concept, business intelligence, can be done to aid public policy making too, for instance in establishing new and improved national strategic R&D funded programmes[23] or educational programmes for universities.

The biggest difference between business intelligence and strategic foresight is not necessarily in methods or in the information that is gathered, but instead in the time frame applied and the levels in which it operates. The used time frame in strategic foresight is usually many years, but in business intelligence it is usually much shorter as this is meant to increase the company's competitiveness in a short- or mid-range time. Yet, even the concepts short and mid-range mean quite different things in business and foresight domain. When, for example, mid-range time in foresight means something between three and 15 years, mid-range in business planning may refer to the quarter after this one (three to six months out). Furthermore, business intelligence may be considered to function more in the input, analysis and interpretation levels of market information, and less in prospection, change in thinking and strategy formulation levels of the strategic foresight process.

The other concept, corporate foresight[24] can be considered to be about the same as strategic foresight, except that the concept's focus on the 'corporate' leaves public organizations and NGO's out of its scope and, in the same way as in business intelligence, it has less emphasis on strategy development and planning, and more on the earlier parts of the strategic foresight process.

The core parts of methodologies related to business intelligence and corporate foresight are usually trade secrets and, therefore, classified information in the same way as many core parts of the methodologies of the military and especially the intelligence agencies are kept secret.[25] This means that only an overview can be given to just a few well known and easily accessible business intelligence methodologies, namely to customer and consumer behaviour pattern recognizing methods, which are based on either software or qualitative tools.

---

22 See Brown (2007); Piercy and Giles (1989).
23 See, for example, the National Strategic R&D Funding Programme Work of www.sitra.fi or www.tekes.fi
24 C.f. Ratcliffe, John S. (2006): Challenges for corporate foresight: Towards strategic prospective through scenario thinking. *Foresight*, 8 (1), 39–54.
25 Most US military foresight methods are open source and in most cases US Government willingly present the results of these public foresight activities, though other militaries may keep their methods secret. C.f. Geis (2009); Englebrecht et al. (1996).

One example of a business intelligence service which provides an insight into current changes in the markets, is IBM's and Google's data mining software tools for drawing rising peaks of value or general interest changes from large databases. IBM uses several methods, such as Public Image Monitoring, OmniFind, and Web Fountain,[26] for pinpointing the rise or lowering of discussion topics in internet discussion forums or for drawing the most interesting internet sites from up-to-date download statistics. Google uses its own database, which is collected from its own search engine service, in order to make sense of the changes in topics that people are interested in regionally, nationally or internationally. One of the newest solutions that can be used in business intelligence is based on the use of self-organized maps (SOM), developed by Teuvo Kohonen. SOM is software that analyses large quantities of versatile written material and produces clusters of interrelated concepts and visualized 'neural networks' of the hidden storylines without any human intervention during the process.

Another example of business intelligence of emerging patterns is found in trend analysis from fashion houses or the general clothing industry. Here, we can utilize Naomi Klein's[27] description of the work of trend analysts or cool hunters in fashion houses like Nike and Tommy Hilfiger. According to Klein, such fashion houses have hired signals' detectors who observe and interview especially young avant-garde individuals from marginal groups. They also observe music videos on MTV and hip hop magazines such as Vibe. By young avant-garde individuals from marginal groups Klein refers to, for instance, poor young men in the big cities' black ghettos', or strong figures who hang around basketball courts. They are influencing opinion shapers in their communities. When these people start representing something, using certain colours, styles, patterns, shapes, designs in their community first, their style is believed to be gradually adopted by the entire community, as people are group animals. Later on, the fashion of the ghetto will have an effect on the fashion of the whole country and even international clothing markets.[28] What is fashionable among avant-gardist groups in the spring might be fashion on the national or international level in the following fall. This synthesizing of rational and inductive processes made by the trend detectors, of course, requires very diverse observation work. The company could not trust observations from just one 'ghetto' or the results of just one observation method.[29] There has to be lots

26 IBM uses several methods, such as Public Image Monitoring, OmniFind, Web Fountain.
27 Klein (2001).
28 Gladwell (2000, 3–9).
29 Klein (2001).

of information collected from different sources, which needs to be embedded in the available theories of fashion and group behaviour.

Such trend detectors are used not only within the fashion business. For instance Nokia[30] uses anthropologists for observing people and their lifestyles in for example, parks, streets and shopping malls. The observers are required to identify early information about psychological changes in human behaviour, individual value systems, key drivers of customers – what excites and motivates people and what are the ways that people want to communicate and establish groups? By synthesizing this information at an early stage, there is a better chance of the mobile phone company being prepared for emerging or immerging (declining) consumer needs.[31]

What is Strategic Intelligence?

> *Knowledge of the higher parts of war is acquired only through the study*
> *of history of the wars and battles of the Great Captains.*
>
>   *Napoleon*

Strategic intelligence is strongly linked to strategic foresight, and national business intelligence, but it has clear differences too. In mainstream literature, it has been common to describe strategic intelligence as the collection, process, analysis, and dissemination of information that has a high strategic relevance. More specifically, strategic intelligence has mostly been related to military planning, to national security intelligence, and to the strategic decision making and intelligence of large companies or public policy. It has been used as a concept which is closely related to business strategy, business intelligence, state security and military intelligence, strategic foresight, strategic sourcing, strategic competition observation and analysis, strategic alliances, strategic management, strategic thinking, strategic consulting, and to strategic development or planning.[32]

A broader view of the concept of strategic intelligence can also be taken. We can argue that strategic intelligence should not be considered only as a characteristic of military, state security and corporate or public policy strategies, but as a more general way of managing knowledge. It is an

---

30 Merriden (2001).
31 Merriden (2001).
32 C.f. Russell (2007); Hamel and Prahalad (2004).

umbrella concept for any set of tools, services or consulting that can help us to understand strategically important and complex issues. It may either help us to reveal large, complex or complicated issues or transformations in a more understandable form, or to get the most valid and up-to-date information on time, and it can refer to any procedure which helps us to reveal something that is unseen from plain information alone. In this broader sense we may say that the methods that can be used for obtaining strategic intelligence contain, not only all the methods that will be mentioned in Figure 3.1, but also methods of modelling, simulations, visualizations, art, narrative, semiotics, fractal or statistical mathematics, graphs, metaphors and analogies etc. because these all are in some way able to help express complicated or complex issues in a simplified way.[33] In that sense, we can say that strategic intelligence operates equally strongly in levels one and two of strategic foresight's process as shown in Figure 3.1, and as described in the next chapter.

What is Strategic Foresight?

> Strategic foresight is about producing foreknowledge and strategic options for someone who wants to win a political, military or business battle.
>
> *Kuosa*

Strategic foresight relates to foresight of strategic issues. Namely, it is a process that enhances a person's or organization's ability to understand the emerging risks and opportunities, path-dependencies, drivers, motivations, resources, evolution or co-evolution, and causalities that are linked to alternative decisions, that form the space of possible, plausible, probable or preferred futures paths, so that they can make better informed and prepared decisions on issues, which are 'concerned with the organisation's overall strategic plans and means of achieving its long-term objectives'. In other words, what differentiates strategic foresight from other types of foresight is its ability to help a (large) organization to 'define the terms and conditions in which the "battle" is fought, and whether it should be fought at all'.

Strategic foresight is something which Sun Tzu held in high esteem in his book *The Art of War*[34] – 'Foreknowledge enables a wise general to achieve things

---

33   Kuosa (2011b).
34   Sun Tzu (2004, 59).

beyond the reach of ordinary men'. According to Sun Tzu,[35] before you decide to go to war you must determine all the military conditions as objectively as possible, and in the following order:

1. Which of the two sovereigns has the stronger determination to win?

2. Which of the two generals is more skilful?

3. Which side has advantage of the topography, weather and light conditions?

4. Which side has a stronger discipline?

5. Which army is bigger and better equipped?[36]

6. Which side has better trained officers and men?

7. Which side is more consistent in its punishments and rewards?

Sun Tzu said:

> *after studying these seven conditions I can forecast which side wins and loses (…). If you know the enemy and yourself, you need not to fear the result of a hundred battles. If you know yourself but not the enemy, for every victory gained you will also suffer a defeat. If you know neither the enemy nor yourself, you will lose in every battle.*[37]

---

35 Sun Tzu (2004, 7–17).
36 It has been said that before WWII, Josef Stalin believed only on the number of men and equipments of the army. When someone talked about the power of the Pope, Stalin replied 'how many tanks and guns has the Pope?' When the answer was none, he bluntly stated 'then the Pope has no power'. Then, at the beginning of WWII, Stalin attacked Finland on 30 September 1939 (according Molotov-Ribbentrop pact). Finland had a small poorly equipped army, which even lacked ammunition. Soviet Union had astonishing superiority in numbers of tanks (over a hundred times more), artillery guns and airplanes (both about thirty times more), men (three times more) that they used in the war, and it had better discipline, but Finland had quite absolute superiority in almost all other aspects that Sun Tzu mentions. What happened was that Finland got prevention victories in both 'Stalin's' wars, caused heavy damages to the Red army, and kept its sovereign independency. There were only three capitals of European countries, whom took part in WWII, which were not occupied in the war: London, Moscow and Helsinki. In comparison, Poland, which had much bigger and better equipped army by numbers/on paper could barely resist two weeks of the German and Russian army attacks at the same time.
37 Sun Tzu (2004, 17).

To be able to make such judgements, you need reliable knowledge of the enemy and:

> *this knowledge cannot be elicited from spirits, it cannot be obtained inductively from experience, nor by any deductive calculation. It can only be obtained from other men.*[38] *(...) Hence, spies are the most important element in war, because on them depends an army's ability to move. (...) It is always necessary to begin by finding out the names of the attendants, the aides-de-camp, the door-keepers and guards of the general in command. Our spies must be commissioned to ascertain these.*[39]

According to Sun Tzu, there are five classes of spies, and all of these should be used at the same time:

1.   local inhabitants of the district;

2.   long-term infiltrated spies (inward spies), making use of officials of the enemy;

3.   double agents (converted spies), getting hold of enemy's spies and using them for your own purposes;

4.   doomed spies, for deception, they carry false information and are reported to the enemy;

5.   surveillance spies (surviving spies), are those who have been sent to enemy's camps and who come back with news.[40]

All forms of spies and scouts were highly important factors in the success of the Mongol art of war. Maybe their role was even bigger in Mongol's army than in Sun Tzu's army as discussed by Timothy May (2007).[41] The major strategy of the Chinggis Khan's army was based on strict discipline, highly skilled and extremely mobile archer-riders, good management and administration in all levels, selection of the best generals based on skills

---

38 See the sub-chapter 'What is Intelligence?', in this chapter, where there are examples of current spying and surveillance activities.
39 Sun Tzu (2004, 59–61).
40 Sun Tzu (2004, 59–61).
41 May, Timothy (2007): *The Mongol Art of War: Chinggis Khan and the Mongol Military System.* Barnsley, Pen & Sword Military.

alone, a fair reward system, true utilization of the concurred armies, use of an undefeatable series of tactics and counter tactics, production of rapid messages across the Empire, and the use of the best intelligence and spies of their time. All mobile merchants were practically some form of spy for the Mongols. And finally, Mongol armies had lots of big and small scout units that went in all directions. They were constantly doing scouting work and frightening the enemy and their allies in attacks, giving no rest, causing damage and stealing all possible supplies. And most importantly the scout units were often able to draw in their enemies to chase them, which always ended up in a devastating ambush. Even the big joint knight armies of Germany, Poland, Lithuania and Hungary were destroyed this way to the last man in the battles of Legnica and Muhin in 1241 by a relatively small number of Mongolian archer-rider units.

Hines and Bishop[42] have defined strategic foresight as 'an ability to create a variety of high quality forward views and to apply the emerging insights in organisationally useful ways; for example to detect adverse conditions, guide policy, shape strategy; to explore new markets, products and services'. This is to say that strategic foresight operates in several stages of strategy work. As already discussed in the strategic and foresight chapters, Henry Mintzberg has defined the difference between *strategic thinking* (alternatives and 'what if' questions), and *strategic planning* (breaking the objectives into steps); and Averil Horton[43] has identified the three phases of all (strategic) foresight processes: *input* (its sub-steps: collation and summarization), *foresight* (its sub-steps: translation and interpretation), and *outputs* (its sub-steps: assimilation and evaluation). And Richard Slaughter[44] has defined the four types of methodologies that can be employed in (strategic) foresight in general:

1.   Input methods, which are used to gather intelligence from various sources.

2.   Analytic methods, which are used to analyse and assess factors and their interrelationships, usually as a first step towards deeper and more detailed work.

3.   Paradigmatic methods, which seek to deepen understanding.

---

42   Hines and Bishop (2006).
43   Horton (1999, 6–8).
44   Slaughter (1999, 287).

> 4.   Iterative and exploratory methods, which are used to explore future states and to create 'forward views' so they are 'prospective' in nature.

Based on these three classifications, Joseph Voros[45] has made his *generic foresight process framework*, which attempts to specify the universal levels, functions and methodologies of strategic foresight processes. Voros suggests several methods or methodologies for use in each level. The framework is adapted and modified in Figure 3.1.

Furthermore, Hines and Bishop[46] define the six steps of strategic foresight as follows:

> 1.   Framing contains guidelines regarding attitude, teams, rationale and objectives.

> 2.   Scanning contains guidelines concerning the system, history, context and how to scan information regarding the future of an issue.

> 3.   Forecasting uses the information from scanning and outlines guidelines regarding drivers, uncertainties, tools and alternatives.

> 4.   Visioning contains guidelines focused on thinking through the implications of the forecast and envisioning the desired outcome for the organization.

> 5.   Planning contains guidelines that develop the strategy and options for carrying out the vision.

> 6.   Acting contains guidelines for communicating the results, developing action agendas, and institutionalizing strategic thinking and intelligence systems.

Sohail Inayatullah[47] has identified the six pillars of futures thinking to transform the futures. The pillars are:

---

45 Voros (2003, 14–15).
46 Hines and Bishop (2006).
47 Inayatullah (2008).

1.   Mapping (futures triangle).

2.   Anticipation (futures wheel, emerging issues analysis).

3.   Timing (macrohistorical analysis).

4.   Deepening the futures (Four-Quadrant Model, Causal Layered Analysis).[48]

5.   Creating alternatives (scenarios).

6.   Transforming the future (backcasting, transcend method).

The methodology presented by Inayatullah has many similarities with both the Hines and Bishop's six steps, and the generic strategic foresight framework of Voros, but it is different in many senses too. The objective of the six pillars is to present the pragmatic pro-active process, how one can grasp and change the future with multiple cumulative methods. In that sense it seems like a strategic foresight process, but it does not aim to form a strategy. Instead it aims to find a mutually desirable future objective or image, and it can be said to operate almost only on the foresight and output boxes of Figure 3.1. Specifically, it does not really operate even in all parts of foresight, as it merely operates in Interpretation, Prospection, and Outputs, and not so much in analysis. Hence, six pillars is merely a methodological framework or strategy of participatory foresight or an integrated meta-framework of futures studies,[49] and not so much a strategic foresight framework.

However, the concept *integrated foresight*[50] refers to the idea of combining many foresight approaches together into a systematic process from A–Z. And this approach is common with both participatory and strategic foresight approaches.

The methods, methodologies and questions that are given in Figure 3.1 as examples of working in each of the six levels of the strategic foresight process, originate mainly from the five sources mentioned above. However, there are some additional parts which have not been explained yet, such as Future

---

48   See Wilber (1997, 2000).
49   Kuosa (2009).
50   See Schultz (2006).

```
┌─────────────────────────────────────────────────────────────────────┐
│                              INPUTS                                   │
│ Detect what is happening: Strategic intelligence, data / web mining,  │
│ early warning systems, environmental scanning, emerging issues        │
│ detection, systematic reading, surveys, Delphi, brainstorming         │
│ sessions, spying, surveillance, and simply talking to people.         │
└─────────────────────────────────────────────────────────────────────┘
```

```
┌─────────────────────────────────────────────────────────────────────┐
│                            ANALYSIS                                 F │
│ What seems to be happening: Trend and cross-impact analysis,        O │
│ social network analysis, data management, FSSF, futures triangle,   R │
│ futures wheel, self-organized map, abduction.                       E │
│                          INTERPRETATION                             S │
│ What is really happening: Causal layered analysis, F-Q mapping,     I │
│ SIF-model, systems thinking, macrohistorical analysis, pattern      G │
│ management, synthesis, induction, falsification.                    H │
│                          PROSPECTION                                T │
│ How things could go: Scenarios, visioning, what 'ifs', wild cards,    │
│ visualizing options, normative methods, backcasting, strategic        │
│ thinking.                                                             │
└─────────────────────────────────────────────────────────────────────┘
```

```
┌─────────────────────────────────────────────────────────────────────┐
│                             OUTPUTS                                   │
│ Tangibles: Getting across insight, logic-deductive conclusions,       │
│ range of options created. Intangibles: Changes in thinking,           │
│ perception of the minds involved in strategy work, altering the       │
│ very process of strategy development, new questions.                  │
└─────────────────────────────────────────────────────────────────────┘
```

```
┌─────────────────────────────────────────────────────────────────────┐
│                             STRATEGY                                  │
│       Policy making, strategy development and strategic planning      │
└─────────────────────────────────────────────────────────────────────┘
```

Figure 3.1   Six phases of strategic foresight process[51]

Signals Sense-making Framework (FSSF),[52] which is a specific knowledge management method for sense-making and outlining various forms of input information into six categories, and SIF-model, which is a framework of strategies for inferring knowledge in foresight. Most of the methods in Figure 3.1 are explained in Chapter 6. The other parts in the Figure, which have not been explained yet, are related to inferring methods (abductive, inductive, deductive), intelligence methods, data and pattern management methodologies, and to inferring methods of foresight in general that are discussed in the following chapters.

Figure 3.1 represents a universal strategic foresight process, but it should be acknowledged that strategic foresight can also be practised in several different

---

51   Figure 3.1 is mostly adapted and modified from Figure 3 in Voros (2003); and partly from Figure 1 in Horton (1999); Figure 1 in Habegger (2010); Figure 1 in Costanzo (2010); Inayatullah's (2008) six pillars; Mintzberg (1994); and Slaughter (1995, 1999); and also partly from Major et al. (2001); Voros (2001); and Liebl and Schwarz (2010).

52   Kuosa (2011c).

domains, as listed below,[53] which all have quite different objectives, contexts and epistemologies.

- Pragmatic foresight – 'Carrying out tomorrows' business better'.[54]

- Progressive foresight – 'Going beyond conventional thinking and practices and reformulating processes, products, and services using quite different assumptions'.[55]

- Civilizational foresight – 'Seeking to understand the aspects of the next civilization – the one that lies beyond the current impasse, the prevailing hegemony of techno/industrial/capitalist interests'.[56]

This means that the methods and the emphasis of different levels may vary. In some domains it is possible to have in foresight level's analysis only some quantitative or economic data analysis practices, and in its interpretation only some data clustering and funnelling practises, leaving no room for alternative views, paths and out-of-the-box thinking creation, in its prospection, participatory elements, or changing the thinking in its outputs. However, I would argue that we should not use the word foresight when we talk about such a narrow intelligence process. It is merely a strategic intelligence or business intelligence process or more narrow surveillance process, not foresight. But it can still be a part of the strategic foresight process.

Summary of Foresight and Intelligence Concepts

What is the most remarkable thing in the English language is the number of its descriptive futures-related words. Words such as foresight, forecasting, prospect, probe, insight, foreknowledge, fore-thinking, vision, visionary, pre-, future-oriented, next, coming, intelligence, estimation, long-range, long-run, futures, futures thinking, futurist, futures studies, futures research, and futuring, all refer to different aspects of sense-making knowledge of undeterministic futures. And the words prediction, anticipation, foreseeing, foretelling, prognosis, projection, prophesy, fortune-telling, extrapolation,

---

53 These three domains were listed in Wikipedia of strategic foresight in July 2010. I believe that this list is not exhaustive, but it gives some insight. Furthermore, I think that the current (July 2010) form of definition of strategic foresight given in Wikipedia is not accurate.
54 Hamel and Prahalad (2004).
55 Slaughter (2004, 217).
56 Ibid.

oracle, animalism, shamanism, crystal ball gazing, psychic seeing, all refer to different aspects of getting 'direct' to a more or less deterministic future.

To give a point of reference, in Finnish language there are basically just five real futures words and half of them offer no serious use. (Ennakointi) Fore-thinking 'anticipating + forecasting + scanning + reasoning + being vigilant' or in other words 'scanning to get insight, and being vigilant and ready to adapt and act based on situational awareness' which is a vague word used basically for referring to all things in the undeterministic words group that were mentioned first as there is no other word for these things; (Ennustaminen) Prediction which refers to all things in the last group of words; (Tuleva) coming which refers to one specific future and it cannot be made to form the idea of futures or 'coming(s)'; (Selvännäkeminen) psychic seeing; and (Povaus) fortune-telling which refers only to commercial palm reading that is done by gipsies – other fortune-telling techniques are referred to as predictions as are so many other things that have not been mentioned yet such as astrology statements. Finnish futurists have to manage with just these three to five words when they speak of futures work related things. Other words can be combined with these words, which are quite pre-industrial age terms, and these words can be modified a little bit, but the lack of useful concepts is the fact which makes many things much more difficult for the futurists. When you speak of specific foresight methodology, or intuitive anticipation, or when you speak of being just 'vigilant in vehicular traffic' you use the same word, which is 'ennakointi'. That is why Finnish futurists prefer to use English concepts as often as they can, but the problem is that people outside the futurists community do not usually understand these words.

Besides these three to five real futures words of Finnish language, there are of course a few other words, which can be used with futures work words, but these are either direct loan words from the English language or from other societal contexts. This list contains the words such as estimation, vision, long-time-planning, surveillance, shamanism, extrapolation, projecting and prophesy. From this group basically only estimation has a useful meaning. Hence, to become understood by the general public with Finnish words, one must speak of 'being alert and ready to act', 'giving estimation' or 'predicting', to which one can combine genitives or words such as 'coming', 'next', 'research', 'method', 'image', 'surveillance' or 'long-time'.

The following table describes and differentiates the specific meanings of the twelve most common futures field-related concepts and practises. The idea in this table is to give the three most focal functions, aims or aspects of each concept. Function A is the primary content of a concept, B is secondary, and C is tertiary. Naturally most of the concepts and practices in the table contain many additional aspects and functions that are not mentioned here. Thus, the aim is not to give an exhaustive list of things that each concept stands for, but to give a list of each concept's viable focal points that differentiate it from the other futures field concepts.

Table 3.1   Meaning of concepts in futures domain

Concept	Function A	Function C	Function C
Participatory foresight =	participation	+ alternatives	+ insight
Strategic foresight =	policy orientation	+ insight	+ alternatives
Corporate foresight =	policy orientation	+ visions	+ insight
Intelligence =	insight	+ predictions	+ alternatives
Horizons scanning =	insight	+ assessment	+ participation
Technological assessment =	assessment	+ participation	+ planning
Forecasting =	assessment	+ predictions	+ insight
Predicting =	predictions	+ visions	+ assessment
Long-range planning =	planning	+ assessment	+ policy orientation
Scenarios =	alternatives	+ planning	+ visions
Futures studies =	visions	+ pro-activity	+ alternatives
Futurology =	pro-activity	+ visions	+ planning

4

Evolutionary Concepts

The unpredictable and the predetermined unfold together to make everything the way it is. It's how nature creates itself, on every scale, the snowflake and the snowstorm.

Tom Sheppard

This chapter introduces evolutionary and systemic concepts for showing the nature of the complex and co-evolutive 'game situations' which must be dealt with by strategic foresight projects. All that knowledge is needed in contemporary strategic foresight, in order to obtain good situational awareness, as discussed in previous chapters.

What is Evolution and Co-evolution?

Biological evolution is a process through which species change progressively over a long period of time that is caused by a combination of natural selection, a process in which there is differential survival and/or reproduction of organisms that differ in one or more inherited traits, by genetic drift, a process in which there are random changes to the proportions of two or more inherited traits within a population, by quite random and rare genetic mutation or genetic recombination, and by spontaneous 'internal self-renewal' caused by self-organization and emergence of order.[1]

The evolution of a social organization or *cultural evolution* is quite different from the evolution of a biological organization as there are no genes at the base of it and it is more an outcome of social agreements, path-dependence and learning. On the other hand the base of a social organization can be seen analogically as a *meme,* which is something similar to a *gene.* When biological genes transmit biological information, memes can be said to transmit idea and belief information. According to the developer of the meme theory Richard

---

1   C.f. Kauffman (1995, 2000, 2003).

Dawkins,[2] a meme is the basic unit of imitating and it carries a certain social idea, symbol or practice. It can be transmitted from one mind to another through writing, speech, gestures, rituals or other imitable phenomena, and it constantly goes through a process of natural selection in cultural evolution.

When biological evolution refers to the progressive change of one species over a long period of time, co-evolution is the long-term change that takes place between interrelated species or entities in an ecosystem. To go back to a social context, here the term co-evolution means the simultaneous co-lateral transformation of the entire social ecosystem. A social ecosystem may contain a few or many strongly interconnected agents that can be either economic, socio-cultural, public or private, or all of these at the same time. Basically, alongside the alteration of autopoiesis, autocatalysis, and dynamical types of evolving, a social co-evolutionary system can be characterized to evolve as a complex adaptive system or complex evolving system, as discussed in Chapter 15. Nevertheless, in order to be able to use the concept of co-evolution in any context, the affecting and effecting between the agents of an ecosystem must be two-way and it needs to happen in a long enough time span. According to complexity researcher Eve Mitleton-Kelly, if such interaction is just short-term, the type of change is merely a matter of adaptation rather than co-evolution.[3] The system which functions in a co-evolutionary situation is further discussed in Chapter 15.

What is Complexity?

The word complexity originates from the Latin word *complexio*, which means assembly, embrace or containing. *Complexity theory* seeks to understand how organization and stability can arise from the interactions of many agents according a few simple rules. In other words; how order emerges out of chaos.[4] The emergence of order from chaotic material and a chemical world is a vital precondition for the emergence of all life forms. Hence, complexity theory is at the deep roots of both biology, and social and organizational studies which are basically the two sides of the same coin.

When we talk about complexity, it is very important to differentiate the meaning of the concept complex from concepts complicated and simple.

---

2   Dawkins (1989).
3   Mitleton-Kelly (2003, 29–32).
4   Kauffman (1993).

Many things such as a living leaf appear simple to us, but are revealed to be extremely complex when examined closely. Others seem complex at first glance, but can be described simply if we have enough time and knowledge to study it. If a system consisting of a huge number of components can be given a complete description in terms of its individual constituents, it should be described as a complicated system instead of complex. Things like jumbo jets or computers are complicated, as we do not expect them to evolve in time. In complexity the interaction between the different constituents of the system and the interaction between the system and its environment are of such a nature that the system as a whole cannot be fully understood simply by analysing its components. Moreover, these relationships are not fixed, but shift and change, often as a result of self-organization. The interactions in complexity do not need to be physical, they can also be based purely on the transference of information as can be seen in the autopoiesis type of self-renewal. Complex systems are usually associated with living things that have dense non-linear and often multidimensional interactions with their neighbours and they are bound to historicity, which means that they change and evolve in time such as a bacterium or a natural language.[5] Therefore complex systems cannot be studied scientifically by breaking them down into parts for analysis.[6] Breaking down a complex system would kill the system, like in the story in which the king wanted to immediately get all the gold from the golden egg laying hen, but after opening the hen's body the king's servant did not find any gold at all.

From a historical point of view, it can be said that even though the complexity study is a quite new discipline, the main themes of complexity have been studied by physicists, chemists and mathematicians for over a hundred years, and these scientists have evolved a toolkit of concepts and techniques to which the complexity theory has added only a handful of new items.[7] The biggest item of those added may be computer modelling to find the patterns within complexity which reveal the complex system in motion and in great detail. During the 1980s, more and more attempts to gather and merge the contribution of various disciplines into one unified theory of complexity started to emerge. These endeavours established both the new science of complexity and the chaos theory as its neighbouring science. In the 1990s, the union between complexity science and evolution biology,

---

5   See the discussion of functions of Complex adaptive systems and complex evolving systems in
    Chapter 15. See also the U-curve of complexity from Figure 4.2.
6   Cilliers (1998, viii–ix, 2–4).
7   Ball (2004, 3–5).

biochemistry, computer simulations including cellular automata, and social sciences started to establish new sciences of life and bioinformatics, and new theories of organizational complexity,[8] which will be discussed from various angles in the coming sub-chapters.

What is Conservative Self-organization and Autocatalysis?

The axis of systemic self-renewal of any social, biological or mechanical system is defined in Figure 4.1. The axis starts from stable, dead 'systems' that are in full thermal equilibrium like a cold stone, where there is no energy consumption or flows, no velocities or accelerations of material particles, no information flows, and thus no life or self-renewal. Such full stability is followed by conservative self-organization, which means the phase transition of reversible structures in thermal equilibrium or near it, such as the ice water in an ice cube, which can revert to water or steam and back to ice if the temperature is changed

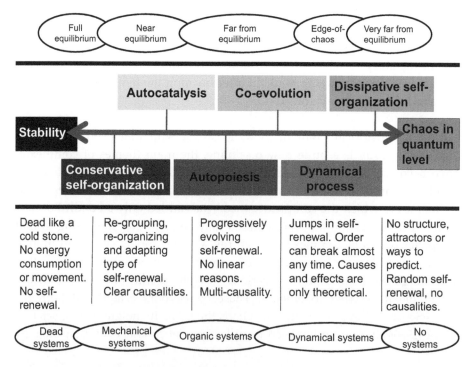

Figure 4.1   Axis of systemic self-renewal

8   C.f. Kauffman (2007, 2003, 2000, 1995); Mitleton-Kelly (2003); Cilliers (1998).

back and forth.[9] An entity, which goes through this kind of conservative self-organization process achieves some form of modest self-renewal which means that it is not as dead as a fully stable entity, and can be called an isolated or closed system. In the axis of Figure 4.1 such 'modest' conservative self-organization is followed by 'augmented' conservative self-organization in which an entity consumes very little energy in its re-organizations and adaptations such as the process of computers' memory saving functions or the workings of a pendulum, but it is still a closed system. This means that 'augmented' conservative self-organization is in a thermodynamical sense nearer equilibrium instead of being in full equilibrium. Both the 'augmented' and 'modest' conservative self-organizations belong to the class of mechanical systems, which have clear causalities and are therefore fully predictable. Such mechanical systems are most likely closed systems that undergo exogenously oriented phase transition, shape transition, or complex branching of growing colony types of transformations.[10]

Social systems are always organically or dynamically open systems, and never fully stable or only conservatively self-organizing as the actors of a social ecosystem are alive, unless we speak of dead or past systems such as the Soviet Union. However, if we observe the system from afar, meaning that we look only at the top level of social organization, we may say that a certain 'alive' system functions, self-renews and organizes its structures as a mechanical system. From that top level a social organization may seem to have a clear homogenous or well-defined hierarchical and even predictable structure, and a closed, or open, causal process with simple input, throughput and output functions. To give an example of such phenomenon in a social context, a queue to a service desk, or distributing an order in a hierarchical chain of command, may seem a form of conservative self-organization. To give an example of zooming up and down, our entire ecosystem on earth is both an organically and dynamically open system at local level, but at the same time, it is only a small part of our whole solar system, which is a 'mechanical' and therefore 'less open system'[11] at its own level, despite the nature of it parts.

---

9   Nicolis and Prigogine (1989, 14, 50–52) give an example of growth of snow crystals, which can revert to water or steam if the temperature is changed back and forth. The same water can change back to snow crystals in later water cycles as well.

10 Ball (2004, 90–160).

11 The solar system is also an open system. It is an interactive part of a larger system, called the Milky Way Galaxy, and more than 90 percent of our solar system's momentum comes from galactic rotation. Our galaxy is also an open system, as it interacts with other galaxies. Thankfully, for the moment, most of this interaction is benign, but our galaxy will collide with the Andromeda Galaxy in the future, probably resulting in numerous collisions of stars and planets – but not within our lifetime. The entire Universe may be a totally closed system,

The next level in the axis of systemic self-renewal is *autocatalysis* or *self-catalysis*, which is located partly in the domain of mechanical systems and partly in organic systems. It derives from the Greek word *autos* = self, and *catalysis*, which refers to an increase in the rate of a given reaction or transformation. In a biological sense autocatalysis refers to self-production or autonomous replication, which is the result of an autocatalytic cycle in which genetic material is replicated by the intervention of specific proteins, themselves synthesized through the instructions contained in the genetic material. Such self-production is the fundamental property of all biological life.[12] A nuclear explosion, albeit different from biological gene-based replication, is probably one of the most commonly known autocatalytic processes. According to Jeff Vézina,[13] the self-catalytic component is vital in understanding how a network becomes creative. It refers to the ability of a system to develop creative shortcuts in order to grow. As the network dynamics for several phenomena are the same at various levels, we can comprehend the dynamics of a network of neurons in ants or the human brain using the same concepts. The network of neurons in the brain is self-catalytic as it is constantly re-organizing itself using 'facilitating' neurons. By organizing themselves through networks, neurons facilitate the reaction of other neurons, ants facilitate the organization of the ant colony, and humans facilitate personal and collective growth.

In a social context autocatalysis refers to transformation, which can be considered as an effect of a single cause such as the push of a driver, a trend or an idea. Autocatalytic process usually has a certain type of dominating centre, the idea or the order, as a gene or mitochondria operate as local 'pushing agents' in biology. An example of a social autocatalysis could be a political decision to significantly increase the maintenance budget allocated to a certain area's railways and roads that is taken from the national budget, which naturally gives a direct push to the transportation cluster in that particular area, plus an additional indirect push to the whole economy in that area. Hence, social autocatalysis is understood as a macro-level phenomenon and process that is more likely caused top-down, or from other external clear effects. On the other hand, autocatalysis may be a fractal process, which means that we may have autocatalytic processes in all levels of the social world. In that sense autocatalysis may be the form of a local and short-term function, the process

---

though there are mathematicians who argue that point. To go even further, actually the solar system, galaxies and the Universe can be described as mechanical systems only if we observe them from human size perspective. From Universal perspective they generate attractors, strange attractors, and they co-evolve and thus behave dynamically.

12 Nicolis and Prigogine (1989, 18).
13 Vézina (2009, 110).

of spreading an idea or meme in the immediate interaction of two or more people. That local interaction is connected to a larger constructivist process, which progressively creates meanings or language in a larger social context, is discussed next.

What is Autopoiesis and Self-renewal?

To go further along the axis, the mid-point of systemic complexity is reached in the concept of *autopoiesis*. When autocatalysis was understood as a short-term process of spreading an order, idea or meme in immediate interaction, either with a top-down push or local discussion, autopoiesis is understood as a larger and longer term endogenous or grass-root level pull to a systemic transformation. Thus, autopoiesis is an internal self-renewal process within a system, but it also defines the existence of the system. Basically it makes one otherwise 'loose' entity an autonomous agent that can define its own laws and is able to pursue to its own good ends, so to speak.[14] A social autopoietic system is more complex and therefore more 'alive' than a system which goes through just an autocatalytic process, which could be defined as a sub-set of larger autopoiesis or social construction of language and meanings.

The word autopoiesis originates from the Greek words *autos* = self, and *poiein* = to create, to do, to produce, to maintain existence, to do again, to conceptualize. The concept of autopoiesis was originally coined in the early 1970s by Chilean biologists Humberto Maturana and Francisco Varela,[15] who defined autopoiesis as follows:

> Being aware that living beings are autonomous unities helps to show how their autonomy – usually seen as mysterious and elusive – becomes explicit, for we realize that what defines them as unities is their autopoietic organization, and it is in this autopoietic organization that they become real and specify themselves at the same time.

In other words all autonomous unities have one thing in common which is life and this life is organized in autopoiesis. According to Maturana and Varela[16] autopoiesis comes from certain relations that we can outline and view more easily on the cellular level, where molecular components of a cellular autopoietic

---

14 Maturana and Varela (1992, 47–8).
15 Ibid.
16 Maturana and Varela (1992, 43–6).

unity must be dynamically related in a network of on-going interactions. The fact that this relation is dynamical instead of mechanical, interestingly, produces components, which make up the network of transformations that produce them.

Some of these components form a boundary such as a cell membrane, a limit to this network of transformations. This membrane is not only limited to the system's transformation network's extension, but it also participates in this network. If cell did not have this spatial arrangement, cell metabolism would disintegrate in a molecular mess that would spread out all over and would not constitute a discrete unity such as a cell.

Hence, autopoiesis is at the same time about self-production, self-maintenance, self-renewal, and self-definition of the existence of the domain of the system. And it is related to a more autocatalysis type of *reproduction*, which refers to the process where a cell originates from another similar cell through division. In autopoiesis the 'creation of internal understanding' or self-definition of the system's domain is done in many loops of transfers of information between the system's locally interconnected elements.

As explained in the complexity part, a complex system can evolve either through physical transfer or transfer of information, or a combination of both. Autopoiesis contains both, but it is more a process of transfer of information in dense communication between the system's immediate neighbours. Usually the internal elements in an autopoietic system are ignorant of the behaviour of the system as a whole, and they respond only to information that is available to them locally. Long-range interactions are possible too, but since the interactions in a local system are usually dense, and as messages can be easily altered in a number of ways in multi-step communication, the practical constraints usually force an autopoietic system to rely on as few steps as possible in its communication.[17] This kind of local communication defines the system's members' mutual objectives, division of labour, and particularly in a case of open social systems such as natural language, it somehow excludes the areas that do not belong to the system. Hence, an autopoietic system reproduces its life systems, understanding and communication in a network interaction of its internal interconnected elements. It acts as an autonomous entity, which separates itself from its surrounding environment and functions.

---

17 Cilliers (1998, 4–5).

Originally the concept of autopoiesis was coined to describe the capacity of cells for self-reproduction,[18] but quite soon it was understood that most autonomous systems do much of their self-renewal through principles that can be called autopoiesis. Both living biological and living social organizations mostly renew themselves through constantly running autopoiesis, but in comparison to biological organizations, social organizations are able to select faster and more open and dynamical ways of self-renewal, as is discussed in the following chapters.

German sociologist Niklas Luhmann is considered to be the founder of autopoiesis in social systems. According to Luhmann,[19] a society is a co-evolutive and indeterministic system, which has no dominating centres.[20] The society contains several simultaneous autopoietic systems such as economy, politics, culture, language, and religion, which all have only one function. The whole society self-organizes itself through interactions between these function systems. The complexity may emerge in the function systems/sub-systems of society only if communication in the society sets boundaries and rules that define them as sub-systems. The actual process of complexity increases following the principles of autopoiesis where all elements of a system are reproduced in a communicating network interaction of the same kind of elements. Such autopoiesis is a functionally isolated self-referring process, which means that all operations in the system are explained by referring first to something outside its own sub-system, and then referring back to its own operations. Hence, for Luhmann, autopoiesis in society is a way to describe how the sub-systems are strongly dependent of the combined performance of the other sub-systems and are therefore co-evolutive and self-referring, to describe how sub-systems are self-reproducing in such autopoiesis, and to explain how these processes together increase the overall complexity and interdependency of the society. In other words, Luhmann's theory explains how a society defines itself, how it renews and reproduces itself through communication, how it does certain work cycles, does multiple feedback loops, how it adapts to evolution, and how it establishes internal gating mechanisms. Economy is an example of autopoietic organization in a society, which means that everything in the society can be explained and defined through the concepts and principles of the economy.[21]

---

18 Maturana and Varela (1992, 43–52).
19 Luhmann (1990a, 1990b).
20 Of course countries, companies and even cultural sectors have their leaders, but this sentence doesn't refer to that kind of affective power. Here, the phrase 'dominating centre' refers to the relationships between the simultaneous autopoietic systems – as none of them really dominates the others in societal co-evolution.
21 Ibid.

Luhmann published his theory in 1990 in his book *Ökologische Kommukation*, just a few years after the discoveries of Maturana and Varela were published.

What should be noted here is the fact that Finnish futurist Pentti Malaska had come pretty much to the same conclusions as Luhmann, at the same time as Luhmann, without knowing his work. Malaska was talking about autopoietic + co-evolutive self-renewal of the society and economy particularly in his synchronic threefold model, but he didn't ever use the concept of autopoiesis. This came out in 2007 when I asked Malaska to comment on my article manuscript.[22] When he read the part in which I discussed the difference and similarities between his, Brian W. Arthur's[23] and Niklas Luhman's theories, Malaska became surprised by the similarities between the theories and asked me to send him the whole Luhman's work which he considered to be extremely interesting. Hence, Malaska doesn't use the concept autopoiesis in his theories, but instead he speaks about the process of societal transition, diachronic model of transformation of societies, or the synchronic threefold model of society.[24] Yet, neither does Brian W. Arthur use the concept of autopoiesis in his 'economical transition' theory, which is highly similar to Malaska's theory of 'economical transition'. Malaska appears to understand the social emergence pretty much in the same way as Arthur – meaning that in both theories there are new seeds of transformation, which cluster and then start to change the entire market logic through local interactions, increasing returns and positive or negative feedback loops, if the time is favourable to it. However, Malaska's point of view regarding path-dependence deviates from Arthur's, as Malaska emphasizes the social transformation's necessity to have alternating extensive, intensive, and regenerative growth periods, which also go partly in parallel. Nevertheless, one could argue that all three futurists came to similar conclusions regarding the autopoiesis + co-evolution logic of the society's transformation, and pretty much in the same year, but only Luhmann named the process after the biological concept of autopoiesis, which has become the best known of all.

To go back to the axis of systemic self-renewal, the next step away from stability, which has been partly discussed already, is co-evolution. Autopoiesis is a process which defines the character and borders of one particular entity or system, co-evolution is a process which defines the character and borders of the whole ecosystem which contains many entities or autonomous and autopoietic systems that are both aiding and competing with all the other

---

22 Kuosa (2007).
23 Arthur (1990).
24 Malaska (1989, 1991); Kuosa (2005).

members of the ecosystem at the same time. As the self-renewal in autopoiesis is based on endogenous communication and feedback loops, the self-renewal in co-evolution is created by the simultaneous adaptation and effecting process in a changing ecosystem. The effects and communication in co-evolution is multi-causal and such multi-causality in it is generated both exogenously and endogenously. In the sense of the system's evolutionary ability to go through rapid self-renewals, and its abilities to produce new life forms (propagate to adjacent ecological niches), co-evolution has many characteristics of the edge-of-chaos where most of the new life forms are generated.[25]

What is Open System and Dynamical Process?

By definition, open system means a system, which continuously interacts with its environment. The interaction can take the form of information, energy, or material transfers into or out of the system boundary. Open system is in contrast with closed and isolated systems, that don't continuously interact with their environment as explained in the examples of the previous sub-chapter. Organic and dynamical systems are most likely open, but mechanical systems can be open as well.

What differentiates dynamical systems from other types of open systems is the increased sensitivity to initial conditions, which can lead to occasional and quite unpredictable fluctuations. All non-linear dynamical systems are unpredictable due in part to occasionally occurring endogenous sensitivity to initial conditions, and due to their generation of strange attractors, which lead to trajectories or orbits that converge to chaotic regions. However, in most cases such chaotic behaviour, sudden fluctuations or the dissipative self-organizations, are found only in a subset of the phase space of a dynamical system. In other words, usually only local chaotic processes exist inside a system which is most of the time dynamical in an evolving way.

As discussed in the autopoiesis chapter, certain processes in any living system must be dynamical in order to provide the networks of transformation inside the system. Without such dynamical fluctuations a system could not obtain its necessary metabolism and self-renewal. On the other hand, in order to provide an internal gating mechanism that guarantees the resilient systemic structure, some of the processes of any living system must be autocatalytic and mechanical in their type at the same time.

---

25 Kauffman (2000).

The difference between a dynamical process and dynamical system is basically in the duration. A system by definition has to be quite long-term as it must have a structure, which evolves in time, but a process can be either a short-term or long-term event. Basically a process can be dynamical in an evolving way or in a chaotic or dissipative way. Being dynamical in a steady way refers to local dynamical processes that are binding to a larger co-evolutive or autopoietic system where the dynamics cannot make radical changes to the whole system. On the contrary, a dynamical process must have the following properties in order to be defined as fully chaotic: It must be constantly sensitive to initial conditions, it must be topologically mixing, and its periodic orbits must be dense.[26] That kind of process can obtain sudden jumps, collapse and emergence in self-renewal and is discussed in more detail in the next sub-chapter.

Alongside strange attractors, occasional sensitivity to initial conditions, high level of complexity, living at the edge-of-chaos,[27] and relatively high energy consumption, are other characteristics that are linked to dynamical systems which are called *self-organized criticality*. The term refers to the discovery of many types of composite systems that naturally evolve to a critical state in which simple local interactions can spontaneously start a chain reaction that can affect any number of elements in the system.

Self-organized criticality is a mechanism that logically describes how a large organization can spontaneously self-organize complexity and triggering points from simple local interactions inside its systemic structure. Consequently, global features of the system cannot be understood by analysing the parts separately as the behaviour is scale invariant. As discovered, emerging criticality does not depend on the finely-tuned details of a system as variable parameters in the model can be changed widely without affecting the emergence of critical behaviour. That mechanism was discovered and put forward by Per Bak, Chao Tang and Kurt Wiesenfeld (BTW) in 1987. They discovered self-organized criticality functions especially in dynamical systems have a critical triggering point as an attractor,[28] but this does not only function in dynamical systems. The most well-known example of the mechanism is presented in BTW's metaphorical visualization of a pile of sand on which new sand grains were being slowly sprinkled to cause 'avalanches'. That initial experimental work tended to focus on examining the logic of real avalanches, but it showcased

---

26 Hasselblatt and Anatole (2003).
27 Kauffman (1995).
28 Bak, Chao and Wiesenfeld (1987); Bak and Chen (1991, 26).

after thousands of repetitions the random nature of emergence of triggering points in a large system.

The self-organized criticality has been explained here as it has much value in explaining social phenomena and our abilities to predict some events. Usually, when we have to explain, for example, the crash of the stock market, we try to find a number of factors that combined to cause it, often with the hope of showing that the chances of the same combination of factors occurring again are slim. This kind of analysis, however, is the result of trying to explain the behaviour of large complex systems by extrapolating from the behaviour of small, simple systems. Unfortunately this extrapolation fails. Thus, any analysis that ignores the possibility of self-organizing critical behaviour by a complex system will be seriously lacking in explanation power.[29]

What is Dissipative Self-organization and Emergence?

Dissipative self-organization means almost the same as emergence. When the word self-organization means spontaneous emergence of order, for example, molecules may spontaneously organize themselves into right-handed and left-handed cells, the word emergence refers to the types of self-organization which creates the new order.[30] Furthermore, dissipative self-organization refers to a phase transition, where order or systemic structures are suddenly destroyed and reshaped into a new form through a cascade of bifurcations or through phase transition.[31] In such processes, the macroscopic patterns emerge from the complex non-linear cooperation of microscopic elements when the energetic interaction between the system and its environment reaches a critical value.[32]

Dissipative systems give rise to irreversible processes and structures (very) far-from-thermal-equilibrium. They have open ways to exchange energy, matter, or information with their environment, and which – when pushed far-from-equilibrium (driven to crisis point) – create new structures and order.[33]

The phenomenon of break or dissipation of an old structure and creation of a new structure through a cascade of bifurcations was first discovered by the Russian chemist Ilya Prigogine (1917–2003), who published his revolutionary

---

29 Cilliers (1998, 96).
30 Kauffman (1995, 1993).
31 Nicolis and Prigogine (1989, 50–52).
32 Nicolis and Prigogine (1989, 51–2); Mitleton-Kelly (2003, 41); Mainzer (1996, 4).
33 Nicolis and Prigogine (1989, 50–52.)

discoveries in 1967, and 10 years later received a Nobel Prize in chemistry for his discovery. Prigogine suggests that systems are capable of self-organization without any external control.[34] At the time of the discovery, this marked a radical departure from general systems theory, and the emergence of a new open, and dissipative or dynamic systems theory. Prigogine showed that self-organization was not in fact an exception, but on the contrary quite a common systemic characteristic for non-equilibrium systems. Once the driving force of a non-equilibrium system is increased beyond a bifurcation point, it can force the system into a dissipative state, which produces a cascade of bifurcations that switch the system to another steady state. In other words, when a critical point is reached, a bifurcation offers two equivalent choices of steady state. A critical phase transition that leads to a novel non-equilibrium steady state may include many branching points, and at each point the options are well-defined but the choice is determined by random fluctuations.[35]

The role of dissipative self-organization in Figure 4.1 marks the stage in the axis of self-renewal, which is between a dynamical process, and total chaos without any structure. There is much less order in dissipative self-organization in comparison to dynamical process, but much more order in comparison to chaos in local or quantum level.

What is Chaos Theory and Chaos in Quantum and Macro-level?

> *Science is born when errors, failures and unpleasant surprises prompt us to look a little closer at reality.*
>
> *René Thom*

Etymologically speaking, the word chaos derives from an ancient Greek verb 'to gape wide open, to yawn, to open'. It is an opening, an ability for change, just as occurs in synchronicity.[36] Chaos theory describes non-linear dynamics based on the iteration of either a mathematical algorithm or a set of simple rules of interaction, both of which can give rise to extraordinarily intricate behaviour such as the intricate beauty of fractals or the turbulence of a river.[37] Whereas complexity theory attempts to explain how order emerges out of chaos, chaos theory focuses on the opposite logic of the same phenomena, how ever-shifting

---

34 See, for example, Nicolis and Prigogine (1989); Prigogine and Stengers (1984).
35 Nicolis and Prigogine (1989, 72).
36 Vézina (2009, 108).
37 Mitleton-Kelly (2003, 43).

deterministic systems rapidly cease to be precisely predictable even if their initial conditions are known in great detail. In other words, how chaos emerges out of deterministic linearity, or how total randomness suddenly emerges out of total predictability.[38] One of the earliest pioneers of the chaos theory was Edward Lorenz whose interest in chaos came about accidentally through his work on computer-based weather prediction in 1961. Lorenz wanted to see a sequence of weather prediction data again and to save time he started the simulation in the middle of its course. To his surprise the weather that the machine began to predict was completely different from the weather calculated before. As a conclusion of the work, Lorenz[39] had discovered that small changes in the initial conditions produced large changes in the long-term outcome of the weather, and that such chaos is not just a system malfunction but its normal state. Thus, weather and many other systems, such as the market economy or stock markets, are sensitive to initial conditions and thus are constantly changing dynamical systems.

Another important pioneer of chaos theory was Benoit Mandelbrot (1977) who discovered the fractal nature of many structures and systems. The theory of fractals means that inside a system the same geometric shape can be found within the system at different levels, that is, that the patterns of a system repeat themselves at the micro level, at the macro level, and in all levels between. The most well-known examples of fractals from nature are snowflakes, river networks and coastlines. Thus, chaotic systems can also be bound which means that they can have clearly defined structures as the fractals show (Ibid.). As the outcomes of chaotic systems are totally indeterministic, at least in quantum level, due to sensitivity to the initial conditions, the branch of mathematics which deals with the long-term qualitative behaviour of such (hyperbolic) dynamical systems does not attempt to answer precisely which points converge on the orbit towards stable manifold or which points diverge from it. It merely attempts to answer questions like: 'Will the dynamic system settle down to a steady state in the long term and, if so, what are the possible attractors?'

Alongside sensitivity to initial conditions and the fractal nature of order, the discovery and explanation of the *attractors* in systems has been one of the key achievements of chaos theory. An attractor itself is a centre mass or a point which starts to generate certain types of trajectories or orbits to a system. When enough time has passed, the trajectories around the attractors remain close even if slightly disturbed. In physics, there are three types of attractors.

---

38 For example, Strogatz (1994); Waldrop (1992).
39 Lorenz (1963).

Mechanical systems contain two simple types of attractors, which are the fixed point and the limit cycle. A *fixed point* attractor is an easily predictable point that a mechanical system evolves towards, such as the final states of a falling pebble or a damped pendulum. Furthermore, a pendulum is a subject to friction forces, tending towards an imaginary point located at the centre of a surface, and will eventually stop at this point.[40] The other type of attractor of a predictable mechanical system is a *limit cycle*, which is a periodic orbit of the system that is isolated and which oscillates without end. In a limit cycle's ideal pendulum, each point of a periodic orbit is close to another point that belongs to a different periodic orbit, which can generate several types of topographical organizations.

The third type of attractor in physics is a fractal attractor, more commonly referred to as a *strange attractor*. It models the behaviour of non-linear complex, dynamical systems such as economy, weather, or the fast flow of a river that hitherto appeared totally unpredictable. Strange attractors continually exchange energy with the environment, they are genuinely open-ended, and they contain complex patterns and dynamism, which is hard to describe, visualize and predict. A strange attractor allows us to understand how a form of nature can be repeated while displaying creative variation.[41] Basically, strange attractor gives the scientific explanation to the idea that you can never cross the same river twice, as the river is constantly changing in local level, but on the bigger scale we can still call it the same river.

The visual map of a strange attractor and its evolution over time arose from an artificial computer model in so called phase space, which generated a moving system's chaotic motion from plain numbers. The *Lorenz attractor* which explains the unpredictability of the weather is 'perhaps one of the best-known chaotic system diagrams of strange attractor, probably because not only was it one of the first, but it is one of the most complex and as such gives rise to a very interesting pattern which looks like the wings of a butterfly.[42]

The ability to reveal a strange attractor in a system allows us to observe the boundaries that constrain the seemingly unpredictable behaviour of complex systems. In other words, such understanding helps us to keep chaos within certain limits. The discovery of strange attractor in chaos theory tells us that on a bigger scale, an observable order emerges even though at the local quantum

---

40 Vézina (2009, 101–3).
41 Ibid.
42 Mandelbrot (1977).

level, everything appears chaotic.[43] This effect can be seen, for instance, when atmospheric disturbances invariably produce, for example, two-point ice needles with random variations at their centre.[44]

Regarding the axis of self-renewal in Figure 4.1 all these new discoveries of strange attractors are merely explaining the principles that make a system dynamical. The extreme case of being dynamical is chaos in quantum level, which refers to the total unpredictability of random fluctuations, which are triggered by changes to small to be observed in local interactions. There is some order, structure and therefore system in dynamical process and even in dissipative self-organization or in chaos in macro-level, but none in chaos in local or quantum level.

What is Far-from-equilibrium and Laws of Thermodynamics?

Thermal equilibrium is a state in which the velocities and the accelerations of all the material points of a system are equal to zero. In equilibrium the system is in a state of rest.[45] In far from equilibrium conditions, non-linear relationships prevail, and a system becomes inordinately sensitive to external influence. In far-from-equilibrium conditions we find that very small perturbations or fluctuations can become amplified into gigantic, structure-breaking waves, which is in contradiction to mechanical systems which are usually near equilibrium, as already discussed.[46]

The laws of thermodynamics determine the general foundations of all transformations of any mechanical, organic, open or dynamical systems. However, they can only provide a prescription for the start and end points, and remain silent on the processes that take place in-between. The first law of Thermodynamics is often called the *Law of Conservation of Energy*. This law suggests that energy can be transferred from one system to another in many forms. However, it cannot be *created* nor *destroyed*. Thus, the total amount of energy available in the universe is constant. The second law of thermodynamics

---

43 C.f. Vézina (2009, 101–3).
44 According to meteorologist John P. Geis, if the atmosphere is cold enough, it will produce ice needles (sometimes called 'diamond dust'); these are 'snowflakes' that can fall on a very cold day without visible moisture. The most common shape of these crystals is linear – a single linear hexagonal bar in the shape of a needle, hence the name. These are very different from 'needle ice', which forms on the ground.
45 Nicolis and Prigogine (1989, 54–6).
46 Mitleton-Kelly (2003, 32–7).

states that heat can never pass spontaneously from a colder to a hotter body. As a result, natural processes that involve energy transfer must have one direction, and all natural processes are irreversible. This law also predicts that the *entropy* of an isolated system always increases with time. Entropy is the measure of the disorder or randomness of energy and matter in a system. Because of the second law of thermodynamics, both energy and matter in the universe are becoming less useful as time goes on. Perfect order existed in the universe only in the instant after the Big Bang when energy and matter and all of the forces of the universe were unified.

What is Causality and Correlations in Different Types of Systems?

> *Everyone affects us; that's the affective domain.*
>
> *Réjean Duchame*

Causality refers to the direct cause and effect relationship between events. For instance x happens directly before y, and as y could not happen without the affect of x, and as there is no other thing affecting what happens to y except x, it can be said that x is the causal reason for y. There are some causal phenomena in our environment, but usually things are much more interrelated, multi-causal and complex. What we tend to confuse in our minds too often, is the difference between causality and correlation. Causality is the correct word when we talk about deterministic, linear and mechanical systems such as pendulums or clock workings. Their causes are proportional to their effects. Small causes cause small effects and big causes cause big effects in a predictable way. With mechanical systems, causality allows us to accurately predict many linearly evolving phenomena, particularly the movement of the planets, the forces of gravity, and the trajectories of comets several hundred years in advance.[47] In other words, mechanical systems are most likely closed systems that undergo exogenously oriented phase transition, shape transition, or complex branching of growing colony types of transformations.[48]

When we speak of open organic systems, the causality is usually non-linear or even multi-causal, which means for instance that there are many simultaneous causes for certain effects, which then effect both back to their original causes, and forward to new things in the system. There the causes and

---

47 Vézina (2009, 94).
48 Ball (2004, 90–160).

effects may even formulate big loops, and then it is not correct to talk about causality any more, which requires the element of predictability.

With dynamical systems, which are sensitive to initial conditions and which renew through strange attractors, we should be careful in using the word causality, although some things seem so strongly interlinked. There is no long-term predictability between causes and effects inside dynamical systems, but as almost all things in the world correlate to some extent, there are correlations even in long-term chaotic dynamism. The price of bananas in Haiti in 2008 may correlate with the popularity of Vladimir Putin in Russia in 2012, and the shipbuilding rates in Brazil in the 1990s may correlate with global climate change in the 2020s. All such long-term correlations however have nothing to do with internal causality, which requires the element of predictability. On the other hand, as discussed in the autocatalysis and chaos theory chapters, when systems are highly dynamical or even chaotic in local level, they may be quite predictable and even causal if we look at the system from afar. But this requires that we go to a level where dynamical processes are not affecting the higher mechanical systemic level anymore. There needs to be a real step to another type of system logic, which does break the otherwise ubiquitous systemic self-organizing criticality. For instance, the earth's ecosystem is highly dynamical and complex and there is no long-term causality. Although it is a direct part of our solar system, the ecosystem's random fluctuations and emergence don't affect the predictable and perfectly causal order of the whole mechanical solar system. In a fractal sense, this same division is true in the case of a river, which is dynamical in the local level, but quite predictable in the higher level.

Summary of Evolutionary and Systemic Concepts

The key concepts of evolutionary transformation, complexity studies and systemic processes that were defined in previous chapters are summarized in Table 4.1. Some concepts, such as strange attractor, chaos theory, self-organized criticality or open system, that are not that focal in the previously presented axis of systemic self-renewal, have not been added to this table.

The figure following Table 4.1 binds both the table and the axis of systemic self-renewal shown in Figure 4.1, to the other concepts and knowledge that have been discussed so far, and establishes a new dimension to the complex life that surrounds us. The main idea behind that dimension or U-curve is to clearly present how all the basic processes of life and self-organization that surround

Table 4.1   Evolutionary and systemic concepts

Concept	Function A	Function C	Function C
Stability =	no energy consumption	+ no movements	+ no life or self-renewal
Conservative self-organisation =	very little energy consumption	+ predictable and causal movments	+ modest and automatic self-renewal
Autocatalysis =	spread of information or order in local and immediate interaction	+ local sub-set of a larger systemic process	+ has centres which dominate the local self-renewal where information is put into use
Autopoisis =	endogenous, stable and longer term self-renewal process	+ loops of information flow inside and entire single system	+ defines the character and borders of one particular entity
Co-evolution =	Long term change of an entire ecosystem without any dominating centres	+ entities of an ecosystem are competing and co-operating at the same time	+ simultaneous adaption and affecting process combined to exogenous affects generate together the multi-causality
Dynamical pocess =	provides the networks of transformation in living systems	+ only theoretical causalities	+ contains strange attractors that may divert the processes fast
Dissipative self-organisation =	order suddenly breaks and then gets fast and randomly re-assembled	+ re-assembling through cascade of bifurcations	+ synonym to emergence which is self-organisation plus establishment of new order
Chaos in quantum level =	totally unpredictable in local level	+ no causalities, order or structure	+ ultimate sensitivity to initial conditions cause random fluctuations
Complexity =	order that emerges out of chaos from the interactions of many agents according to a few simple rules	+ highly interlinked, multi-causal, multi-dimensional and non-linear	+ alive and evolving, cannot be studied analytically as not the same as complicated which is only the sum of its parts

us are interconnected into a chain, which allows us to name three levels of complexity. In the low level of complexity the process of a 'system' is either stagnated or dead, or is in total chaos without a form. In both cases the 'system' has no characteristics of complex structures.

In the mid-level of complexity the system starts to have some form, but the system is still not living or evolving and is bound to historicity. Here the system is either mechanically or predictably self-organizing or is in a phase of dissipative emergence, which destroys the systemic complexity and historicity and creates a new form of existence.

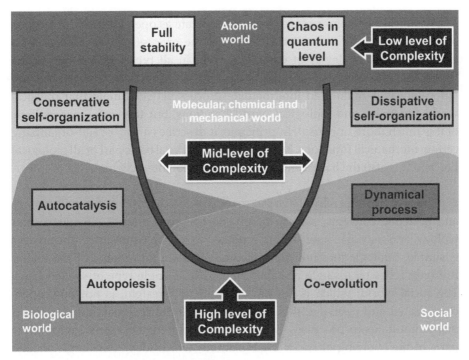

Figure 4.2   U-curve of complexity

Finally we come to the high level of complexity at the bottom of the U-curve. That is the level of either biological or social worlds where all real life exists. In the biological side of the U-curve, we have organic systemic structures that have clear borders or membranes with historicity and metabolism, which make them autonomous entities. On the right side of the U-curve we have social organizations, which operate mainly as open systems where the borders or membranes of the system need to be constantly negotiated and re-negotiated. Open social systems are highly multi-dimensional small worlds that are autonomously learning and adaptive in complex ways. They need to consume energy in their processes to remove the system's internal entropy, which reminds the open organic systems' metabolism in many ways. Therefore, open systems are strongly bound to historicity, but some open mechanical systems such as autocatalysis may be more ad hoc by nature.

All forms of highly complex life contain all of the systemic characteristics at the same time. In that sense, there could be a third dimension in Figure 4.2. Such a dimension could highlight the fractal nature of all the fundamental processes in the U-curve. For instance social organizations don't only operate as dynamical systems, as sometimes they operate as open mechanical or open organic systems. To give another example, the process type of autocatalysis exists in almost all levels of complexity and in all types of systems. In the figure, the autocatalysis is located to the mid-left part of the U-curve because autocatalysis is mainly an intermediate process between molecular-physical world functions, and biological world functions, but the basic process logic of it is much more universal. In principle, it describes a way of self-organizing certain mechanical functions, but in practice it is a vital basic part of all biological life, and it is also the basic function of many social interactions.

One may wonder why I have put so much effort discussing the evolutionary and systemic concepts, which mainly derive from physics, chemistry and biology, and may ask, how is all that related to strategic foresight? The answer is simple. Strategic foresight doesn't produce valid knowledge of the reality if it only relies on a single research method or a single type of system logic. The social world, which is studied in strategic foresight, is not only open, complicated and evolving, it is also highly multidimensional and it contains many simultaneous processes, which may have different systemic logics. Some parts of the evolving of social organizations, which may seem large, chaotic and complicated are actually quite predictable, when some parts, which seem quite simple and linear actually undergo randomly sudden fluctuations and re-assembling, which cannot be predicted. Such complexity of the research objective is a double edged sword for strategic foresight. We can know a lot about the future if we are able to look at the processes from afar, but at the same time we are blind to small changes that may act as triggers in dynamical systems, which should be acknowledged when we do strategic foresight. We need to be multi-disciplinary as our world is the product of all the sciences, interacting with each other to produce the reality that strategic planning and foresight seek to foresee/predict/forecast. Multiple methods, dimensions and system logics need to be used simultaneously, and the knowledge must cumulate into an inferred understanding of viable alternative scenarios and strategies that can be used or changed anytime; just as relying on a single method or view would leave us blind in the complex world. The relationship between systems thinking, evolutionary processes, strategic management and foresight methods are further discussed from different angles in the book's final chapters in Part IV.

5

Inferring in Theory

Men willingly believe what they wish.

Gaius Julius Caesar

This chapter discusses the ontology of knowledge – how can we argue that something like a risk exists or is emerging? It defines the interests of knowledge, the principles of producing and verifying scientific knowledge according falsification, the scientific method and optional forms of reasoning, the difference between research strategy and methodological principle, and finally the parts that constitute a fully-fledged methodology. These philosophical aspects are presented in this chapter because they form the foundation for producing any reliable strategic foresight or intelligence knowledge. Hence, these aspects need to be defined and discussed in some level in any fully-fledged methodological theory that we want to make for strategic or foresight purposes. In this sense, this chapter is a prelude for the sixth chapter where the methodologies, principles and practices of inferring in foresight are discussed.

What is Reasoning?

Reasoning or inferring is an old field of philosophy. The study of it is called either logic, or formal reasoning, which is one form of critical thinking.

The field of formal reasoning was founded by ancient philosophers such as Aristotle[1] (384 BC–322 BC) and goes under epistemology, which is one part of methodology in philosophy – 'meaning the study of ways to produce knowledge'. Aristotelianism has been followed and partly modified by many religious philosophers such as St. Augustine, many philosophical schools such as Peripatetics in antiquity, Stoicism of the sixteenth century, and many late modern philosophers such as Immanuel Kant (1724–1804) and Georg Wilhelm Friedrich Hegel (1770–1831). One of the most well-known philosophical, or logical, statements is Rene Descartes' (1596–1650) 'Cogito ergo sum' which

---

1 Aristotle (1999, org. 350 BC): *Metaphysics*; Aristotle (1995, org. 350 BC): *Nicomachean Ethics*.

translates as 'I think, therefore I am',[2] which he presented in his book *Discourse on the Methods*.[3]

Today, when we speak of reasoning we usually divide the act into two different branches, formal logic,[4] and everyday inferring. The first one is practiced through theoretical philosophy, mathematics, political science and computer science, and the last is practiced through everyday life and general scientific procedures. The concepts and theories developed under formal reasoning apply in everyday reasoning, but their meaning is often a little bit different. In formal reasoning, inductive reasoning and deductive reasoning have very specific meanings which may be defined simply as, drawing general conclusions from specific examples (probable inferences – induction), and drawing logical conclusions from definitions and axioms (necessary inferences – deduction). However, in everyday reasoning we tend to say that inductive reasoning is going from specifics towards the general, and deductive is going from the general towards specifics. Anyway these are the two basic forms of inferring, and they are related to two of Aristotle's dichotomies, analysis which takes an object of study and examines its component parts, and synthesis, which considers how parts can be combined to form a whole.[5] Alongside these two forms of inferring there are some special approaches, such as analogies and their prominent everyday forms, like case-based reasoning, and abductive reasoning which were discovered by Charles Sanders Peirce (1839–1914). Peirce's[6] discovery was made in 1865, when he tried to reformulate the Kantian question, of how synthetical reasoning is possible at all? From this point of view, abductive reasoning is a particularly valuable approach, which will be discussed next.

Abduction can be characterized as reasoning from surprising ideas and questions to the best explanatory hypothesis. Therefore, abduction can be characterized as a weak form of inference, as it starts with clue-like signs, and reaches tentative hypotheses, which have to be tested through subsequent inquiry.[7] Jaakko Hintikka[8] has even suggested that abduction is not actually a form of reasoning at all, but rather a (why)-question-answer step in the

---

2   It also translates as, 'think or die', as 'sum' can mean totality of existence, or the totality (end) of life.
3   This description is over simplified in many sense. See more accurate description of the branches of philosophy and epistemology from Niiniluoto, Ilkka (2002).
4   Formal, informal, symbolic and mathematical logic.
5   C.f. Kirwin (1995): *The Role of Analysis and Synthesis in Strategy Work*.
6   Peirce (1992, 1905, 1903).
7   Paavola et al. (2006, 138–9); Paavola (2004).
8   Hintikka (1998, 523).

process of an inquiry. Hence, abduction can be seen to be closely related to the interrogative model of inquiry (I-model), as both see epistemology as a sort of a game where inferential and question-answer steps are intertwined.[9] On the other hand, abduction is closely related to the process of making innovations, as innovation refers to a novel and useful thing (which may be commercialized), which is made by combining very different (old) things together. Furthermore, we may even say that the freely heuristic nature of abductive reasoning provides the unique opportunity of approaching true inter-disciplinarity under a single aspect.

The discovery or merely the scientific formulation of abductive reasoning was a gift from Peirce to the philosophy of science. Peirce did not stop at defining the principle of abductive reasoning, he pushed it further in order to discuss the *scientific method*.[10] The scientific method itself was originally discovered and successfully used by Galileo Galilei (1564–1642) and Johannes Kepler (1571–1630) in their scientific investigations.[11] What Peirce wanted to do was to reformulate these early discoveries and principles into a revisited description of a process that all scientific methods follow.

The Peirce's description of the process starts with abduction: why-questions, setting hypothesis, and a conjecture about what actually is going on. Then, by means of deductive inference, conclusions are drawn from the hypothesis – what other things must be obtained if the hypothesis is assumed to be true. Finally, when applicable, inductive hypothesis-testing is performed by seeking experimentally to detect something that has been deduced and obtained from the hypothesis. In other words, can we find reliable evidence, which would verify the hypothesis? Going back to Figure 3.1, the abduction phase takes place in the analysis part, and both deductive and inductive phases take place in the interpretation part of the figure.

What is Fallibilism?

Karl Popper (1902–94) is another philosopher of science who has contributed greatly to our contemporary understanding of scientific methods, theories

---

9   Ibid.
10 See the discussion around the concept of method and methodology in Chapter 6.
11 Galileo and Kepler introduced the process by which one observes a phenomenon, forms a hypothesis and then scientifically tests the hypothesis via experimentation. The description of the used method was added to the margins of the Galileo's study, which makes it the earliest known formulation of scientific method.

and reasoning. Popper, an advocate of freedom of thinking, and a diehard opponent of all pseudo-sciences and fundamental dogmas, introduced the principle of *falsifiability or fallibilism*,[12] which eventually replaced the principle of induction as the characteristic method of scientific investigation. In many pseudo-sciences the concept of scientific (theory or method) is understood as a synonym to systematic (theory or method). According *fallibilism*, a theory is scientific only if it is refutable by a conceivable event. Every genuine test of a scientific theory, is therefore, a logical attempt to refute or to falsify it, and a single genuine counter-instance falsifies the whole theory.

> *Theory is scientific only if it divides the class of basic statements into the following two non-empty sub-classes: (a) the class of all those basic statements with which it is inconsistent, or which it prohibits – this is the class of its potential falsifiers (i.e., those statements which, if true, falsify the whole theory), and (b) the class of those basic statements with which it is consistent, or which it permits (i.e., those statements which, if true, corroborate it, or bear it out).*[13]

Hence, according to Popper, it is logically impossible to conclusively verify a universal proposition by reference to experience, but a single counter-instance conclusively falsifies the corresponding universal law.

Through combining Peirce's description of the scientific method and Popper's fallibilism, Roland Omnes[14] has defined the falsification or verification as the fourth step in the use of any scientific method. The first three steps in his description of scientific method are:

1.   Empiricism (to see what happens, observing empirical rules);

2.   Concept formation (inventing or selecting concepts for representing reality, and principles that organize the facts); and

3.   Development (imagining and examining all possible consequences of the principles and linking them together).

Some practical foresight applications of these theories are discussed in the SIF-model in Chapter 5.

---

12 Popper (1979).
13 Thornton (2009).
14 Omnes (1999).

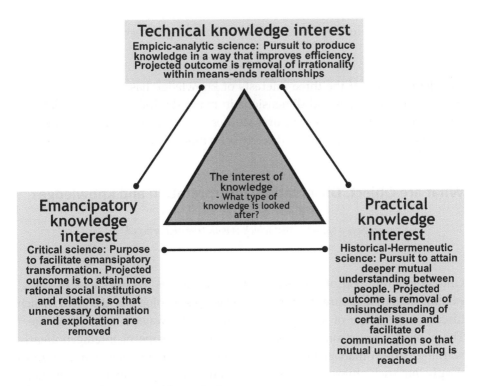

Technical knowledge interest
Empicic-analytic science: Pursuit to produce knowledge in a way that improves efficiency. Projected outcome is removal of irrationality within means-ends realtionships

The interest of knowledge - What type of knowledge is looked after?

Emancipatory knowledge interest
Critical science: Purpose to facilitate emansipatory transformation. Projected outcome is to attain more rational social institutions and relations, so that unnecessary domination and exploitation are removed

Practical knowledge interest
Historical-Hermeneutic science: Pursuit to attain deeper mutual understanding between people. Projected outcome is removal of misunderstanding of certain issue and facilitate of communication so that mutual understanding is reached

Figure 5.1   Interests of knowledge

What are the Interests of Knowledge?

Another key philosopher of science whose contribution to scientific reasoning should be mentioned here is Jürgen Habermas (1929–) who introduced the theory of knowledge-constitutive interests in his systematic framework for critical social theory.[15] According to Habermas, there are three knowledge-constitutive interests, which are technical, hermeneutical, and emancipatory interests. Technical refers to human nature's deep-seated need to classify, predict and control the natural environment. Positivism sees knowledge in these terms, and naturalistic accounts of human possibilities often regard human history only from this point of view. Second is practical interest, which is contemporarily modified to form hermeneutical interest of knowledge.[16] This refers to our deep-seated need to more deeply understand life, nature and ourselves. Third is emancipatory interest, which refers to

---

15   Habermas (1972).
16   See Willmot (2003).

our deep-seated need to reveal and overcome dogmatism, compulsion, and domination.[17]

Identification of the three interests of knowledge has helped to organize the research strategies and dimensions in many disciplines. For instance, the three research dimensions of futures studies, which were discussed in the sub-chapter critical futures studies, directly echo this division.

What are Object, Observation, Interpretation and Knowledge?

> *Knowledge is a subset of that which is both true and believed.*
>
> *Plato*

Ontology is the field of philosophy which discusses the questions of being, existing and the nature of reality, whilst epistemology is the field which discusses the scope of knowledge, truth, and the ways to get knowledge.[18] These aspects are strongly intertwined with the scope of intelligence/early warning/pattern management methodologies, but as my aim is not to go to deeply into such philosophical dilemmas, I have only presented the main logic and difficulty behind pattern recognizing.

In a simple 'epistemological' sense, the chain of getting knowledge from the world starts from the object (the more or less tangible things that exist), and ends with the knowledge of the object in our understanding. Between these two ends of the chain or axle is the process of observing, sense-making and clustering of observations. In reality this process is much more complicated.

First, there are at least three kinds of objects: 'existing', 'invented' and 'emerging'.[19] Existing refers to things like a terrorist group in action, or a loaded bomb, which are very tangible in our minds and quite tangible in the physical world too. Invented refers to things that are subjective or collective constructions[20] of things that we have observed, like a form of fundamentalism, or North-Korea's

---

17 As discussed in Chapter 2, the interest of knowledge in foresight is a little bit more technical and the interest of knowledge of futures studies is a little bit more both, hermeneutical and emancipatory.

18 See more accurate description of the branches of philosophy and epistemology from Niiniluoto, Ilkka (2002).

19 This sub-chapter is based on Kuosa (2011b).

20 Social constructivism is explained in Potter, Jonathan (1996): *Representing Reality: Discourse, Rhetoric and Social Construction*. London, Sage; and in Fairclough, Norman (1992): *Discourse and Social Change*. Cambridge, Polity Press; the idea of seeing the invisible 'risk' is explained

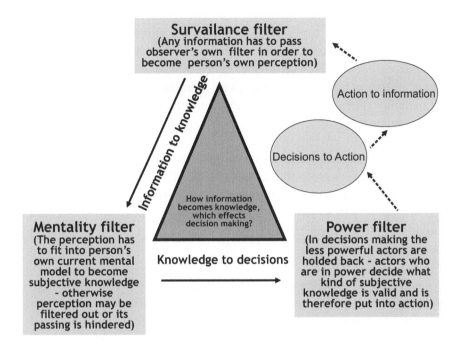

Figure 5.2   Filters of knowledge

unpredictable regime. A sub-set of invented objects are 'discovered' objects that are mathematically reasoned clusters of things that are interlinked. Emerging refers to objects that do not exist yet, but which will possibly or probably become reality based on our knowledge, such as the idea of Israel's pre-emptive strike on Iran's nuclear facilities. Despite the different levels of concreteness, all of these types of objects may be called, for example, risks.

Second, there is the step of observing, which is highly unconscious and subjective. Every individual sees and senses the same stimulus in their individual way. Our brains build images, that we see, in a process which combines 'direct' visual stimulus, that we obtain, into patterns (e.g. basic matrix of a face), which are rapidly compared to downloaded images or memories in our long term memory (like faces that we have seen before). Hence, things that we see mainly come unconsciously from our own long term data base, which is a highly subjective process. This is why those researching the brain say that we see what we are ready to believe.[21] This can be called the surveillance filter.

in Quiggin, Thomas (2007): *Seeing the Invisible: National Security Intelligence in an Uncertain Age.* Singapore, World Scientific Publishing.

21 Lindeman-Viitasalo (1995); Dawkins (2006).

Third, the various types of observations are subjectively sense-made in heuristic and abductive processes, which are highly susceptible to many types of cognitive filters, such as values and ethics, taboos and social norms, beliefs, cultural historical burdens and scars, and identification filters, which we can call mentality filters.[22] This is a particularly acute problem in so called weak signals[23] analysis.

Fourth, the sense-made issues are usually clustered in social (or electronic) processes which are susceptible to power filters. It matters who presents what, and in what context (or what programming algorithms or indicators have been selected). Some people or views have more power in defining things than should (logically) go into certain clusters, or are a more or less plausible thing or argument.

Finally, our knowledge of the objects/the things that we are interested in is based on the outcome of linking and filtering information in a long chain. As Plato put it, 'Knowledge is a subset of that which is both true and believed'.

However, what is 'true' is a controversial issue, and it is a matter of our selection of inferring methodologies, as discussed with the three kinds of objects. What is believed is an easier concept – what we are ready to believe, or what fits to our existing mental models, is what we tend to take as 'truths'.

What is Methodology and Research Strategy?

> *A theory is something nobody believes, except the person who made it.*
> *An experiment is something everybody believes, except the person who made it.*
>
> *Albert Einstein*

In the *Concise Oxford English Dictionary*,[24] the word method is defined as:

---

22 C.f. Ansoff (1975); Voros (2001).
23 The concept of weak signals refers to observations of the surrounding world which someone has subjectively reasoned to have some special foresight value. It should be noticed that there are many ontological and epistemological problems in the theory of weak signals analysis. Therefore, the value of one single signal should not be overemphasized in foresight. The reasoning of emergence of a certain issue requires clustering of many different types of signals and history knowledge. See Kuosa (2010a).
24 *Concise Oxford English Dictionary* (2002).

1. A particular procedure for accomplishing or approaching something; and 2. Order lines of thought or behaviour.

In the same publication, the definition of 'methodology' is:

1. A system of methods used in particular area in a particular study of activity; and 2. A methodology for investigating the concept of focal points.

In the *Webster's New Twentieth Century Dictionary of the English Language*,[25] which represents the US English side, the word methodology is defined as:

1. The science of method, or orderly arrangement, specifically, the branch of logic concerned with the application of the principles of reasoning to scientific and philosophical inquiry; and 2. A system of methods, as in any particular science.

Here, the origin of the concept is presented as 'Methodology [Gr. *Methodos*, method, and *logia*]' which means that it is a combination of the concept of method or methodos (*a way to pursue knowledge*), and the concept of logia (*expressing the understanding*). To be specific, the word methodology refers to two things:

1. To methodology as an area of philosophy which studies the ways to produce knowledge – it contains studies of epistemology, ontology, interests of knowledge, ways of inferring etc.; and

2. To 'a system of methods' – a specific well-argued theory for how knowledge of certain well defined researched themes can be obtained, such as social constructivism.

As methodologies are a combination of both critical discussions on the ways to produce knowledge, and well defined alternative ways of obtaining knowledge, they cannot be true or false, only better or worse argued, and more or less useful, in the same way as any other theory. In the social sciences, the word methodology can be used when broadly referring, for example, to selecting between general research strategies, such as qualitative or quantitative approaches, or more narrowly naming, for example, grounded theory or conversation analysis as a methodology, or it can refer to an exhaustive list

---

25 *Webster's New Twentieth Century Dictionary of the English Language* (1971, 1134).

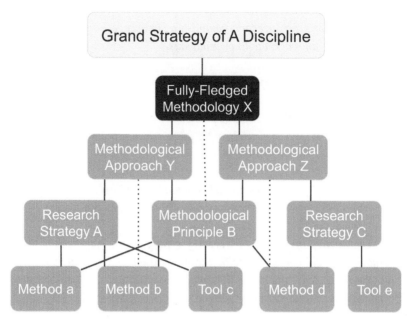

Figure 5.3   Methodological levels

of suitable methods in one well defined research area with descriptions of the ideas behind the methods, such as *Futures Research Methodology*.[26]

Kyösti Raunio and Sirkka Hirsjärvi et al.[27] describe methodology as a meta-level of research, a strategic decision, which remains somewhere between the disciplines' or the individual's own world view, and a separate decision to use a certain type of technique, tool, or method. Methodology is related to strategic questions such as: 'should I travel via sea, land or air' and when a method is related to the selection of a specific vehicle after one has decided to travel, for example via land 'should I now take a car, bus, train, bicycle or should I walk'. Hence, methodology is at a higher strategic level, and methodological approaches and research strategies are at a lower strategic or operational level, when methods and tools are at a tactical or operational level. However, there are some exceptions to this due to the use of the term method in the English language, where it can refer to a more common way of doing something. For instance Charles S. Peirce introduced in his pragmatism[28] the *scientific method*, which refers to the general principles that any scientific work should follow.

---

26 C.f. Glenn (2009a).
27 Raunio (1999); Hirsjärvi et al. (1997).
28 Charles S. Peirce introduced the abductive reasoning in his pragmatism (1992, 1905, 1903).

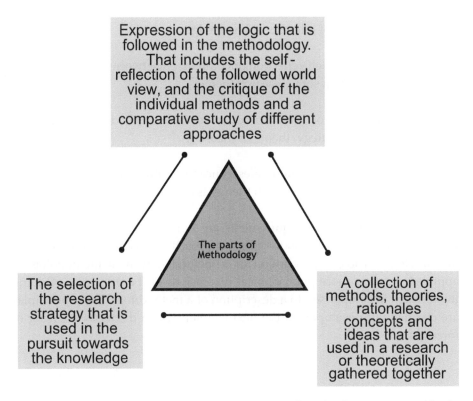

Expression of the logic that is followed in the methodology. That includes the self-reflection of the followed world view, and the critique of the individual methods and a comparative study of different approaches

The parts of Methodology

The selection of the research strategy that is used in the pursuit towards the knowledge

A collection of methods, theories, rationales concepts and ideas that are used in a research or theoretically gathered together

Figure 5.4   Parts of methodology – collection of methods, strategy and logic

In a simple hierarchical sense, such a grand strategy of science is at a higher level than grand strategies of disciplines and methodologies, but it is still called a method, as it refers to 'a particular procedure for accomplishing scientific knowledge'.[29]

The difference between methods, research strategies and methodologies are explained through practical examples in Chapter 6. The description of the SIF-model particularly opens up ideas regarding what alternative research strategies stand for.

Figure 5.4 defines the parts that should be discussed in a fully-fledged definition of a methodology:

    1.   selection of research strategy;

---

29 *Concise Oxford English Dictionary* (2002).

2.   discussion of interests of knowledge;

3.   discussion, self-reflection or comparison between alternative logics of inquiry in some research theme;

4.   some level of identification of useable methods in the defined research strategy, theme or theories;

5.   discussion of the rationales, concepts, hypothesis, models, findings and ideas in the research theme, as discussed by David Silverman.[30]

If only some of these five requirements are fulfilled in the description, one may use the words 'methodological approach' instead of 'fully-fledged methodology'. Thus, a description of a methodology or a methodological approach requires more philosophical discussions of the principles of doing the research in comparison to a description of a method/tool. These principles are clarified with examples in the next chapter, which discusses inferring in foresight.

---

30 Silverman (2000, 76–101).

6

Inferring in Foresight

If I would have asked the customers what they want, they would have said a faster horse.

Henry Ford, the developer of T-model Ford

Foresight and futures studies have a special interest on futures knowledge as discussed in the second chapter. They seek to connect together various driving forces, trends, emerging issues and conditioning factors in order to envisage alternative futures (rather than predict the future). They have a broader scope of research than the normal sciences, as their research objective does not exist in an empirical sense, because it is contingent and undefined by nature. Yet, this does not mean that we could not get relevant futures knowledge from our present environment, in the same way as we can get, for example, history or marketing knowledge. Hence, this unusual research objective has led the research field into a unique epistemology which differentiates it from principles and methodologies of all normal sciences.

How many methods are there in futures domain? There is no simple answer to this. The millennium project's futures research methodology v.3.0 names and describes 39 futures research methods, but that list is certainly not exhaustive. It is easy to name dozens of methods that are not mentioned in the book, and it can be argued that many of the methods in the v.3.0 are not well-known applications that would be in serious use in the field. I could estimate, that from an operational point of view, there are about ten specific fully-fledged methodologies or methodological approaches in futures domain, which will be discussed in this chapter. Then there are about 30 to 50 research strategies or methodological principles such as explorative and normative scenario approach, Delphi approach, trend-analysis approach, weak signals approach, participatory approach and so on. And then there are these various practical applications that can be used in these methodological principles. No one really knows how many of these there are in the world, as most of the applications are not published anywhere. They may have been used only by one researcher on one project, or some methods may be direct combinations of two or more old methods such as Q2,[1] or a method may be directly borrowed from another discipline such as interviews, SWOT and surveys, or there may be small variations in applying an old method to a certain research case or context, or there may be an old method in use but a new idea to showcase the analysis results or to gather expert panels such as real-time Delphi, and so on. There are probably over 50 method applications for the scenario approach. I have used over ten different ways to do scenarios myself. Therefore I would estimate that there are about 400 to 1,000 genuinely different applications of futures domain methods, which all are in principle methods of the domain.

This chapter discusses my understanding of the ten fully-fledged methodologies of inferring futures knowledge in futures domain. There are two motivations for presenting this list. First I think that a list of methodologies should follow a transparent process logic which allows knowledge to cumulate as described in phases of strategic foresight in Figure 3.1. In other words, this means that I think that one foresight methodology should exist for one epistemological purpose only, and it should be a particular phase in a cumulative futures process chain, as I have discussed in an earlier publication.[2] That is why I call the first fully-fledged methodology 'Environmental scanning and data mining' instead of just, for example, Delphi. Delphi itself is only one approach or strategy for producing environmental scanning knowledge and there are so many other ways to do it. Delphi[3] is more than a method, but it does not cover the whole epistemological need or domain of 'Environmental scanning and data mining' – it is only a sub-set of that.

The other motivation is to present methodological sets to each of these epistemological needs in the futures process chain that follow the five main requirements of a 'fully-fledged methodology' as discussed by David Silverman.[4]

Based on these two motivations I consider the following ten as the fully-fledged methodologies of inferring in futures domain: 'Environmental scanning and data mining, Analysis and categorizing, Pattern management

---

1   Tapio et al. (2011): The unholy marriage? Integrating qualitative and quantitative information in Delphi process. *Technological Forecasting and Social Change*, doi:10.1016/j.techfore.2011.03.016.
2   Kuosa (2009).
3   Delphi was invented in RAND in the 1950s and it was first thoroughly discussed by Linstone and Turoff (1975). In their book they define the Delphi technique as a group communication process structuring technique that helps a group of individuals to grasp a complicated problem. See also Kuusi (1999); Tapio et al. (2011); Tapio (2003); Bell (2005).
4   Silverman (2000, 76–101).

and synthesizing, Roadmapping and technological forecasting, Creative visioning, Early warning and emerging issues analysis, Holistic sense-making, Alternative objectives and future mindsets, Scenarios to alternative futures, and Strategic management'. These ten fully-fledged methodologies are put into a logically cumulative order, which means that if one pursues affective futures process, one should start with the first one, then go to the second, and finally end with the last one. However, when needed the order can also be exchanged.[5] Each of the ten methodologies are discussed in separate sub-chapters, which contain a brief description of the principles behind each methodology, and in some cases a few examples of the methodological approaches, strategies and specific methods that belong to this group of approaches.

As my intention has not been to create an encyclopaedia of futures domain methods but to emphasize new methods that I believe deserve more publicity, many old or more commonly known methods are not discussed in these sub-chapters as thoroughly as they could be. However, the references to sources where the older methods are well described are provided as often as possible.

There are two methods, forecasting radar and the SIF-model, which haven't been published before. Power vectors triangle (PVT-method) and assessment through future mindsets (ATF-lenses) are new methods which are based on ideas presented previously, and two methods, namely FSSF and Mixed scenario approach, are new practical applications for existing futures methods. The strategic SWOT was originally created in the 1970s but, as it has been largely forgotten, it has been presented in its old format. Finally there is a table at the end of this chapter which concludes the practical usability and the preparatory requirements of each of the example methods.

Environmental Scanning and Data Mining

Environmental scanning, also known as horizons scanning, combined with knowledge gathering and assessing with experts and data mining approaches, is the first methodology of futures domain to be discussed here. It is not a method in the sense of being one particular procedure or tool for accomplishing or approaching something, and not just a single strategy in the sense of being an option to do scanning work, but a broader way of organizing research as discussed in a previous chapter. It is a specific and well-argued theory for how

---

5   The discussion of the principles behind the methodologies and techniques continues in
     Chapter 15.

knowledge of certain well-defined research themes can be obtained through gathering knowledge from the environment as broadly and as systematically as possible.

As already discussed in Figures 5.3 and 5.4, a full-fledged methodology should contain the following elements:

1.   a selection of research strategy;

2.   discussion of interests of knowledge;

3.   discussion, self-reflection or comparison between alternative logics of inquiry in some research theme;

4.   some level of identification of possibly useable methods in the defined research strategy, theme or theories;

5.   discussion of the rationales, concepts, hypothesis, models, findings and ideas in the research theme.

Based on the following presentation, one can assess if these five requirements are fulfilled through environmental scanning. In other words, is it a full-fledged methodology or only a research strategy or principle, or a narrower methodological approach to futures domain?

According to Theodor Gordon and Jeremy C. Glenn,[6] the following seven principles should be considered when creating environmental scanning systems:

1.   Expert panels can be created to 'look out' for changes on the horizon that could be important to implement or accomplish plans via Delphis, listservs, and various other forms of collaboration software. It is probably worth considering a host of emerging technologies that are similar in terms of promoting potential 'active' participation (e.g. Delphi). There are candidates such as facilitated dialogue mapped face-to-face meetings, 'world cafés', and even prediction markets (see the chapter on this method in this series).

---

6   Gordon and Glenn (2009, 3–4).

2.   Database literature reviews provide access to a broad range of information useful to policy makers, planners and strategists.

3.   Alarming databases such as 'Google Alerts' (see http://www. googlealert.com) which allows one to pre-select terms that are searched daily and delivered to your e-mail address. 'Web crawlers' can search for sites with new versions that can provide early warnings or alerts to new information.

4.   Many websites offer press releases available to the public. You should know the ones most suitable for your interests, as these identify issue-related information and emerging trends.

5.   Hard-copy literature reviews of selected periodicals could also be scanned to detect important incipient changes; however, they are increasingly being replaced by electronic versions.

6.   Essays by experts could explore critical long-term issues for recommendations on policy and strategy. These essays could use contemporary software such as issues maps.

7.   Key person tracking (who knows the most, and how do you keep track of their new insights) and monitoring of key conferences on your special interests, in person or online via streaming or archived video.

Discussion of the methodology of environmental scanning can be continued with Wendy L. Schultz's description of an integrated foresight process,[7] which locates the environment scanning to the early stage of the work where it operates most effectively. Schultz[8] portrays the movement and transformation of data derived from environmental scanning through five key activities of integrated foresight, and offers a few example research methods affiliated with each activity:

1.   Trends, drivers, and emerging issues of change (weak signals) are collected via scanning diverse data sources.

---

7   Integrated Foresight refers to the idea of combining many foresight approaches together into a systematic process from A to Z. This approach is common for both participatory and strategic foresight, e.g. Sohail Inayatullah's Six pillars approach. See Wendy L. Schultz's description from (2008, 5).
8   Schultz (2008, 5).

2.   The change data is extrapolated using a variety of statistical computations as well as qualitative impact assessment techniques.

3.   The change data, the extrapolations, and the impacts can then be assembled into scenarios of alternative possible outcomes, neither wholly good nor wholly bad but expressing both opportunities and threats in each scenario.

4.   Those possibilities seen as contributing to the most desired outcomes are built into a preferred future, or vision.

5.   Strategies to realize this vision are devised which both build on the positive trends of change, and counter or ameliorate the negatives.

In my opinion environmental scanning is very much a fully-fledged methodology of futures domain based on well-defined objectives, applicable processes, and theoretical principles that were used to describe it. Environmental scanning is strongly linked to early warning system and emerging issues analysis, which can either be seen as special sub-approaches of environmental scanning, or as independent methodological approaches that benefit the knowledge that is produced in a separate environmental scanning process. In this book the view taken on this issue is the latter.

Environmental scanning as a fully-fledged methodology and research principle, allows one to use many alternative research strategies to fulfil the objective of systematic knowledge gathering. The most commonly used research strategies or principles in it are Delphi,[9] surveys, literature reviews, dialogue mapped face-to-face meetings, world cafés, in-depth interviews, automated data mining from internet, and subjective weak signals analysis. A self-organized map (SOM), that was discussed in Chapter 3 (Business Intelligence and Corporate Foresight) is a new approach to data mining, but it can also be counted as pattern management. Then there are various practical methods and tools that can be utilized and applied under each of these strategies and principles as already discussed in Figure 5.4.

---

9   Sometimes Delphi and scenarios are called the only genuine methods or methodologies of futures domain. All the other futures domain methods have at least some origins in other disciplines. True or not, Delphi is a very meaningful method in the field. That is why naming Delphi as a methodological approach instead of a fully-fledged methodology may seem degrading to some professionals. My logic behind this division was discussed in the introduction to this chapter.

Analysis and Categorizing

The second fully-fledged methodology of futures domain is analysis and categorizing. It is a specific principle for how knowledge of certain well-defined futures domain research themes can be obtained through breaking the issue into smaller parts, categorizing and studying the contents of each part, and studying the interactions between the parts. Analysis is a coherent way of obtaining futures knowledge and there are lots of alternative methods and strategies that can be utilized in this approach, therefore it is called a methodology or methodological approach in this book.

Critical futures studies, which was discussed in the second chapter, can be seen as one methodological principle or approach of analysis methodology. The special methods that can be utilized in it are, for example, causal layered analysis and four-quadrant model. The basic principle in it is to go deeper towards the roots of the phenomenon.[10]

Another methodological approach or research strategy of the analysis methodology is *trend* or *issue analysis*, which was discussed in the second chapter as well. It contains for example, the methods of trend-impact-analysis, S-curve analysis, issue management and futures wheel.[11] All of the four break one trend or divide the issue into parts like sub-trends and study the interactions and implications of each sub-trend. These methods should not be confused with trend-extrapolation, which belongs to the methods of forecasting methodology.

The third research strategy or sub-approach of the analysis methodology is categorizing and classifying information. The newest method for categorizing diversified futures knowledge is 'Future Signals Sense-Making Framework' (FSSF),[12] which is discussed next.

FSSF is a framework that suits four types of futures knowledge categorizing and assessing tasks. First it helps to assess if you have enough futures knowledge of the theme that you are studying and is it diverse enough – should you continue knowledge gathering?

Second it helps to assess if a particular signal is a true anomaly in the theme and therefore a real weak signal (A1), or is it other type of interesting signal

---

10 Inayatullah (2008).
11 For example, Gordon (2009a): Trend impact analysis.
12 Kuosa (2010a).

within the theme that you are able to link to existing trends or phenomena (A2), or is it an observation that does not have any relevance as a futures knowledge in the theme (does not fit into any category).

Third, it helps to assess if a particular change factor is a true pushing driver (B3), or a pulling driver (B4) of the theme area.

Fourth, it helps to assess if a particular change factor is a true weight of history, which blocks the change in the theme (C5), or an existing trend that brings an inevitable transformation process forward (C6).

Fifth, it helps to assess how much change power a weak signal from (A1) has to all other categories of knowledge in the theme area. To do this you must first try to fit as many true weak signals into (A1) as you can. Then you fill all other FSSF categories with your knowledge of the theme. After that all signals in (A1) are assessed one by one in each other category (B2–C6). The question is; how could any particular weak signal challenge things that were named in this category?

Table 6.1   Future Signals Sense-making Framework

The levels of futures knowledge	Six categories of change factors in futures	
A. Weak signals (Observations and intuitive feelings of anomalies)	**A1. Novel observation which is totally surprising, amusing, ridiculous, or annoying to you** (You believe that there is something novel in this observation, but the others don't see the same. This 'thing' may be hard to put into words)	**A2. Interesting observation which tells you that something is increasing or decreasing** (Useful strong or weak signals that you can link to trends, drivers or phenomena)
B. Drivers (Agents or things that push or pull the change forward)	**B3. Pushing drivers** (Top-down political decisions: 'we will put a man to the moon before the end of the decade'. Other pushing ideas, decisions or 'agents' that push the change forward)	**B4. Pulling drivers** (Needs that arise from grass-root-level – What is needed, socially, politically, technically, economically 'etc' and therefore can be expected)
C. Trends (Long-term paths of transformation and weights of history)	**C5. Blockers of change** (Factors which slow down or prevent the otherwise emerging change – Laws, values, interests, bureaucracy, taboos, borderlines, technical bottle necks etc)	**C6. Trends and inevitable large change processes** (The flowing river of change – Megatrends, path-dependence, direction of change that can be proven basing on statistics)
	Disrupting the linear	**Promoting the linear**

Sixth, a similar assessment as in the fifth example can be done with wild cards in each category (B2–C6) as well. In this case you start by creating wild cards for the theme (small probability – high impact). Then you do a similar assessment as you did with the weak signals in the fifth example as described above.

Seventh, it can be used as an interview platform in a particular theme. In this case you can begin with an empty FSSF platform and ask the interviewee to tell you what should be in the category, or you can present more general questions and fill the platform later with the results, or you can fill the platform first with your literature review knowledge and ask the interviewee to comment on the information you already have in each category.

In practical terms the FSSF platform is, for example, a plain sheet of A4 paper, which you divide into six boxes that you name simply A1–C6 as in Table 6.2. To the top of the paper you name the theme that you are analyzing, for example, 'Energy Security of Europe'. After that the method is ready for using and applying to almost any context.

Table 6.2   **FSSF platform**

Theme:		
A. Weak signals (Direct observations of anomalies)	A1.	A2.
B. Drivers (Agents or things that push or pull the change forward)	B3.	B4.
C. Trends (Long-term trends and paths of transformation or weights of history)	C5.	C6.
	Disrupting the linear	**Promoting the linear**

Pattern Management and Synthesizing

The third fully-fledged methodology of futures domain is pattern management and synthesizing. It is a specific principle for how knowledge of certain well-defined futures domain research theme can be obtained through clustering, synthesizing and managing patterns of information. Pattern management and synthesizing is a coherent way of obtaining futures knowledge and there are lots of alternative methods and strategies that can be utilized in this approach, therefore it is called a fully-fledged methodology in this book.

Pattern management[13] (PM) is an ancient practice, but a fairly new concept. One of the first developments in this concept was Kamran Parsaye's article,[14] where he drew a line between data management and pattern management. According to Parsaye, when recent data is put into an operational system and merged with historical data gathered over time, we have data management. When all this data is analysed over time it is merged with historical *patterns* we have in pattern management. Thus, PM is not data management, data mining or construction of knowledge-based systems. PM deals with patterns after they have been discovered by data mining and management. Parsaye gives a simple analogy, 'consider data as grapes and patterns of knowledge as wine. Data mining is then the wine-making process, (…) and the data mining tools are like wine-making equipment'. Hence, what makes data management something called pattern management is the way already identified smaller clusters/ patterns or proven sub-hypothesis are re-clustered and used in falsification, in order to make the final conclusion in the theme.

There are many ways or methodological approaches of doing knowledge or pattern management. One way is statistical or so called '*Empirical Calculation* (EC)'[15] which starts from ICT or statistical 'data cracking or mining', where rising peaks or data clusters are created from quantitative data, and which continues to combine recent data to historical data. Patterns created that way were used for instance to detect changes in consumer behaviour or immigration patterns. If such recent patterns of, for example, immigration are benchmarked and

---

13 In Figure 3.1 of Chapter 3, Pattern management methodologies are named as interpretation methods under the level of foresight. However, pattern management methodologies (EC, TPO and RC) can be considered as alternative sets, how the whole process from Input to Analysis and Interpretation can go. In the same way, strategic intelligence, business intelligence or intelligence agencies methodologies or procedures can be considered as alternatives to handle all these four first steps of the strategic foresight process.

14 Parsaye, Kamran (1999).

15 These categorizations of the methodologies of pattern management, and Figures 6.1 and 6.2, are based on definition in my article (2010b).

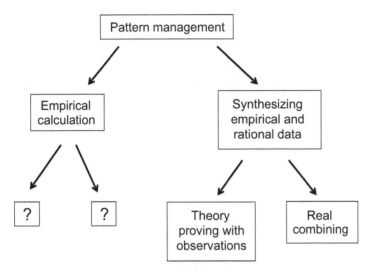

Figure 6.1   Main categories of pattern management here

merged with historical patterns of immigration, we have empirical software based pattern management. Another method applied in EC is the ICT tool, the self-organized map.[16] The 'object', as described in Chapter 5, that is looked after in EC is usually 'invented', or its sub-set – 'discovered' object, that are mathematically reasoned clusters of things that are highly interlinked.

Another general way starts from 'data cracking or mining' of both empirically and rationally produced data, and attempts to identify or prove certain hypothesis or pattern as 'existing or non-existing' with any available evidence. In my article,[17] I have called this methodological approach '*Synthesizing empirical and rational data*' (SER). The two most common ways of SER are abductive inferring or so called '*Theory proving with observations* (TPO)', and Qualitative inferring or so called '*Real combining* (RC)'. Practical examples of SER type of approach in revealing, for example, a spy or mole may be found in Chapter 3 '*What is intelligence?*'

The 'Theory proving with observations (TPO)' is basically the second methodological approach of pattern management. The idea of the approach was introduced as Peirce's description of scientific method in Chapter 2. It starts with the abductive process of asking 'why-questions' and linking pieces of information together. It then proceeds to making many plausible hypotheses

---

16 For example, Fountain Park Ltd and Data Rangers Ltd have focused on this method.
17 Kuosa (2010b).

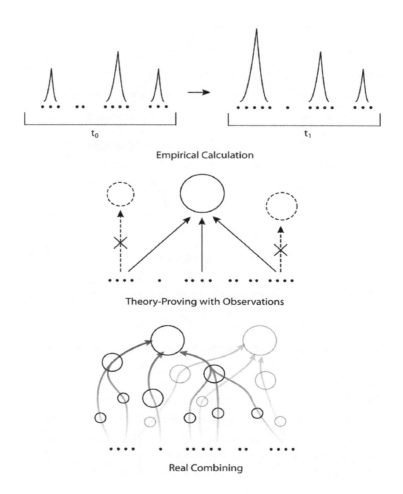

Empirical Calculation

Theory-Proving with Observations

Real Combining

Figure 6.2   Three methodologies of reasoning in pattern management

to the problem. It is followed by deductive conclusions, which are finally verified inductively. Popper's idea of fallibilism is very important in TPO. The 'object', as described in Chapter 5, that is looked after in such TPO is usually 'existing' by its type.

The other form of SER, which is the third methodological approach of pattern management, I have called either '*Real combining* (RC)', or qualitative inferring as discussed in the SIF-model part of this chapter. RC is the process of fully qualitative but systematic research. It relies mainly on the use of analogies, metaphors and other approaches for finding interconnectedness, similarities and possibilities to combine qualitative data into meta-knowledge, with a common storyline and understanding. As described in Figure 6.2, RC is highly subjective work of combining things that are interrelated according one selected logic. In RC, as in any qualitative research, one researcher can end up at a different conclusion than another researcher, even if the research materials are the same, but both can be equally right on the issue.

RC is a valid methodological approach of reasoning when both the 'object' and the system under research, are very complex. The 'object', as described in Chapter 5, as looked after in such RC is usually 'emerging' or 'invented' by its type.

Roadmapping and Technological Forecasting

The fourth fully-fledged methodology of futures domain is roadmapping and technological forecasting.[18] It is a specific principle involving ways through which knowledge of certain well-defined futures domain research themes can be obtained through building systematic what-to-do steps from the present to the objective in the future. Roadmapping breaks the objective into smaller parts that should be obtained on the way to the ultimate objective. It establishes a concrete timetable of actions and showcases what things are linked and effecting on the path that has been designed.

The other 'branch' of this methodology is technological forecasting, which aims to showcase systematically and with empirical data that certain developments are proceeding in a certain way with high probability. I have combined both roadmapping and technological forecasting into a single methodology as the fundamental philosophy behind them is the same – to remove systematically all possible ambiguity, to increase control and to get to a conclusion as directly as possible. One is about 'knowing with certainty' and the other is about planning and designing based on the knowledge gathered.

The principles behind technological forecasting are discussed in Chapter 2 and the specific methods of this methodology can be found in J. Scott Armstrong's (2001) book *Principles of Forecasting*. Further readings on practical cases in technological forecasting can be found in the journal of *Technological Forecasting and Social Change*.

---

18   Gordon (2009b): Science and technology roadmapping.

Creative Visioning

Imagination is more important than knowledge.

Albert Einstein

One of the key qualities of futurists is their ability to imagine the future as being different from the past. Those without such imagination can only extrapolate trends, something less than useful in providing the necessary vision for long-term planning. Herman Kahn taught that the biggest surprise would be that the 'surprise-free scenario' from extrapolation would actually occur. How then do we move the mind beyond extrapolation to analysis, synthesis, and speculation about alternative futures? There are several ways to do that, which together establish the foundation for the fifth fully-fledged methodology of futures domain – creative visioning. This is a specific set of principles and ways through which out-of-the-box thinking on certain well-defined futures domain research themes can be obtained through creative thinking.

The foundation of going beyond extrapolation is through the inclusion of intuitive processes within it. The word intuition derives from the Latin 'in + tuere' which literally means 'looking into oneself' in order to gain insight. Intuition is thus like inner vision. One of the most well-known methodological principles for this is *Genius forecasting*[19] or creative imaginary or intuitive visioning, which was a term coined by Ralph Lenz in the late 1950s. As a subjective approach to creating and/or finding insight about the future, the term is most closely associated with Herman Kahn, who was considered to be a genius futurist. The term has been used less among futurists since the death of Kahn in 1983.[20] According to Jerome C. Glenn, Kahn's pronouncements about the future often showed great insight.

Somehow an individual, seasoned by experience and history, integrates all that is obvious and implicit – through internal processes that are not necessarily obvious – and argues for a particular future or set of developments. How do they do it? Not by making decision trees like computers, but by some other internal genius process.

Note that the method is called genius forecasting instead of 'genius predicting, prophesy or foresight', as is the case with many methods in futures

---

19 Ibid.
20 Glenn (2009b).

domain. There are two basic reasons for this. First any serious endeavours in futures domain cannot be called predictions for sure because the term refers to a belief in one deterministic future, which contradicts everything that foresight and futures studies stand for. Second genius forecasting cannot be called foresight either, as intuitive visioning attempts to describe what the future will be like. Whether this is done by a group of experts or by an individual, it is in contradiction with most of the principles of fully-fledged foresight.

Another methodological principle for going beyond extrapolation is innovating, which refers to the notion of applying and linking two or more things or ideas that seem strange in the first place, but then prove to be a novel, highly useable and even profitable combination for some particular purpose. One particular research strategy under creative visioning, is the principle of getting smartly over power and expertise filters in large innovating groups. Innovating strategy's basic principle is the establishment of three autonomous and very different teams that take turns in circulating information in a well-designed innovating process that is steered by one director. The original idea behind the strategy was created by Reginald Victor Jones during World War II when he worked in Scientific Intelligence for Air Staff and later for British Intelligence. This research strategy is further discussed in Ilan Mitzrahi's interview in Chapter 13. A direct modification of it, which is named ALT3, is used in the AlternativeFutures Ltd[21] consulting company as a heuristic method for innovating according to the Blue Sea strategy. Alongside ALT3, there have been many types of heuristic methods used in the creation of alternative futures to make the leap forward. The most well-known are probably those carried out by Shell Oil in 1970s and RAND in 1950s and 1960s.

Third all other heuristic methods,[22] including brainstorming, brain writing and future workshops, that have not been mentioned yet can be viewed together as an independent methodological principle of creative visioning. These methods can be linked to the two principles mentioned previously, but such an 'inventing approach' has genuine differences too, as it is not innovating or forecasting, which allows us to call it the third methodological principle.

---

21 AlternativeFutures Ltd is a company and a joint service with YATTA Ltd, a concept design company. Available at: www.alternativefutures.fi
22 Schwarz (2006).

Visualizing knowledge regarding futures knowledge and options through graphs, images or maps can be named the fourth methodological principle of creative visioning, as it makes ideas more concrete and enhances all the participants' creativity during the process. Finally the fifth methodological principle of creative visioning is known as pure science fiction.

Early Warning and Emerging Issues Analysis

Early warning systems and emerging issues analysis are particular types of environmental scanning systems that aim to detect alarming issues as soon as the first signs immerge. They can either be seen as special autonomous methodological approaches of more general environmental scanning, or they can be seen as independent methodologies that utilize the knowledge that is produced in a separate environmental scanning process prior to it. In this book early warning systems are considered to be the sixth independent fully-fledged methodology due to its specific interest in knowledge. Suggestions for developing national early warning systems[23] can be found in the third part of this book and in Helene Lavoix's interview.

A good example of the principles behind the building of an early warning system is provided by Theodor Gordon and Jerome C. Glenn[24] in their work on the principles of environmental scanning methodology that includes an example of a process they completed for the Kuwait Oil Company. The task for which the Kuwait Oil Company contracted the Millennium Project was to produce an 'Early Warning System' for them to help track global change that might affect their long-term strategy.

The method that was followed by Gordon and Glenn,[25] was an environmental scanning approach where each piece of detected information or record involved their assessment through the following ten fields that could only be edited by preselected individuals:

---

23 For example, Lavoix (2006).
24 The Kuwait Oil Company contracted with the Millennium Project to produce their 'Early Warning System' to help track global change that might affect their long-term strategy. Software was produced that integrated the advantages of relational data bases with the ability to comment like blogs to produce a dynamic system that could 'learn' through feedback with multiple definitions of users and authors for the entire organization. See Gordon and Glenn (2009, 3–4).
25 Gordon and Glenn (2009, 3–4): *Environmental Scanning*.

1.   *Category or Domain*: Technological, Economical, Environmental, Political, and Social Assumptions and Risks?

2.   *Leading Indicator*: What would tell you that change in this item is possible?

3.   *Source*: Where did the information come from?

4.   *How to access the source*: A person, their office telephone number, or e-mail, and is there anything special one should know, like she goes to the annual meeting of the strategy institute and is open to discussion at their meetings?

5.   *Other Comments*: Anything that should be included, but which did not fit in any of the other fields?

6.   *Significance or importance*: Even if completely obvious, include it anyway, so that it shows up in a database search later when the item could be important in a pattern analysis for an early warning report.

7.   *Potential consequences or impacts*: We don't know the future, but we can make educated guesses. What is the range of possible consequences for the item? You might do a Futures Wheel (as an individual or in a group) on the item.

8.   *Current and future status*: What is the current status of the item; for example, early social movement, laboratory tests, sales volume, percentage of the public involved, or are there any other ways to specify its current status? Future status (will there be some event planned in the future that is relevant to the item; for example, a date on which it is to be addressed at a WTO meeting, a date of a conference, a date that a UN treaty is to go into force, a date of an election etc.)?

9.   *Actors*: Who are the actors affecting the indicator? If it is a new line item in an R&D budget, then the actor would be the research lab that conducts the research. If it is an environmental terrorist act, then it would be the organization that initiated the act. Where possible, one should add the network(s) in which the actors act.

10. *Date*: The day the information was entered and the name of the scanner are automatically entered by most software.

As identified, the core aim of early warning methodology is to detect alarming issues as soon as the first signs appear. Therefore, the research strategies or principles that should be linked to early warning methodology are environmental scanning, emerging issues analysis or management, risk assessment, impact analysis, anomalies, non-linearities or weak signals detection and wild cards analysis.

One method that can be utilized in early warning and emerging issues analysis is the forecasting radar,[26] which has been developed by myself, Jari Koskinen and Mika Ilari Koskinen through the AlternativeFutures[27] group of Yatta Ltd. The basic principle of the radar is first to scan large quantities

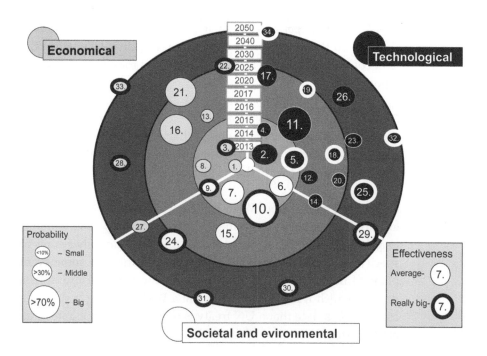

Figure 6.3   Forecasting radar

---

26 Forecasting radar (also called Forecasting map) is used in AlternativeFutures' toolkit. Available at: www.alternativefutures.fi
27 AlternativeFutures is a service of YATTA concept company. Available at: www.alternative futures.fi

foresight databases and other relevant sources of futures knowledge and, based on the scanning and analysis, identify the most important affecting issues and emerging phenomena that a company will possibly face during a certain interval; for example, between now and 2050. Each emerging issue and phenomenon is split into its individual components, for example, its driver, trends and other change factors. Weak signals that can be used to justify either the component or the emerging phenomena are linked within the system. Next, identified important phenomena or issues in each five year period are clustered and, based on the findings, conclusions of hot spots or dangerous junctions and non-linearities within that particular interval are given to the company. After that, the actual consultation begins.

Holistic Sense-making

Holistic sense-making is the seventh methodology of futures domain discussed here. It is not a method in the sense of being one particular procedure or tool for accomplishing or approaching something, neither is it a methodological principle such as an idea that 'synthesis enhances holistic understanding', and it is not a single research strategy either, as a research strategy refers to a single way through which to approach something. Holistic sense-making is a broader way of organizing research as discussed in the methodology chapter. It is a specific well-argued theory for alternative ways through which knowledge of certain well-defined research themes can be obtained by gathering knowledge from different sources as broadly and as systematically as possible, and then clustering and synthesizing that knowledge into a better holistic understanding.

Research strategies or methodological principles under the holistic sense-making approach are:

1.   The transformation of analysis, which refers to a method where emerging issues, trends, drivers, and 'paradigm' shifts are merged with the knowledge of synchronous levels of transformation.[28]

2.   Macrohistorical analysis,[29] which refers to the idea of identifying repeating macro patterns from transformation such as cyclical,

---

28 C.f. Molitor (2003); Toffler (1981 and 1991).
29 Galtung, Johan and Inayatullah, Sohail (1997): *Macrohistory and Macrohistorians*. Westport, CT, Praeger.

linear, hermeneutical processes etc. and understanding the logic of change from that point of view.[30]

3.   Cross-impact analysis.[31]

4.   Futures landscape analysis, which refers to the idea of identifying the 'big strategic' game, such as jungle, chess, mountain, star, in which a player or company is in during a particular moment.

5.   Power vector triangle (PVT-method), which is a larger and more systematic version of Sohail Inayatullah's[32] idea of futures triangle. The idea behind futures triangle is to list and compare the pushes of the present, pulls of the future and the weights of history and, based on that, make a conclusion regarding the plausible direction of the transformation. Inayatullah however, did not open up this method further in his article.

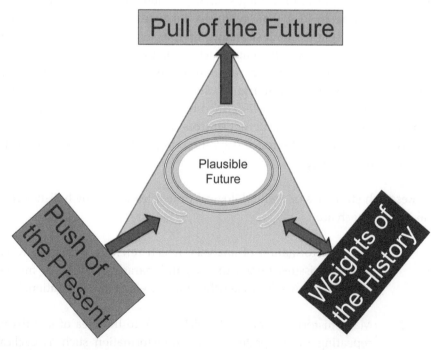

Figure 6.4   Futures triangle

30 Inayatullah (1998a); Kuosa (2005).
31 Gordon (2009c): Cross-impact analysis.
32 Inayatullah (2008): Six pillars.

Because PVT-method is the newest method in the list above, it will be presented next as an example of holistic sense-making.

Discussion of the use of PVT should begin with environment scanning, for example, use of forecasting radar or interviews of a particular theme, which are followed by FSSF categorizing of the knowledge gathered. All knowledge in FSSF categories is then sorted into three boxes 'pull of present trends and actions; pull of objectives and futures images; and pull of blocker of change/ weights of history'. All the issues in each of the boxes are then rated with points from 0 to 10. Next the points attributed to each box are totalled and the final figure is the amount of pulling power that the box has towards the 'ball of the future'. The 'ball of the future' was first conceived as being the low right corner of the triangle as it will stay there unless the two other corners have a combined pulling power that is more than the history and blockers of change. If the low left corner has a pulling power of 0 then the ball would be located to the right side straight edge between the top corner and low right hand corner. If the low left hand corner has a pulling power of 10 and the other two corners have a pulling power of just 1 then the ball would move towards the low left hand corner.

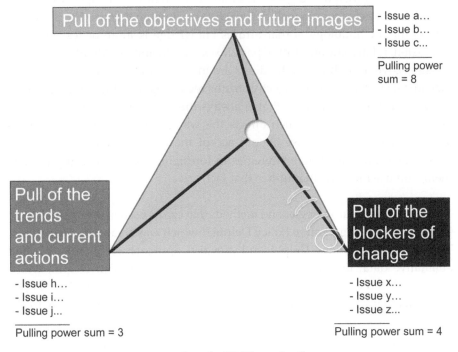

Figure 6.5   Power vectors triangle (PVT-method)

Note that things that seem small may have more influencing power on the future of a theme than the others that seem overwhelmingly large in the first instance. You can rate weak signals or any intuitive knowledge regarding the issue in each box with points as high or as low as you deem relevant. Objectivity comes from combining the many assessments. Remember that all factors, even weights of history such as a forbidding law, are considered to be equal pulling issues here.

In other words, PVT-method should be done autonomously by several people or groups and the conclusions drawn from these should be merged and synthesized so as to gain a deeper understanding of the power vectors pulling power and the direction of the plausible future. One method that can be utilized alongside the PVT-method is ATF-lenses, which is presented in the next methodology.

Alternative Objectives and Mindsets Towards the Future

The eighth fully-fledged methodology of futures domain is alternative objectives and future mindsets. It is a specific principle for how and why knowledge is gathered and generated and of different views, aspects, opinions and alternatives for certain well-defined futures domain themes. The basic idea behind the methodology is that futures knowledge is more or less open for discussion, relativistic and full of paradoxes and dilemmas. All interpretations are subjective and all understandings are in relation to the views and values that are taken. There are no objective truths regarding the future nor any single research or inferring strategy that is always the right one. Research is always done in certain context, which affects the way we nominate our objectives and strategies. Therefore we should accept the idea of multiple alternative perspectives and alternative strategies in foresight, instead of trying to deny them, and use methods that utilize that fact.

There are several strategies and methods that can be used in the methodology. One is Q2 or Disaggregative Policy Delphi,[33] which was created by Petri Tapio. This method combines Delphi and scenario approaches, quantitative and qualitative data, into a new type of formula. It begins with Delphi, which contains closed questions that are measured on a scale from 1 to 7, and open questions that ask the informant to argue certain issues. The answers to the

---

33 Tapio, Petri (2003): Disaggregative policy Delphi – Using cluster analysis as a tool for systematic scenario formation; and Tapio et al. (2011).

closed questions are statistically clustered (into value clusters) in the SPSS's disaggregative programme through tree diagrams. In other words, people whose value profiles are the most similar are put together. Next, all answers to open questions in each value cluster are merged into one 'stereotype' set of opinions or vision to the theme. Finally, based on the merged knowledge, the researcher is able to write alternative grounded 'value based' normative scenarios to the theme.

Another possible research strategy of the methodology is Harold Linstone's *Multiple Perspective Concept*,[34] which is discussed in the Futures Research Methodology v.3.0. The third alternative is to use the research strategy and method of assessment through futures mindsets (ATF-lenses). The idea behind it is briefly introduced by Sohail Inayatullah in his article, the *Six Pillars*. The following list, adopted when using this method, introduces nine ultimately different world views and unconscious beliefs of the factors and logics that make the future. Some people are fixed to only one of the beliefs in the list, but the world views of others are combinations of several of these. The five listed first are introduced by Inayatullah,[35] but modified by myself, and the remaining four are introduced by me only.

1. We need progress and growth – more technology, man as the centre of the world, and a belief in rationality. The growth of economy and investment in research solve all our problems and make the world better day by day.

2. We need to go back to the good old days – we are past our prime; we need to return to simpler times, when hierarchy was clearer, when technology was less disruptive, when the Empire was clear. Change is too overwhelming; we have lost our way, and must return.

3. We need to stop – we cannot continue like this or there is a collapse ahead. Man has reached his limits, indeed he has overshot them: world inequity, fundamentalism, tribalism, nuclear holocaust, climate disasters all point to a worsening of the future. We do not need to go back to the future as it was not as glorious as the present

---

34 Linstone (2009).
35 Inayatullah (2008); Micic, Pero (2010): *The Five Futures Glasses: How to See and Understand More of the Future with the Eltville Model* has some similarities too.

time, but given the current pace we are heading towards a collapse of everything that is dear to us.

4. We need to break barriers and get more understanding of differences – we need to focus on ways to come closer as economies and as cultures. Borders need to break down; technology and the free flow of capital can bring riches to all. All humans are the same no matter what their skin colour, sex or religion. Traditionalisms and dogmas are the barriers stopping us from achieving a new world.

5. We need to save nature and it will save us – the world is a garden, cultures are its flowers, we need social technologies to repair the damage we have caused to ourselves, to nature and to others, becoming more and more inclusive is what is important. We should stop using natural resources and find sustainable ways of living. Gaia – partnership between women and men, humans and nature and humans and technology is needed. This is challenging the very notion of 'man'.

6. We need a dictator – we need an enlightened dictator to rule the change for the better. Ordinary people are merely sheep without vision. They should not be asked what to do. We need a strong leader who has visions of a better future.

7. We need to accept that the future is deterministic – the future is written to a 'big book' and it can be read from the stars. Almost everything is fixed and decided and we can only follow the big plan.

8. We need to accept that the future is steered by masses and big trends – small incidences and even political decisions fade under the big pressure of overall transformation. The future can be forecast from the knowledge of the big trends and the transformation logic that we see.

9. We need to accept that the future is a chain of random small incidences in the same way as history was – the supposedly inevitable direction of transformation is radically converted time after time by small incidences. Being affective in the right place at the right time makes a larger difference than any great plans.

The idea in the ATF-lenses[36] method is to assess sets of futures knowledge through these nine views or lenses to obtain truly alternative aspects on the issue. The futures knowledge that is produced through these 'assessment through futures mindsets' lenses is greater than we tend to understand. ATF-lenses are particularly suited to assessing, from various angles, any material that is produced through the PVT-method. Hence, ATF-lenses are a method for increasing any assessment's objectivity and it helps to avoid possible blind spots.

The fourth possible research strategy of the alternative objectives and future mindsets methodology is the SIF-model, which has two dimensions. The first dimension is based on the Future Signals Sense-making Framework (FSSF) from analysis and categorizing methodology, which introduces the different levels of futures knowledge: A: *Weak signals* level which refers to the level of gathering and analysing raw data or interpretations of perceptions; B: *Drivers* level which refers to cumulative reasoning of the causalities or effective factors for change, and C: *Trends* level which refers to the reasoning of trends from time series, subjectively inferring complex or relativistic phenomena, and identifying large clusters or hidden patterns from various sources of information, as explained in the second chapter.

The second dimension of the SIF-model is constructed from the idea behind the three general strategies of pattern management; empirical calculation, theory proving with observations, and real combining. The second dimension opens up the spectrum of inferring from quantitative to abductive to qualitative, which adapts to the types of information that are looked at in each case: existing, invented or detected, and emerging objects, as discussed in the fifth chapter.

When these two dimensions are put together, we get the following three vertical categories of inferring answers in foresight, namely strategies: X, Y and Z. These three strategies represent independent and alternative ways to handle the entire process of reasoning the reality, the change, and the future. One can select any of these three SIF strategies, based on their objectives, methods, context, and the type of phenomena with which they are working,or alternatively the strategies can be combined.

Strategy X is particularly suitable for quantitative, statistic and software based analysis. The answer that is searched for is a snapshot of the truth, that

---

36   ATF-lenses of the nine world views are used in AlternativeFutures' toolkit. Available at: www.alternativefutures.fi

Table 6.3   SIF-model

The levels of change factors: A, B and C	Strategies of Inferring in Foresight: X, Y and Z		
A. Weak signals/anomolies	Anomolies in data	Anomolies in existing hypothesis	Anomolies in social environment or in our concepts' abilities to explain new observations
B. Drivers	Underlying causal factors that have explanatory power	Underlying links and alternative hypothesis for explaining	Underlying social forces and needs
C. Trends	Pattern management, time series analysis and trend-extrapolation	Verifying hypothesis of the real world	Indentifying large social phenomena
	X: Quantitative inferring Conclusion through automated calculation/ data-analysis. 'Snapshop truth' to limited set of data. For 'detected or invented issues'.	**Y: Abductive inferring** Anomalies -> Abductive hypothesis -> falsification -> conclusion. 'Universal truths for tangible existing issues'.	**Z: Qualitative inferring** Subjective and constructivistic conclusions for issues that are too complex for hard science methods. For 'invented and emerging issues'.

Table 6.4   Conclusion of the research strategies in SIF-model

Strategy	Data/evidence	Reasoning/method	Objective/answer
X: Quantitative Inferring/ Empirical Calculation	Mostly quantitative and statistics raw data.	Mostly inductive. Calculations, statistic, variable or factor analysis, clustering and pattern management, correlations, modelling.	Snapshot 'truths' that constantly change alongside with the data. The objective of reasoning is a quantified answer.
Y: Abductive Inferring/Theory Proving with Observations	All relevant data and perceptions can be equally used as evidence. The objectives determinate the required or relevant data sources.	Abductive, which can utilize any form of reasoning. Test sets or comparisons. Creation of new hypothesis and falsification of existing hypothesis as long as necessary.	Reasoned 'undeniable truth'. The objective of reasoning is a tangible and permanent answer, 'e.g., virus x causes this illness'.
Z: Qualitative Inferring/Real Combining	Mostly qualitative, perceptions, literature, talk, tacit knowledge, weak signals, intuition, wisdom, interpretations, social agreements.	Mixture of all forms of reasoning, e.g., analogies and case-based reasoning. Creating linkages, possible causalities and synthesis. Holistic and autopoietic sense-making.	Invented or emerging 'truths'. Fuzzy logic. Subjectively or socially constructed answer to complex or relativistic issue. The objective of reasoning is to understand very complex issues.

is, something which is true for that particular moment only. Therefore, the user of this strategy accepts that the answer or truth changes over time. In level A of strategy X, one should gather all relevant raw data or perceptions. The interpretations are made according to statistical rules. In level B, knowledge is cumulated and causalities are searched for – the proximate and ultimate drivers and the interrelations should be revealed. In level C, the discovered snapshot path, peak or trend that were located in level A are mapped, as well as the causalities discovered in level B (interrelations and drivers). Thus, in level C, all the conclusions from levels A and B are combined and based on these, one can extrapolate how trends or phenomena may change over time. Such extrapolation in X may follow, for example, time series analysis or multi-causal analysis. Basically strategy X is common in technological forecasting, modelling, and in environmental scanning and early warning systems.

Strategy Y is common in natural sciences, forensic and medical research, history, engineering, astronomy or any other type of research where the expected outcomes are believed to be more or less permanent truths or answers to certain questions. For instance, based on all the evidence, there must logically be a planet in a given solar system, person x must be the murderer, all swans cannot be white, there must be an unknown virus causing this illness etc. In strategy Y, the three levels of knowledge (A, B and C) are merely different sides of one research process, not independent research phases as is the case with X and Z. In Y, the role of A is to map the evidence, the role of B is to carry out the abductive research, and the role of C is to conclude the final answers to the research questions. In foresight strategy, Y can be applied to research, which attempts to solve tangible problems or gather cumulative knowledge of certain themes. It may be applied in environmental futures studies, regional foresight or in any research which requires the systematic phases of detection -> generation of hypothesis -> falsification of wrong hypothesis basing on evidence -> verifying the right hypothesis.

Strategy Z is suitable for any qualitative research, and it is common in all social sciences, humanities, arts, and any holistic, synthesizing, or constructivist reality or discourse building. All users of Z usually realize that the outcomes of the process are more or less subjective (or collective) interpretations. Thus, the concluded 'true' answer, the discourse, the futures knowledge, or the extension or existence of a phenomenon – whatever it is that is looked after – is understood as something that is genuinely invented or constructed in the human mind. In other words, the users of Z, as well as the general audience, should realize that some other person, some other research group, or some other culture, would end up with another set of conclusions from the same research material. Here, the expected outcomes of the reasoning are always approximate, subjective, or even completely invented. Z, and especially the philosophy behind it, can be seen to have similarities with the idea of fuzzy logic,[37] where answers are not precise and solutions vary somewhere in the grey zone, being almost never black or white. According to fuzzy logic, if a network or structure is large enough, there are always many alternative ways from one point to another. And social phenomena are always full of paradoxes and alternative angles and views on the issues. In practice, this kind of an approach makes, for example, a corporate strategy, an electrical network, or even a washing machine more robust in comparison with a single solution approach. To go back to the use of the levels of knowledge in the SIF-model, strategy Z starts with the mapping and interpreting of subjective discoveries or believed qualitative characteristics, discoveries, anomalies, weak signals, tacit knowledge etc. of certain phenomena in level A. In level B, believed causalities and drivers behind the complex phenomenon or a trend are qualitatively reasoned. In level C, all the evidence and the subjective conclusions are combined in order to get a holistic view over the complex, large or relativistic issue or phenomenon.

Alternative Futures Scenarios

Alternative futures scenarios is the ninth methodology of the futures domain. It is a specific principle that shows how knowledge of certain well-defined futures domain research themes can be obtained through building systematically alternative futures scenarios. This methodology refers to a broad way of thinking about the future, and it can be said to be the foundation of both participative foresight, and strategic foresight, as can be seen in Figure 6.2. The philosophy of this methodology states that the future is not just one, but a set of alternative futures. We can systematically assess the probabilities, desirability and links for each option of transformation with certain principles and methods, and this knowledge is crucial for understanding the future.[38]

As already explained in the second chapter, there are two basic methodological approaches that fall under scenario methodology; normative and explorative. Then there are various strategies such as 'critical action scenarios', methods such as 'futures table', and combinations that can be applied in either of the approaches. And then there are methods, which

---

37 Vliet, Kok and Veldkamp (2010).
38 For example, Biloslavo and Slavko (2009); Bezold (2010).

combine quantitative and qualitative approaches with scenario work such as Dissaggregative Policy Delphi and Fuzzy Cognitive Maps.[39]

One combination of scenario work's methodological approaches is the mixed scenarios approach.[40] It is actually a realistic strategy of doing explorative scenarios in a project, which does not begin from an 'empty table', as in a pure explorative approach, and it does not begin with pure normative visions or objectives generation work either. This approach follows the idea that in reality we always have some background information of the theme before we start any research, and thus we always do have some work hypothesis, which affects the organization of our work. In other words, in most cases we mix normative visioning with any type of explorative work. One reason for mixing normative visioning with explorative scenario work is that it is known for characteristic or quality of scenario work. Useful scenario work should deliberately present 'a situation radically at odds with traditional thinking', as defined in Coates and Glenn's[41] third application of scenarios.

Strategic Management

Finally strategic management is the tenth methodology of futures domain. It is not a method in a sense of being one particular procedure or tool for accomplishing or approaching something as is the case with many of its methods, for example, with a strategic SWOT, relevance tree,[42] and morphological analysis futures memorizing. It is not just a methodological principle such as the idea of 'visionary management', nor a methodological approach such as the process of strategic foresight, the core theme of this book, and it is not a single research strategy either, as a research strategy refers to only one way of approaching something. The most common research strategy under strategic management is the normative (management) approach that was discussed in the second chapter. Hence strategic management is a broader way of organizing the research as discussed in the methodology chapter. It is a specific well-argued theory of affective ways to gather strategic intelligence for strategic decision making.

---

39 C.f. Vliet, Kok and Veldkamp (2010).
40 Kuosa (2010b): Future of U.S. power: Is China going to eclipse the United States? Two possible scenarios to 2040. *RSIS Working paper No. 203.* Nanyang Technological University, Singapore. Available at: http://www.rsis.edu.sg/publications/WorkingPapers/WP203.pdf
41 See scenarios part in Chapter 2; Coates and Glenn (2009).
42 Futures Group International (2009). Relevance Tree. See Bell (2005) and other articles of *Futures Research Methodology – Version 3.0* as well.

Irrespective of which management doctrine or style is in vogue, for a manager the purpose of any strategic intelligence is always to make strategically better decisions. In most cases achieving such an aim requires the use of many systematic intelligence, analysis and assessing methods. As discussed earlier in this book, strategic foresight is one good integrated way to produce such strategic intelligence material for use in strategic management. It attempts to explain how knowledge of certain well-defined research themes can be obtained through gathering knowledge from different sources as broadly and as systematically as possible, and how to then cluster and synthesize that knowledge systematically into better holistic understanding. And finally, it attempts to define the 'what-if' questions, outside-of-the-box views and to build alternative strategic scenarios for decision makers.

Alongside strategic foresight, there are many other alternative principles, strategies and useful methods of strategic management, such as relevance trees and backcasting, which unfortunately cannot be discussed here due to limited space, and my decision to focus on new methods, or methods that are very useful but forgotten as is the case with the strategic SWOT, which will be presented next.

The strategic SWOT, or eight field SWOT in its original form, was introduced by Nigel Piercy and William Giles in 1989 in their article 'Making SWOT Analysis Work'.[43] This method is based on two elements. The first is SWOT analysis, which had already been developed by business consultant Albert S. Humphrey in the 1960s, and the other is the idea of combining SWOTs into business strategy and development work, which was introduced by D.F. Abell and J.S Hammond in 1979.

A strategic SWOT attempts to improve the use of SWOTs in strategy work by assigning the following five rules:

1.   Focused SWOTs;

2.   Shared vision;

3.   Customer orientation;

---

43 Piercy, Nigel and Giles, William (1989): Making SWOT analysis work. *Marketing Intelligence & Planning*, 7 (5/6), 5–7; and Abell, Derek F. and Hammond, John S. (1979): *Strategic Market Planning: Problems and Analytical Approach*, Englewood Cliffs, Prentice-Hall; Kai Koski of KyAMK, and Kotler and Payne (1993, 101–2).

4. Environmental analysis;

5. Structured strategy generation.

Focused SWOTs refer to the need to do several different SWOT analyses and to limit the scope of each so as to concentrate on parts of a business strategy, instead of looking at the whole company from a single global perspective.

Shared vision refers to the rule for basing SWOT analysis on the diverse sources and opinions inside a company, and not just on the company's executives or planning teams' views.

Customer orientation refers to the rule for basing SWOT analysis only on realistic information that comes directly from customers. If a company restricts itself to its own internal understanding of its strengths and weaknesses, this is most likely to be misleading. Furthermore, each issue that is looked at from a customer point of view has both strengths and weaknesses. This means that there should be separate customer view assessments that cover all aspects of the company, for example, 'an old established firm' – strengths and weaknesses of this; 'a large supplier' – strengths and weaknesses of this.

Environmental analysis refers to the rule that all opportunities and threats exist only in the outside world – the things we propose to do about them are our

Table 6.5   Strategic SWOT

		Internal components	
	Aligning SWOT with strategy work into 'Eight field SWOT'	**Strengths** - Products/services - Competenecies - Customer relationships - Financing	**Weaknesses** - Qualtity of products/services - Market understanding - After-sales marketing - Lacking planning - Competitive advantage
External components	**Opportunities** - New markets - New customer groups - New ways of marketing - New supply source	STRATEGY 1 'Match'	STRATEGY 2 'Improve'
	Threats - Competition - Future competition (new solutions) - Changing buying behaviour - Change	STRATEGY 3 'Convert'	STRATEGY 4 'Catastrophy plan'

strategies. For example it may be suggested that price-cutting is an opportunity. This is not an opportunity in a strategic SWOT – it is a price strategy, which we may adopt. However, according to Piercy and Giles (1989), we would only accept the desirability of a price-cutting strategy if, for example, our size gave us greater cost-economies than our competitors, and there was an identified opportunity in terms of there being a price-sensitive segment of the market, or the need to meet a competitor's threatened entry to the market with low prices.

Structured strategy generation refers to the idea that, when we are able to complete all four cells of the strategic SWOT matrix, and we have ranked each item in each category in terms of its importance, then the matrix automatically acts as a generator of supplement strategies.

The second example of strategic management methodology of futures domain is the methodological principle of visionary management. It was created by Pentti Malaska and Karin Holstius in 1999 as a next generation response to the needs of business leadership following its predecessor, scenario approaches. According to Malaska and Holstius the reason for introducing both approaches was the fact that the business environment has become more complex, unpredictable and turbulent.

According to Malaska and Holstius[44] the basis for visionary management is in visionary decisions, which are very different from opportunistic and strategic decisions. When an *opportunistic decision* is made the situation is known with certainty and it is evaluated in the short-term, the resources are fixed and the purpose is to maximize immediate profit and cash flow. In the case of *strategic decisions* the situation is assumed to be changing but still predictable in the time frame of the decision. Beneficial reallocation of resources is a reaction to the predicted changes and the purpose of adaptation is to strive for growth and improved return on investment, that is, to improve the conditions of opportunistic management. *Visionary decisions* become appropriate when the situation is assumed to include discontinuities and to be unpredictable in the long term. New skills are needed to reframe and envision the business, and the purposes aimed at are: maintaining excellence of performance and creating novel options, or survival in the long run.[45]

However, the question of good public decision making, whether opportunistic, strategic or visionary, and the ideas behind the necessary

---

44 Malaska and Holstius (1999, 354).
45 Ibid.

components of these, are not new by any means. According to Malaska and Holstius[46] a modern view of good decision making can be found in the teachings and thoughts of Aristotle. His first rule for making a good decision was to define the purpose and objectives clearly. Aristotle's second requirement was a thorough understanding of the situation in question and information about the available means and resources. The third rule was to perceive the future environment and combine it with the three kinds of knowledge at hand, the purpose, situation and resources, by using sound logic. Thus a decision maker can reach a good decision only by deliberating these three kinds of knowledge and the perception of the environment simultaneously.

What is visionary management all about? At first it is of course about good visionary decisions from futures perspectives. Second it is about creating a preferred vision, as introduced in the second chapter. Third it is about reflecting the present situation against the focused vision. This third step enables several basic observations to be made. The first one is to realize how the company's present performance differs from the vision. Then these differences are 'visionarily' adopted as new objectives for the company. The idea behind this 'visionary' logic is the understanding that, present performance has been possible through the company's current core competencies, skills and resources. With these current competences it will not be possible to achieve the objectives of the future vision. For this purpose the company will have to develop new core competencies, skills and resources, and this is what Malaska and Holstius call visionary development, which is at the heart of visionary management.

Alongside the difference between the types of decisions, the other differentiating aspect between visionary, strategic and opportunistic management is in the time range used. The time range for opportunistic management is 1–3 years in the future, whilst the range of strategic management is 3–5 years, but the time range of visionary management is +5 years. However Malaska's and Holstius's[47] original time range is not the only one that has been used to describe the difference. For instance Kaivo–oja et al.[48] have preferred to use different time ranges. Here the operational management operates only in a time range of 0–1 years in the future, strategic management operates in a time range of 1–10 years, and visionary management operates in a time range of 10–50 years in the future.

---

46 Ibid.
47 Ibid.
48 Kaivo-oja et al. (2004, 543).

Despite the fact that Malaska and Holstius emphasize the broad difference between strategic management and visionary management, in this book visionary management is considered an alternative to the methodological principle under the much broader domain of strategic management.

Summary of Futures Domain Methodologies

This chapter presented the ten major methodologies of foresight and futures domain. There are arguably a few other methodological approaches and principles that could also be counted as top level methodologies of the domain. For instance, the soft system methodology[49] is named and introduced as a futures studies methodology in some cases. One could also argue that critical futures studies, time-series analysis, weak signals analysis, predictive methods, modelling, evolutionary futures studies,[50] expert methods, workshop methods, integrated foresight/strategic foresight, explorative forecasting and normative forecasting should all belong to the macro-level of methodologies and not to the meso- or meta-level of principles, strategies, and approaches. Alternatively, the whole list of ten methodologies can be seen to form a sketch of an integrated foresight or strategic foresight process that runs from environmental scanning all the way through to strategic management, which would submit all the methodologies to those research strategies. Hence, we must admit that in some cases the borders between methodologies, approaches, strategies, principles and methods can be confusing. Nevertheless, the descriptive principles of a fully-fledged methodology are quite transparent. Anything that combines a method with a description of the principles behind the use of that method does not pass as a fully-fledged methodology. In most cases such descriptions are merely principles that can be applied in many methodologies, which eventually are just parts of a larger entity in a discipline.

Table 6.6 summarizes the profiles of the methods and principles that have been used as examples in the ten methodologies of futures domain. The list is not exhaustive but it gives a good overview of the different types of methods. One can use the list for assessing what types of methods can be used, for instance, in a short workshop. It tells which methods are large group methods or which require a large group of informants, which suit for smaller boards or teams, and which are merely meant to be used by a single researcher alone. One may also want to assess how much preparation time the method requires.

---

49 Checkland (1981).
50 Laszlo (2003).

Some methods can be used ad hoc whilst some are for larger research projects only. And finally, the methods serve different types of interests of knowledge. Some of the methods are for systematically gathering as much knowledge of a certain theme as possible. Some methods are well suited to obtaining a better understanding and going to roots of a certain phenomenon, and some are meant to be used as assisting methods in strategic work. The logic in profiling each method with x:s or -:s is that I have tried to put as few x:s in the list as possible. The more there are for checking, the less there are for differentiating factors and the less information the list carries, and vice versa. However, in some cases it is necessary to check more than one characteristic for a method.

Table 6.6   Profiles of methods and principles in ten futures domain methodologies

Methods	Time needed			Participants			Preparation			Knowledge		
	Hours	Days (min 1/2 max 2)	Many days	One is enough	A few	Larger group	No need (in advance)	A little bit of need	Requires a lot	More information	Better understaning	Strategic options
Database literature reviews	–	–	x	x	x	–	–	x	–	x	–	–
Delphi	–	–	x	–	x	x	–	–	x	x	x	–
Future Signals Sense-making Framework (FSSF)	x	x	–	x	x	–	–	–	x	x	x	–
Pattern management	–	x	x	x	–	–	–	–	x	–	x	–
Critical futures studies	–	x	–	x	–	–	–	x	–	–	x	–
Disaggregative Policy Delphi	–	–	x	–	–	x	–	–	x	–	x	–
Relevance tree	x	–	–	x	–	–	x	–	–	–	x	–
Forecasting radar in Early warning	–	–	x	x	x	–	–	–	x	–	x	–
Power Vectors Triangle Method	x	–	–	–	x	x	–	x	–	–	x	–
ATF-Lenses (future mindsets)	x	–	–	–	x	x	x	–	–	–	x	–
SIF-Model	x	x	–	–	x	–	–	x	–	–	x	x
Roadmapping	–	–	x	x	x	x	–	–	x	–	x	x
Strategic SWOT	x	–	–	–	x	–	x	–	–	–	x	x
Mixed scenarios	–	–	x	x	–	–	–	–	x	–	–	x
Visionary management	–	x	x	–	x	x	–	x	x	–	–	x
ALT 3, Creative visioning	–	x	–	–	–	x	–	x	–	–	–	x
Backcasting	x	x	–	x	x	–	–	x	–	–	–	x

PART II
Structure

International declaration without military power behind it is like music without instruments.

Carl von Clausewitz

Introduction

This part of the book is named structure as it presents the public strategic foresight organization or system in 23 countries, regions, federations, or other transnational thematic areas. The cases are mainly from Europe as the European Union and some of its member states' agents, such as France's *General du Plan*, and some individual European researchers, have been willing to map the European Union's old and new member states foresight systems for public policy making. Outside Europe, two countries Singapore and the US, are given as examples, as these two countries have put considerable effort into strengthening their national security through various intelligence practices.

The structure part of the book is followed by the process part. It brings together cases from selected countries, and their existing practices and structures into debate, whereby experts from different domains of strategic foresight assess their strengths and weaknesses and suggest ways of improving public strategic foresight systems.

Structure

7

Principles of Strategic Foresight in Public Policy Making

Many governments have realized that focusing on a single-issue is often insufficient in dealing with emerging threats and opportunities. They have therefore started to experiment with strategic foresight that deliberately cuts across the traditional boundaries of policy areas and government departments. In the past, public policy has focused more often on science, technology, and innovation policy, now the focus has started to incorporate societal and economic issues to health, environment or national security, and international initiatives are starting to combine the various national experiences in order to lift them to a higher strategic level.[1]

According to Beat Habegger, there are two ways in which national strategic foresight contributes to public policy making: 'It informs policy by providing more systematic knowledge about relevant trends and developments in an organization's environments; (...) and it acts as a driver of reflexive mutual social learning processes among policy makers that stimulate the generation of common public policy visions'.[2] Another way to view this definition is to say that national strategic foresight can contribute to public policy making at three distinctive levels.

- The first level is intelligence work, where the aim is to gather systematic foreknowledge of changes in trends and potential new issues and risks that should be addressed in public strategy work.

- The second level is enhancing reflexive mutual social learning processes among policy makers, and cutting across traditional boundaries of policy areas and government departments, thus

---

1   Habegger (2010, 50).
2   Habegger (2010, 49).

incorporating societal and economic issues to health, environment or national security, in order to obtain a more holistic understanding of public policy requirements.

- The third level is helping the public decision makers to formulate better informed and better prepared future visions and political grand strategies.

If that statement is translated to real life, we may say that level one is better represented in national strategic foresight than level two, and again level two seems to be better represented than level three. This becomes clear in the interview answers of the policy makers and high ranking government officials in Chapter 12, which gathers their ideas into questions such as 'How could the strategic foresight process better facilitate national decision making?' Hence, one could say that there is still much unused potential in strategic foresight, which could be utilized in public policy making.

8

Strategic Foresight in the European Union's Older Member States' Public Policy Making

Public strategic foresight is about refining foreknowledge and strategic
options for a public actor who wants to win a societal, political, economic
or military battle for a country.

Kuosa

The European Union has 27 member states. The 15 states which were members of the EU prior to its last large enlargement in 2004 are here referred to as the old member states, and the 12 states which have joined the EU during or after that year are referred to as the new member states. The national foresight systems of these old member states[1] are discussed first, and these are followed by a presentation of the new member states systems, and finally there followexamples of strategic foresight systems in Singapore and the US, and in the OECD, UNIDO and IIASA.

Cases from the European Union

Foresight and futures work in the European Union has grown significantly in the past 20 years. Most European Union member states have undertaken national foresight exercises in some form. In the European Union government

---

1   The systems of all 15 old member states are not discussed here, as there have not been sufficient studies of all the systems available. Systems of the UK, France, Germany, Netherlands, Sweden, Finland and Ireland are presented, and systems of Belgium, Luxembourg, Denmark and Mediterranean countries are not. However, it should be noticed that there are many public foresight functions in the list of countries that are not thoroughly discussed. For instance Belgia has its Federal Planning Office in Brussels, which is the capital of both Belgium and the EU, Denmark has among else, for example, its already old Copenhagen Institute for Futures Studies, and Spain, Greece, Portugal and Italy have many foresight functions too.

foresight has steadily gained some institutional structures as well. There are several small units within the government, such as the former Science and Technology Foresight unit within the EU Directorate General for Research,[2] and foresight work within the Institute for Prospective Technological Studies and DIUS in the UK. There are also some institutional networks in the EU government, such as the European Parliamentary Technology Assessment[3] (EPTA), a network of parliamentary and other organizations that includes foresight among its activities examining the impact of new technologies. The European Commission has the Joint Research Centre (JRC) which has seven joint scientific institutes that are located at five different sites in Europe: Geel (BE), Ispra (IT), Karlsruhe (DE), Petten (NL) and Seville (ES). The JRC's Directorate-General is located in Brussels. The JRC provides independent scientific and technical advice to the European Commission and the Member States of the European Union in support of EU policies.[4] Among the JRC joint research institutes, the Institute for Prospective Technological Studies (IPTS)[5] based in Seville plays a major role in foresight in the EU through the Foresight for the European Research Area (FORERA) team. The IPTS has hosted three international seminars on future-oriented technology analysis, and has also been involved in the development and hosting of the online guide to foresight, that is part of Forlearn,[6] a continually developing resource for those wishing to undertake a foresight exercise. The guide outlines the reasons for doing a foresight exercise and the issues involved in setting up, running, and following up a project.[7] The IPTS's strategic foresight system that merges horizons scanning with funnelling the emerging issues into trends which should be tackled in policy making, has not only been utilized in the EU. It has also been adopted by Singapore's strategic foresight system, where it is used as the basic model for Singapore's Emerging Strategic Issues Project (SESIP).

European Foresight Monitoring Network (EFMN)[8] is the EU's on-going project for monitoring its foresight activities. The website provides a searchable database and tools to search foresight activities not only in Europe but worldwide. On the website the initiatives can be searched via basic details such

2   Available at: http://costa22.org
3   European Parliamentary Technology Assessment. Available at: www.eptanetwork.org/EPTA/index.php
4   Available at: http://ec.europa.eu/dgs/jrc/index.cfm [and] http://en.wikipedia.org/wiki/Joint_Research_Centre_(European_Commission)
5   See Institute for Prospective Technological Studies. Available at:http://forera.jrc.es/
6   Available at: http://forlearn.jrc.ec.europa.eu/guide/0_home/index.htm
7   Available at: http://forera.jrc.es/fta/intro.html; May, Graham H. (2009, 58).
8   See European Foresight Monitoring Network. Available at: www.efmn.info/

as title and country; a series of drop down menus under research area, industry, market, audience, output and sponsor; and a further drop down menu that includes 31 different foresight methods. In 2009, the EFMN website listed 1,916 foresight initiatives in the EU. The EFMN also contributes to Forsociety[9] and Forlearn[10] which aim to provide a knowledge sharing platform for foresight practitioners and policy makers in the EU.

One of the newest initiatives is the European Strategy and Policy Analysis System (ESPAS), which the European Union is setting up at the time of writing. It is steered by a 'quadrilateral' inter-institutional task force (BEPA, the Council Secretariat General, the European Parliament, and the European External Action Service). The project is intended to work as an EU inter-institutional strategy, and a policy analysis pilot aims to identify long-term global trends on a whole set of issues across different world regions and how these could influence EU policy. A Paris-based think tank of the EU, the Institute for Security Studies (EUISS) has been identified as the centre for the ESPAS's proposed trend-monitoring system.

Although there are a number of small foresight units and institutional networks within the EU government, most of the EU's foresight work has taken the form of funded projects such as large Framework Programmes,[11] which are run over a number of years by outside contractors and lead to the publication of reports, guides and toolkits. These have been undertaken by a growing number of university departments, research institutes and consultancies that have, in the process, developed capability in foresight and produced several guides on the use of futures methods and techniques.[12]

Examples of the most remarkable foresight projects that have been funded through the EU's large Framework Programmes include COST Action 22:

---

9   See Forsociety. Available at: www.eranet-forsociety.net/ForSociety/index.html
10   See Forlearn. Available at: http://forlearn.jrc.es/index.htm
11   At the Community level, the European Union (see http://cordis.europa.eu/home_en.html) possesses three key funding instruments to support research and innovation: Cohesion policy which is funded through the Structural Funds and Cohesion Fund; the Research Framework Programme and the Competitiveness and Innovation Framework Programme. From the point of view of foresight research funding, the framework programmes are the key funding element. For instance the 7th Framework Programme (2007–2013) funds almost all main sectors of research and society (see http://cordis.europa.eu/fp7/home_en.html). The EU Research Framework Programmes were explicitly designed to support the creation of 'unified' European Research Area (ERA), according the European Commission's strategic grand plan *Towards a European Research Area* of January 2000.
12   May (2009, 63).

Advancing Foresight Methodologies[13] (2004–2007) that focused specifically on foresight methodology. COST Action 22 brought together an international group that included individuals with backgrounds in futures and sustainability and the environment.

Another example is ERA-Net,[14] a sustainable and dynamic network that aimed to build a close relationship between foresight in the EU and its member states. In the ERA-Net national foresight programme, managers co-ordinated their activities and – on the basis of shared knowledge on relevant issues, methodologies, legal and financial frameworks – regularly developed and implemented efficient trans-national foresight programmes that significantly enriched both national and European research and innovation systems.

The objective of the third example, Futures for Regional Development (FUTURREG), was to create a regional policy-making futures toolkit, based on previous projects carried out by the international partners of the project. The Toolkit includes guidance on which tools and approaches may be appropriate according to regional objectives, resources and priorities. It was also developed for wider use in other EU regions. Regions and their public authorities are meant to be able to use the FUTURREG futures tools to deal with important challenges and trends in an intelligent and strategic way.[15]

One the most ambitious foresight and horizons scanning projects under the European Commission's framework programmes is the Blue Sky research project 'Interconnecting Knowledge' (iKNOW). iKNOW intends to become a cornerstone for on-going and future horizon scanning, foresight and forward-looking activities in Europe – advancing knowledge, tools and capacities for the analysis and use of wild cards and weak signals approaches. In particular, iKNOW has developed conceptual and methodological frameworks to identify, classify, cluster and analyse wild cards and weak signals and assess their implications for potential impacts on Europe and the world. As a result, iKNOW puts forward a novel 'horizon scanning 2.0' approach which, on the one hand, promotes participatory and bottom-up scanning supported by web 2.0 technologies, and, on the other, improves information collection, filtering, communication and exploitation.[16]

---

13 Available at: http://costa22.org
14 Available at: www.eranet-forsociety.net/ForSociety/index.html
15 Available at: http://www.interreg3c.net/sixcms/detail.php?id=8109
16 See WI-WE Bank. Available at: http://wiwe.iknowfutures.eu/; iKnow Community. Available at: http://community.iknowfutures.eu/#1

Graham H. May has made an assessment of the potential influence of the various foresight activities to EU policy making. He notes that although in terms of futures and foresight the recent increase in foresight activities has been important, they are small in relation to the activity of both the EU and its member states. Although it is difficult to assess precisely how much influence recent foresight activities have had on the day-to-day work of government, it seems likely that foresight is seen mainly as an additional activity in policy making, leaving little imprint directly on EU policies. May concludes:

> *Despite this extensive practical experience there has been little development in the academic sector of theoretical understanding or education and training in futures.[17] There is little real appreciation of what foresight can and cannot be expected to do, or of critical evaluation of the results, apart from some reviews of national foresight studies with the danger that unrealistic expectations of its capabilities will be disappointed and its value doubted. The growth of foresight and related futures work in Europe has occurred during a period of economic prosperity and growing public expenditure but it may not be sustainable as unrealistic expectations fail to be fulfilled and public spending in the recession is cut back and foresight seen as an expendable luxury. The last 15 years will then prove to be an exception rather than the beginning of the embedding of foresight into society.[18]*

Cases from Finland[19]

There are six more or less stabilized foresight functions or networks in Finland, which together can be called the Finnish foresight system. There is no single unified top-down steered national foresight system in Finland, and never has been. Foresight functions are fragmented between many actors which are public, private, non-governmental and international, or a combination of many of these types. In this sense the Finnish 'system', if we are able to call it a system at all, is typical among developed countries. National foresight systems are

---

17 At the same time it should be noticed that there are approximately two dozen North American universities with graduate programmes in Futures Studies, to include two programmes that now grant Ph.D.s. In the EU area these numbers are about in the same.

18 May (2009, 65).

19 This chapter bases on the interviews of Riitta Kirjavainen, Deputy Head of Policy-analysis Unit, Finland Prime Minister's office; Jyrki Kasvi, the long-term Vice-Chair of the Committee for the Future, and the Committee for the Future's long-term Senior Advisor Osmo Kuusi. See Kuusi (1999), Teknologian arviointeja (2004).

always some kind of complex evolving combinations of many overlapping functions and networks. Some systems just have more top-down features, resources, direct influence, or more actors or functions than the others.

What is characteristic of the Finnish foresight system is its overall flexibility and ability to penetrate the whole of society, and involve so many decision makers, ministry officials, university and sector researchers, corporate organizations, national funding agencies, and other stakeholders. The Finnish system has the following six parts:

- The Government Foresight Report work;

- Government Foresight Network;

- Finnish Parliament's Committee for the Future;

- Foresight consortium for labour force, competence, and educational needs;

- SITRA's Foresight network;

- Finnish futures community and society.

There are three main groups in the Finnish strategic foresight system: functions related to the Finnish parliament, functions related to the Finnish government, and functions related to the Finnish futures or futurists community which functions outside the government. The core of the system is The Government Programme combined with The Government Foresight Report, as that links the government's and parliament's futures work together.

THE GOVERNMENT FORESIGHT REPORT IN THE GOVERNMENT PROGRAMME

Every time a new government begins its work in Finland, it writes a *Government Programme*[20] for its term, which is normally four years. This highly political

---

20 The Government Programme is an action plan agreed by the parties represented in the government and it sets out the main functions of the government. Government Programme of Prime Minister Mari Kiviniemi's government was submitted to Parliament in the form of a government statement on 22 June 2010. The government will proceed with the implementation of decisions of Matti Vanhanen's second government, Government Programme and the Mid-Term Policy Review.Available at: http://www.vn.fi/tietoarkisto/aiemmat-hallitukset/

document defines the government's visions, objectives and the action plan to which all parties and members of the government officially commit. All decisions prepared in ministries should follow the nature of the Government Programme. One thing that was named in the last Government Programme was the theme for the *Government Foresight Report*.[21] It is a large report that discusses the development aspects of a large thematic area usually 20 to 30 years in the future and defines the government's vision as well as its guidelines. The Prime Minister's Office's Policy-Analysis Unit is responsible for the preparation of the report, and is supervised by a group of ministers. Subject experts in ministries and the research community are invited to join the coordination group, set up for the preparation. Background reports are commissioned, and are written by the state's sector research institutes such as the Government Institute for Economic Research (VATT), the National Institute for Health and Welfare (THL), the Technical Research Centre of Finland (VTT), the Agrifood Research Finland (MTT), the Statistics Finland or think tanks etc. The next Government Foresight Report is always on a new theme, so to prepare for this, the PM's Office invites research institutes and Ministries' departments to join the preparation process, in order to always have flexibility and cost efficiently, and the best experts involved in the work. This means that the preparation team is assembled according to the theme of the Report.

The official role of The Government Foresight Report in the Finnish political system is to be the government's long-term visionary document and it is expected to be handed to parliament for comment during its term.[22] Preparation of The Government Foresight Report begins with a phase during which government officials undertake the project planning work, sometimes with the assistance of outside consultants, and the team is then nominated. The team gathers relevant background information and, when needed, orders research reports. These reports can be produced by state sector research institutes, other research units, or think tanks. The team may also organize scenario processes and public hearings. Next the aggregative final report is drafted and the

---

vanhanenII/hallitusohjelma/pdf/en.pdf; and http://www.vn.fi/hallitus/hallitusohjelma/pdf/en.pdf

21 The Government Foresight Reports are academic reports, which discuss the long-term development aspects of one thematic area usually 20 to 30 years ahead in time. The government adopted the Foresight Report on Long-term Climate and Energy Policy in October 2009. Setting a target to reduce Finland's greenhouse gas emissions by at least 80 per cent from the 1990 level by 2050 as part of an international effort, the report marks out the road to a low-carbon Finland in 2050. Available at: http://www.vnk.fi/julkaisukansio/2009/j28-ilmasto-selonteko-j29-klimat-framtidsredogoerelse-j30-climate_/pdf/en.pdf

22 If the government changes during a parliamentary term of four years, the Future report is not changed as a result. It will still be the standing government's Future report.

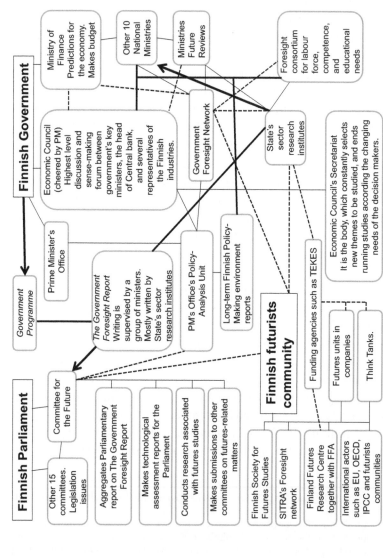

Figure 8.1 Finnish public strategic foresight system

Note: The arrows in Figure 8.1 mark the directions of mandatory reporting relationships. Solid lines mark hierarchical or other direct relationships or permanent duties. Bold solid lines refer to especially strong joint function between the linked units. The dotted line describes unofficial link between the units, such as quite frequent information sharing or ad hoc collaboration.

finished report is submitted to parliament by the government. The PM's Office, together with the Finnish Parliament's Futures Committee then start a series of regional citizens' discussion seminars and learning cafes around the country, where they introduce the report's results and gather citizens' opinions. After that the report, together with the citizens' opinions, goes for comment to the Finnish Parliament's Committees. The Futures Committee is the body in the Finnish parliament which is obligated to gather parliament's opinion on the report.

The implementation of Government Foresight takes much longer than one four year government's term, which means that it also partially binds the work of the next government. In principle, the government's foresight work should set the foundation for the next administration's government programme. Alongside the ministries foresight work and the parties' political programmes, other long-term work which affects the new government's programme is the state's medium-term budget framework that is prepared by the ministry of finance. This framework directs the new government's budget allocations more than anything else. Naturally the government programme must also follow the nature of the constitution.

The Government Foresight Report plays a formal role in work by the Finnish Government and Parliament, but it is not the only foresight report that is prepared under the PM's Office. In addition, the Government Foresight Network prepares a long-term Finnish Policy-Making Environment report (joint operating environment description). A third type of futures-oriented report that is done under the government is the Ministries Future Reviews. Each of the 12 ministries of Finland prepare their sector's Future Reviews at certain intervals (a year before the parliamentary elections). These reviews are vertical overviews of the emerging problems and possible solutions within a particular ministry's domain in the near future. Finally the PM's Office's other units and particularly its Economic Council and the Ministry of Finance, publish various futures-oriented reports every year.[23]

Each ministry prepares development projections and related strategies under its own administrative branch. The PM's Office is an intermediate body between ministries and political decision makers. It coordinates the

---

23 Prime Minister's Office's foresight publications are available in English at: http://www.vnk.fi/julkaisut/julkaisusarja/en.jsp; See the latest: http://www.vnk.fi/julkaisukansio/2010/j11-suomi-2010/pdf/en.pdf; and http://vnk.fi/julkaisukansio/2009/j33-yhdessa-ja-erikseen-j03-together/pdf/en.pdf

collaboration between ministries and prepares issues and agendas for national policy-making. The principle of the foresight work under the PM's Office is to keep the work as flexible and cost-efficient as possible. The number of staff dedicated to foresight work in the Office and in Governmental Ministries is still very small compared to most other developed countries, and this is despite the various tasks and multiple good quality foresight reports that are produced under the government every year.

In the system, other foresight works besides the preparation of the Futures Report as described above, proceeds after the PM's Office, or any ministry, orders studies from either dedicated sector research institutes, think tanks, consulting companies or universities, and supplements this work with its own expertise. Such reviews or assessments are usually done quickly in order to answer the knowledge needs regarding the issues on the government's current agenda. The Economic Council's Secretariat is the operational body which constantly selects new themes to be studied, and runs studies according to the changing needs of the decision makers. This ensures that the budget allocated to foresight work by the PM's Office is always put to efficient use, and does not get spent on fixed costs. The Secretariat doesn't do research itself as it is a joint operational coordinator between the decision makers of the Ministries and the Economic Council and the various research units that actually do the forecasting work. The Secretariat has three permanent members and several floating members, and it has strong ties to the Ministry of Finance. It is a team within the PM's Office's Policy-Analysis Unit, and it assists the PM's Office's highest forum the 'Economic Council', which is chaired by the Prime Minister. The Economic Council is not a decision making body, but it is a high level forum that is comprised of the government's key ministers, the head of the Central Bank, and representatives of Finnish industries and social partners.

GOVERNMENT FORESIGHT NETWORK

Another large foresight process that is coordinated by the Prime Minister's Office is the Government Foresight Network.[24] It is a network between people who either do, order, or coordinate anticipation work between the different ministries. The network has two members from each of Finland's 12 ministries, plus an additional four secretaries which increases the number of members to 28. When it is their turn to chair the network, a ministry will do so for a fixed two year term. The network is intended as a forum for sharing foresight

---

24 Available at: http://www.valtioneuvosto.fi/toiminta/ennakointiverkosto/en.jsp

knowledge, and for discussing substance issues and foresight methods. Duties of the Government Foresight Network include:

- Addressing major-impact change factors, development trends and weak signals in cooperation with other parties involved in anticipation activities, whenever possible.

- Sifting through anticipation data and drawing attention to possible overlaps between the ministries' anticipation work, variations in results and blind spots. Introducing initiatives to promote cooperation between administrative sectors.

- Improving the effectiveness of anticipation data in political decision-making.

- Serving as a ministerial contact forum for the preparations of the Government Foresight Report.

- Preparing a joint operating environment description to be used as background material for the ministries' future reviews.

FINNISH PARLIAMENT'S COMMITTEE FOR THE FUTURE

The Finnish Parliament's Committee for the Future[25] is one of its 17 committees. It was established as the parliament's temporary committee in 1993, and it was made a permanent committee in the year 2000. It has 17 members and nine vice-members plus four civil servants. Originally the Committee for the Future was established to formally produce parliament's answer to The Government Future Report once in its four year term, but it later began to get more parliamentary duties. The Committee for the Future, however, does not have any legislative duties, it does not give parliamentary legislative reports on any matter, it only gives Committee opinions to futures or technology related matters, and it does not have the right to give binding resolutions on the government's proposals or legislative bills, which all other Parliament committees have in their domain. That may make the Committee for the Future a little bit less esteemed in the eyes of ambitious politicians than many others. On the other hand, it conducts research associated with futures studies, including their methodology. The

---

25 This sub-chapter is based on the interviews of Jyrki Kasvi, the long-term vice-chair of the Committee for the Future, and its long-term senior advisor Osmo Kuusi. Available at: http://web.eduskunta.fi/Resource.phx/parliament/committees/future.htx

Committee also functions as a parliamentary body that conducts assessments of technological development and the effects of technology on society.[26] Like other committees, the Committee for the Future has plenty of freedom to choose endogenously new future themes to be studied, which means that a large part of their research themes are highly interesting to their members. Sometimes the Committee for the Future grasps a new research theme that is suggested from outside, sometimes it handles themes that are submitted to it from other Committees, but most of the time it works with the themes that its own members have suggested.

The Committee has been successful in suggesting new issues for debate in parliamentary sessions. It has been very active in publishing good quality technological assessments for parliamentary use, it has been organizing theme seminars for the whole of parliament, and it has a good visibility in the media. Furthermore the Committee is reputed to have a great deal of informal influence inside parliament, owing to the long-term Committee Counsel Paula Tiihonen's, ability to network the Committee so well both inside and outside parliament.

The establishment of the Committee for the Future in 1992–93 owed much to the sudden deep economic recession in Finland in the early 1990s, when almost all trade with the Soviet Union ended without warning. This came as a shock to the government and investors who had expected endless growth. The government had even decided to increase the levels of social benefits just one month before the collapse. The government then had to save the national banks with huge and expensive foreign loans, and it was obligated to make heavy cuts on all budget lines throughout society, including social benefits. That tough shock combined with the coincidence that there happened to be two strong members and real promoters of forecasting in parliament at that time, Martti Tiuri and Eero Paloheimo, generated sufficient support for the establishment of the Committee for the Future.

The decision for establishing a Futures Committee to assist parliament could have gone differently, as there was strong support for a German model too. The principle of the German model was that Parliament Committees did not do foresight research or evaluations. They merely ordered foresight reports from outside and then read, discussed, and commented on the results. The supporters of this model did not think that research was the work of politicians.

---

26 C.f. Teknologian arviointeja 17 (2004). (The practice of technology assessment in the Finnish Parliament).

The advantage of the German model is the fact that the research institute is impartial, non-political, and can provide information to all Parliament Committees without, for instance, the need to consider sensitive domains or territory issues between committees.

The unique thing in the Finnish system's Committee for the Future is that it aims to get beneath the day-to-day politics and party views to uncover the roots of emerging issues, usually the Committee has been successful in this. One of the very few cases when the Committee has been obliged to vote is when it was asked to give its view on establishing new nuclear energy reactors to Finland. This question was too politicized to be studied and argued impartially.

Another unique feature in the Committee is the fact that its members really get involved in the preparation work and research projects that are undertaken, and they aim to use scientific arguments instead of political ones. The idea is that when a politician works with a theme, he/she learns about the subject and is able to ask better questions and make better decisions. The minimum level of a politician's involvement in the Committee is participation in the projects' steering groups' work and writing their comments on the reports. In the best cases they use foresight methods in their research and write entire chapters on the studies. The combination in which an impartial researcher of a certain sector works in collaboration with a politician is said to be fruitful in digging into matters which are novel and have political dimensions. The existence of a parliamentary committee with such a hands-on approach is unique. There have been some attempts to establish something similar in other countries, but so far none of these attempts has prevailed.

FORESIGHT CONSORTIUM FOR LABOUR FORCE, COMPETENCE AND EDUCATIONAL NEEDS

The Ministers group of Finnish Work, Entrepreneurship, and Labour markets decided to establish the foresight consortium for labour force, competence and educational needs on 18 April 2008.[27] The idea of the foresight consortium was to establish a mutual foresight system for coordinating all the Finnish government's actors' decision making regarding issues in vocational education and labour markets competence needs. The steering of the system's work is divided between the Ministry of Employment and the Economy, and the

---

27   See http://www.minedu.fi/export/sites/default/OPM/Koulutus/koulutuspolitiikka/ennakointi/ liitteet/yhteistyoryhmanasettaminen18042008.pdf; and http://www.tem.fi/files/27163/TEM_39 _2010_netti.pdf

Ministry of Education. The domain of the Ministry of Employment and the Economy contains both the short-term foresight of the competence and educational needs, and the labour force needs foresight in general. The domain of the Ministry of Education contains the foresight of the competence and educational needs in the medium- and long-term.

The foresight system orders its basic forecasts and input data of the labour markets and economy from the Government Institute for Economic Research (VATT). This data is further broken down for use at a regional level and in different administrative fields, and it is also utilized in the work of the Government Foresight Network, and in the completed Government Future Report. The VATT's forecasts are complemented with development forecasts from other organizations, and corporative organizations are also participating in foresight in fields that are facing remarkable structural changes. The biggest challenge here is to merge the quantitative forecasts with qualitative foresight into a single storyline.

The consortium says in its statement that, from now on, they should start regulating national foresight activities, due to their societal importance. One solution, the consortium suggests is that foresight work should be added to the list of government regulations, and the Ministries' responsibilities regarding foresight should be clearly defined.

SITRA'S NATIONAL FORESIGHT NETWORK

The Finnish Innovation Fund (SITRA),[28] was set up in conjunction with the Bank of Finland in 1967 in honour of the 50th anniversary of Finnish independence. Today it is an independent public fund, which, under the supervision of the Finnish Parliament, promotes the welfare of Finnish society. SITRA has concentrated its activities into programmes, and it aims to grasp trans-societal challenges, with an emphasis on Finland's future. The strengths of SITRA are in its independence, ability to react quickly, and powerful networking ability between public and private stakeholders.

SITRA's core objectives, as a national development fund, are to enhance the Finnish innovation system and the national competitiveness. According to SITRA, the challenges that Finland faces are taken under discussion and subjected to closer examination in its work, in order to promote

---

28 Foresight: Available at: http://www.foresight.fi/info-in-english/; and http://www.sitra.fi/en/Working+for+the+Future/foresight/foresight.htm

innovation activities that provide the necessary answers to the challenges it faces. The goal for cooperation between many public, private, NGO's and university stakeholders is to promote the long-term perspective in Finnish decision-making and to improve society's ability for a controlled structural renewal.

SITRA's working for the Future goes through the following themes:

- Foresight (including the National Foresight Network);

- Strategy processes;

- Development programmes and decision-makers' training;

- Strategic research;

- Design strategies;

- Working for the information society.

The National Foresight Network, as part of the foresight work undertaken by SITRA, has two primary modes of operation:

- Subject matter experts and policymakers gather together in thematic groups to identify and closely examine change drivers that are relevant for Finland.

- The Foresight.fi website, launched in December 2008, aggregates together foresight insights and relevant information from Finland and abroad.

However, from the point of view of public decision making, SITRA's National Foresight Network has not produced much foresight material or comments that would have been utilized, for example in Government Future report work. The SITRA's National Foresight Network is said to be more of a discussion and sharing network than a policy making network. In this sense, the biggest influence on national policies is that the network exercises come from the network's influence on SITRA's development programmes.

FINNISH FUTURISTS OR FUTURES COMMUNITY AND SOCIETY TOGETHER WITH, FOR EXAMPLE, FFA AND FFRC

The sixth large part of the Finnish foresight system is the various futurists' or futures-oriented networks in Finland. The biggest and most organized network among these is the Finnish Society for Futures studies,[29] which was established in 1980 on the recommendation of the government's Central Board of Research Councils. Fourteen Finnish institutions of higher education were the founding members, and 14 additional institutions and over 700 individuals have since joined the society.

Another large network functions under the Finland Futures Academy (FFA),[30] which is a national education and research network in the field of futures studies for universities. FFA has nine member universities for which it produces futures education modules. The network is coordinated by the University of Turku's, School of Economics' and the Finland Futures Research Centre (FFRC),[31] where the national Masters programme and post-graduate school in futures studies are based. FFRC is the biggest foresight and futures studies actor in Nordic countries and it is among the biggest in the world. It was established at the Turku School of Economics in 1992, where it has functioned as an external funding research centre with very little direct public funding ever since. The project funding of FFRC comes from various types of customer projects, which are mostly paid for by national development funds or by the European Union. The annual number of staff and projects in the FFRC is around 50 at the end of the first decade of the new millennia. The centre's *academic research* focuses mainly on such themes as foresight in development projects, environmental and energy research, innovations, social and cultural research and research on creative industries. Despite the FFRC's large influence on the Finnish futurists community and its international reputation, it has completed few strategic foresight processes for companies or ministries. Such projects are usually ordered from various small Finnish consultation companies which offer services in foresight. Hence, the direct influence of the FFRC's work on public policy making has been mostly limited to a few research reports which have been utilized at some level in the ministries, and to the fact that the centre's researchers are regularly invited to speak at the Finnish Parliament's Committee for the Future. The centre's researchers are sometimes interviewed for television news programmes, or

---

29 Futura society. Available at: http://www.futurasociety.fi/
30 FFA. Available at: http://www.tvanet.fi/default_eng.asp
31 FFRC. Available at: http://www.tse.fi/EN/units/specialunits/ffrc/Pages/default.aspx

they have participated in educational programmes, and this may also have had some influence on public policy making.

Along with such formal network communities or centres, there are several less well-structured networks in Finland and they partially overlap with the previously mentioned networks. These can be referred to as the scientific community of futurists, foresight experts and the practitioner's community, ministries' and other public institutions' foresight oriented people network, network of politicians, and network of citizens debate participants.

SUMMARY OF FINNISH CASES

The Finnish public foresight to the framework that strategic foresight processes usually follow can be summarized as:

- *Guiding rule*: government programme which is a political document that sets themes to be studied in ministries and in Future reports. The Prime Minister's office coordinates and establishes research teams so that they can be flexible in response to the changing needs.

- *Input*: sector research institutes and ministries produce information with regards to their sector. Other stakeholders contribute.

- *Analysis*: sector research institutes produce ordered forecasts. Ministries produce Ministries' Reviews (sectoral).

- *Interpretations*: in government – preparing the PM's Future reports (horizontal), policy-making environment report, and Government Future Network. In parliament – Parliament's Futures Committee's opinions and technology assessments, together with other committees' work and citizens' debate.

- *Prospections*: Scenarios in the PM's Office's Futures report. Some what-if questions come from the Ministries' Reviews (sectoral).

- *Output*: Stakeholders become committed, options are discussed at all levels, and stronger networking.

- *Strategy*: Options go to the PM's Economic Council, to particular Ministry groups that steer government programmes, to political parties, and to Parliament's Committees. Influence on the national budget, which is set by the Ministry of Finance, is indirect via the EC and government network and programmes.

Cases from France

French foresight started to emerge as a field soon after foresight began to be used outside the US military in the early 1960s. Hence, French foresight has a long history even in an international context. However, due to the language barrier, French foresight is not as well known to the international community as the foresight work of many other countries. Today, the French strategic foresight system has three strong pillars; 'Strategic analysis centre', 'DATAR' and 'Futuribles'.[32]

Strategic analysis centre[33] (*Centre d'analyse stratégique*) is a decision-making and expertise institution which aims to advise the government on the creation and application of economic, social, environmental and cultural policy, and it provides forecasts for major governmental reforms. On its own initiative, it carries out studies and analysis as part of an annual working programme. It gives particular attention to the European dimension of the questions it examines. It was established by decree on 6 March 2006, and it operates under the Prime Minister's office in Paris. It is the successor to the Commissariat général du Plan,[34] which was established by Jean Monnet and Charles de Gaulle in 1945–46 (at the time the Plan was called Centralized Commissariat au Plan). According to Jacques Richardson,[35] the reason for establishing the Plan was that de Gaulle and Monnet both believed that such an institution was essential to rebuilding a nation wrecked by war and deprived of normal economic intercourse for half a dozen years. From the start the Plan operated for 60 years almost consistently under the Prime Minister's direct tutelage, theoretically in close coordination with parliament, other ministries (notably the budget, regional planning, education, and industry), senior civil administrators in France's 22 regions, semi-autonomous governmental entities such as the National Scientific Research Centre (CNRS), and leaders of labour and the manufacturing and service sectors. At its height the Plan employed over 150 people.

---

32 See http://www.ek.fi/ek_suomeksi/tulevaisuusluotain/dokumentit/tietotori/matkaraportti_240604.pdf
33 See http://www.strategie.gouv.fr/rubrique.php3?id_rubrique=20
34 See http://www.plan.gouv.fr/; http://www.plan.gouv.fr/mission/historique.php; http://www.sjsu.edu/faculty/watkins/francereg.htm
35 Richardson, Jacques (2006).

In 2006, the Plan was replaced by the Strategic Analysis Centre by Prime Minister Dominique de Villepin, as he declared that France needed an expertise which is both quick and immediately operational, and which better serves the republic's executive arm, especially on questions of mid- and long-term strategy, as we live in a world that is increasingly complex.

DATAR[36] (*Délégation à l'Aménagement du Territoire et à l'Action Régionale*) is, in part, a publically funded regional foresight and policy agency of France, which was established in 1963. It focuses on the regional aspects of national economic plans and it stimulates, guides, and coordinates the regional planning efforts of other agencies. DATAR has various large networking programmes, and it has also developed a network of information offices outside France to encourage foreign investment. In recent years DATAR has employed around 100 people.

Futuribles[37] is divided into three divisions; 'Futuribles Press', 'Futuribles International', and 'Futuribles Research and Consulting'. Futuribles Press publishes two monthly publications: *Futuribles Journal* and *Futuribles Newsletter*. The journal was established in 1975, and its monthly print run is 6,000–8,000 copies (40 per cent of which goes to foreign countries). Futuribles International (formerly Association Internationale Futuribles) is a Paris-based international, independent, private, non-profit, organization network or society on future studies. It works as a research centre, multi-sectoral discussion forum, education centre, and a data bank. It was created in 1960 by Bertrand de Jouvenel while the 'Centre d'études prospectives' was created by Gaston Berger in 1957. Futuribles research and consulting centre employs 15 people and holds a research network of 200 experts. It focuses on foresight, research and consulting in almost all societal sectors, and provides an online databank.

Cases from Germany

Germany does not have any centrally steered planning offices or systems for coordination of foresight projects. Instead it has a fragmented system, with many publicly supported and funded independent organizations located outside governmental structures, many ad hoc committees and scientific councils reporting to the ministries which deal with problems as they arise.[38]

---

36 See http://www.datar.gouv.fr/. See Laboratory for Investigation in Prospective, Strategy and Organisation (LIPSOR). Available at: www.cnam.fr/lipsor/eng/contents.php

37 See http://www.futuribles-revue.com/

38 See for example: Z-punkt, 'The Foresight Agency', (www.z-punkt.de); Institut für Zukunftsstudien und Technologie-bewertung (Institute for Futures Studies and Technology

At the federal level, the major ministries have departments, observatories or scientific councils that can manage these evaluative, futures or strategic studies. For example, the Ministry of the Economy includes an Economic Policy Division that carries out analysis and makes forecasts. It is also worth mentioning that Bundesinstitute and Bundesanstalten are widely recognized official evaluation institutions involved in different fields of public management including: approval, certification, labelling, research, forecasting, futures studies, advice, as well as carrying out executive tasks for the Ministries.[39]

According to Bruno Herault,[40] over the last 20 years the German federal system has increased the haggling among central and regional authorities. As a result, the latter has learnt to use all the strategies available to them to obtain a maximum amount of subsidies. The tools they have used to do this are, carrying out territorial diagnoses and regional futures studies. Hence, Germany includes numerous public and decentralized sources of futures studies, but it has a poor tradition of public planning. In conclusion, according to Herault, Germany has always produced more 'forecasts' than 'futures studies'.

Probably the best known strategic foresight structure in Germany is the council of the 'Five Wise Men' (Sachverständigenrat zur Begutachtung der gesamtwirtschaftlichen Entwicklung, Bundesministerium für Wirtschaft)[41] which was created by decree in 1963. It plays a role similar to that of the Economic Analysis Council in France (CAE – Conseil d'analyse economique), but it differs in its size as it has only five experts, in its years of existence (41 compared with six), and in its method (a search for consensus rather than comparing analyses). According to Herault, it is given the mandate of periodically evaluating the German economy from every angle, and it takes the form of an academic authority that advises the government and parliament on economic policy issues. Every year, the five university experts present a report on the 'overall economic situation' and its 'foreseeable evolution' to the Chancellor, while highlighting the 'risks' that are appearing and the possibilities

---

Assessment, www.izt.de); Netzwerk Zukunft (www.netzwerk-zukunft.de); Zukunftsinstitut (www.zukunftsinstitut.de); Futur (www.futur.de), funded by the Federal Ministry of Education and Research; and Sekretariat für Zukunftsforschung (SFZ, Secretariat for Futures Studies, www.sfz.de); 1. Agenda 2010 was presented by Gerhard Schroder, Chancellor of Germany, to the Bundestag on March 14, 2003; it is available in the form of a brochure (available at: www.bundesregierung.de/Anlage609273/The+brochure+.pdf).

39 Herault, Bruno (2006a, 2006b).
40 Ibid.
41 See www.sachverstaendigenrat-wirtschaft.de; Council of the Five Wise Men (2002/2003), Twenty Proposals for Employment and Growth, Annual report 2002–2003, Chapter 1, Council of the Five Wise Men, Reutlingen.

of controlling them. The report includes a diagnosis, a part devoted to short-term forecasting, and developments that will challenge future public policy. The Council is also tasked with assisting policy makers at all levels (local, regional and federal). Lastly, it is asked to help the general public to have access to 'reliable information on economic matters'.[42]

Cases from Ireland

In Ireland there is no strict equivalent of the French Strategic analysis centre (Centre d'analyse stratégique – formerly the Commissariat general du Plan), the Dutch Centraal Plan Bureau, or the Belgian Federal Planning Office, at least in its current form, nor a single public body dedicated to futures studies. However, according to Celine Mareuge who has mapped the Irish system, there are certain structures in the Irish system[43] which have missions that are close to those entrusted to the CGP either in the past or more recently. She says, in general, futures studies associated with defining political strategy in Ireland are carried out within the framework of public authorities and sometimes involve multiple institutions, which gives an impression of proliferation. These public authorities have common characteristics including an emphasis on the multi-disciplinary nature of analysis methods and, above all, the central position given to consultation and consensus. The approach consists of seeking political strategies based on social consensus (the social partnership approach), which is a legacy of the years of crisis that have deeply marked the Irish system of mobilizing resources to assist public decision. Thus, according to Mareuge, the members of the public advisory bodies systematically represent all those involved and the reasoning that underpins the public order for advisory work is always explicit in the definition of consensus objectives. Moreover, the high degree of centralization of the Irish state, combined with the importance of the

---

42 Herault, Bruno (2006): Public forecasting and futures studies in Germany. *Foresight*, 8 (6), (2006), 71–7.

43 See the recent publications which describe the domain of Irish system, as referred in Mareuge (2006, 60). Publications by the NDP: National Development Plan, 2000–2006, available at: www.ndp.ie/newndp/r/NDP_complete_text.PDF; by NSS: online publications www.irishspatialstrategy.com/NSSDownloads.shtml; by the NESC: An Investment in Quality: Services, Inclusion and Enterprise, November 2002, available at: www.nesc.ie/dynamic/docs/CR181102.pdf; by the NESF: A Strategic Policy Framework for Equality Issues, available at: www.nesf.ie/dynamic/docs/nesf_23.pdf; by the CPA: Policy Submission – Working Towards a Poverty-Free Society, Submission to the National Action Plan Against Poverty and Social Exclusion, 2003–2005, June 2003 available at: www.combatpoverty.ie/downloads/publications/Submissions/2003_Sub_NAPincl.pdf; By the Expert Group: The Fourth Report of the Expert Group on Future Skills Needs, October 2003, available at: www.skillsireland.ie/press/reports/pdf/egfsn0310_4th_skills_report.pdf

structural objectives for catching up that are linked to European integration, explains the special place still given by the State to planning and programming. Since the middle of the 1990s and the return of high growth that generated profound structural changes, planning stricto sensu has lost importance in favour of strategic orientation.[44]

Mareuge summarizes the Irish system by stating that it is highly proliferated between authorities, which gives the advantage of diversity but the disadvantage of resource separation. Most of these foresight institutions in Ireland are young and are distinguished first, by their capacity to combine societal futures studies (all-embracing reflection around the notions of rights and policies of equality, inclusion, etc.) and more operational studies. Second, by their approach which is fundamentally based on consultation and consensus, their desire to get players in the field, 'civil society', and the non-profit sector to join in the specialist work; and third by their approach of promotion and support for recommendations; and their involvement in European research pools.[45]

Cases from the Netherlands

Unlike many other countries such as Germany or Ireland, the Netherlands has a central planning agency under the government. The CPB 'Netherlands Bureau for Economic Policy Analysis' (*Centraal Planbureau, Central Planning Bureau*) was founded in 1945. CPB is funded by the Dutch government but it works as an independent agency. To ensure its independence, the CPB conducts its analysis free of charge. The CPB is only allowed to work for a certain group of clients, and it is obliged to turn down the requests when clients offer to pay for the research.[46]

The objective of the CPB is to make independent economic analyses that are both scientifically sound and up-to-date, and relevant for policymaking in the Netherlands. Through its analyses, the CPB informs not only politicians and policymakers but also societal organizations, the scientific community and the general public. The CPB conducts its research on its own initiative as well as upon request by a limited group. Within this group are the cabinet, government ministries, parliament, individual members or factions of parliament, and political parties (parties in office, as well as opposition parties). Also able to

---

44 Mareuge (2006).
45 Ibid.
46 See http://www.cpb.nl/eng/; Central Planning Bureau, Scanning the Future, A Long Term Scenario Study of the World Economy 1990–2015. Sdu Uitgeverij, The Hague, 1992.

call on the CPB's research efforts are employers' and employees' organizations, the Social Economic Council, and several other institutes and organizations in the field of social economic policy and research. Formally, it is the Minister of Economic Affairs who decides whether or not the CPB will answer a particular request, or may determine that the CPB may participate only to the extent that the request fits within the CPB's common activities.[47]

Alongside the CPB, the Dutch government has three other planning offices; the 'Social and Cultural Planning Office (SCP)', the 'Netherlands Environmental Assessment Agency (MNP)', and the 'Spatial Planning Office (RPB)'.

According to Barend van der Meulen, the Netherland's foresight in science and technology has developed along three lines of science and technology policy. The first line is that of standing panels (the so called advisory sector councils for research) that have a tripartite composition of researchers, research users and government officials. The main task of these panels is to advise ministries on their sector science policies, taking future societal developments and scientific possibilities into account. The second line is that of technology policy. In the 1980s the Ministry of Economic Affairs, which was responsible for technology policy, developed foresight studies in order to identify critical technologies for Dutch small and medium enterprises (SMEs) and help them adopt these technologies.[48] The third line is that of science policy for the sciences. In 1992 the Minister of Education and Sciences established a Foresight Steering Committee to co-ordinate and initiate foresight studies and advise the minister on the consequences for science policy. The Foresight Steering Committee adopted the scenario approach that was developed by the Group Planning of the Shell Company as well as continuing the science policy tradition of disciplinary panels. From 1992 to 1996 the Dutch Foresight Steering Committee initiated and co-ordinated a range of foresight studies in science and technology. In the spring of 1996 the committee published its final report in which it selected ten research themes that were crucial to developing a means for anticipating the future needs of expertise and knowledge in the Netherlands.[49]

One of the most ambitious foresight initiatives in Netherlands has been its Horizon Scan 2007[50] project under the Commission for Consultation of Sector

---

47 Ibid.
48 Dijk (1991).
49 Meulen (1999).
50 Commission for Consultation of Sector Councils (2008): Horizon Scan Report 2007: Towards a Future Oriented Policy and Knowledge Agenda. The Hague. See http://www.horizonscan.nl/uploads/File/COS_binnenwerk%20engels_06 (1).pdf

Councils (COS) which formulates priorities for society-oriented research, focusing in particular on those experts dealing with cross-sector subjects at the interface of policy domains and scientific disciplines. The Horizon Scan 2007 project was carried out by a specially established team consisting of representatives from research, society, industry, government, and think tanks from the Netherlands.[51]

However, according to Habegger, the Netherlands Horizon Scanning Project's strategic scan provided so broad and valuable an input for policymaking by identifying, assessing, and clustering future trends, issues, and developments, the decision makers wanted to continue the project.[52] Hence, when the final report of Horizon Scan 2007 was published, the project was no longer expected to remain a one-time measure: in February 2008, the tasks of the COS were transferred to the Knowledge Directorate of the Netherlands Ministry of Education, Culture and Science, and it is expected that a permanent facility will be created outside the ministry.[53]

Cases from Sweden

Sweden has a permanent Institute for Futures Studies and other planning agencies under the government. Alongside with these official agencies, there are many, varied players involved in foresight or futures studies in Sweden and they work interactively. There is some Futures-oriented work in regional and municipal levels, but foresight is mostly carried out at a national level, where the most important actors are the institutions closest to decision-making powers, such as the planning and prospective units in certain ministries, and the government agencies which are responsible for advisory work in a given field. Swedish foresight projects are frequently characterized by a public/private partnership[54] and big companies often have an active futures studies department.[55]

According to Sandrine Paillard, who has done an interview study[56] on Sweden's foresight system's key actors, the futures study is a decisive

---

51 Habegger (2010, 55).
52 Botterhuis, Lineke, Duin, Patrick van der; Ruijter, Paul de and Wijck, Peter van (2010): Monitoring the future: Building an early warning system for the Dutch Ministry of Justice. *Futures*, 42, (2010), 454–65.
53 Habegger (2010, 55).
54 C.f. www.tekniskframsyn.nu
55 Paillard (2006).
56 Ibid.

part of the public decision process in Sweden. It can be direct in the case of commissions of inquiry. These are officially set up by the government and their results are directly put into use when working out public policies. Apart from the commissions, futures-oriented studies are not generally commissioned by the government, even though the latter may provide support for certain initiatives (funding, legitimacy). Likewise, there is a pretty clear division of labour between the prospective debate on the one hand, which consists of identifying factors of change and future challenges (and for which experts are greatly called upon), and the task of drafting public policies on the other hand which are conducted by the government and ministries.

The biggest success story of foresight in regard to national decision making so far has been the Lindbeck's Commission. It was established in December 1992, during the depths of a brutal and unprecedented economic crisis in Sweden. By then, the government asked Assar Lindbeck, an internationally renowned economist, to chair a commission of inquiry. Its mission was to analyse the causes of the crisis and to suggest solutions for getting out of it. The Commission was made up of seven researchers (a sociologist, a political analyst and five economists including a Norwegian and a Dane) chosen by Assar Lindbeck. It worked on the basis of studies commissioned from researchers and interviews with experts from the political parties, unions and some government agencies. The aim of the Commission was to propose economic rules that were healthy and irrespective of the economic environment Sweden would be faced with in the future. The Lindbeck Commission was a resounding success. The 17 series of recommendations in the report *'Turning Sweden Around* (1993)' were followed by results in the form of reform proposals made by the government to parliament. Over a hundred journalists from the press, radio and television attended the press conference. The media covered the event for several weeks and a series of five television programmes provided the opportunity to present the report's conclusions to the general public. Ten thousand copies of the report were sold. The report therefore reached a wide audience that stretched beyond researchers, students and political and administrative spheres.[57]

Another success story of foresight in regard to national decision making in Sweden is the Institute for Futures Studies (Framtidsstudier).[58] Its mission is to carry out long-term studies with a view to stimulating a broad and open debate on future threats to and opportunities for social development. The establishment of the Institute was initiated by the principle of political independence and by the

---

57 Ibid.
58 Institute for Futures Studies. Available at: www.framtidsstudier.se

need to thwart the overly technocratic direction that futures-oriented analyses had taken in Sweden in the 1970s. The Institute employs about 25 researchers (historians, economists, sociologists, demographers and geographers). It is an independent research foundation but funded 75 per cent by the Ministry for Education and Research, with the remainder being paid for by public and private funds for specific projects (research councils, companies, trade unions, the European Union, etc.). The Institute works particularly on the very long term. Historical or demographic projects are carried out within the context of a 50- to 100-year perspective even though time scales can be shorter (10–30 years).

Irrespective of their authors and sponsors, the Institute's futures-oriented analyses contribute, along with other types of debate, to introducing new questions to public debates and the political agenda. In recent years, these studies have contributed to making many themes public such as, demographic issues and problems related to population ageing, the Swedish labour market in an enlarged Europe, and matters relating to sustainable development, particularly those that focus on climate change and town planning.[59]

As Paillard[60] said, futures study is a genuine public policy instrument in Sweden, and in this respect, it essentially fulfils three aims. First, the futures-oriented analyses contribute to public debate and to making Swedes more aware of future challenges. Second, futures study is a frequently used method for consultation which takes place prior to major social reforms; and third, futures study, in particular through technology and scientific foresight projects, is a tool through which strategic priorities are defined.

Cases from the United Kingdom

One the most well-known foresight systems in Europe is the UK government's Foresight Programme. The UK Foresight Programme is considered to be effective in informing the strategic policy-making of the British government. While it was initially centred on S&T policy – and still places a strong emphasis on these issues – it has continually broadened its scope and today provides policy makers with a perspective on the full public policy agenda. The programme covers the whole spectrum of a comprehensive foresight process – from early detection and the generation of foresight knowledge to

---

59 Paillard (2006).
60 Ibid.

the development of policy options – it links expert knowledge to a long-term perspective, and employs sophisticated techniques of futures analysis to raise the government's strategic policy-making capacity.[61]

According to Ian Miles,[62] the early roots of the UK Foresight Programme go back to the 1960s, when a new focus on science and technology (S&T) policy addressed the widely recognized innovation problem in the UK. The emergence of information technology and the necessity of increased investments in research and development forced policy makers to make choices between competing demands and to set the right priorities in light of the country's economic requirements. In the early 1990s, four academic and private institutions were commissioned to develop methodologies to identify and prioritize emerging technologies that were of importance to the UK. The resulting vision of 'key technologies' paved the way to what in 1994 became the UK Foresight Programme. The programme operates under the Government Office of Science, and one of its key functions is the UK Horizon Scanning Centre (HSC).[63] The HSC began work in December 2004 and aims to 'feed directly into cross-government priority setting and strategy formation, improving government's capacity to deal with cross-departmental and multidisciplinary challenges'.[64]

According to Habegger, the UK Foresight Programme can be roughly grouped into three distinct programmes or activities: the horizon scans, the futures projects, and the public outreach programme.[65] In horizon scanning there are two complementary programmes, the Delta Scan and the Sigma Scan, which provide an intersectoral informational basis to underpin all foresight activities across the UK government. These ongoing scans look ahead over a range of up to 50 years to uncover 'contradictions and ambiguities in mapping the turbulence of change'.[66] The Delta Scan, with more than 250 S&T experts as contributors, gives an overview of future S&T issues. The Sigma Scan is a synthesis of other horizon scanning sources that may be characterized as a

---

61 Habegger (2010, 54).
62 Miles (2005).
63 See http://horizonscanning.defra.gov.uk/; www.hse.gov.uk/horizons; UK Foresight Programme and Horizon Scanning Centre (www.foresight.gov.uk/index.html).
64 United Kingdom HM Treasury, Science and Innovation Investment Framework 2004–2014. London, 2004. Available at: http://www.hm-treasury.gov.uk/spending_sr04_science.htm
65 See www.sigmascan.org; www.deltascan.org. The Delta Scan is an overview of future science and technology issues and trends, with contributions by over 200 science and technology experts from the worlds of government, business, academia and communication in the UK and US.
66 Schultz, Wendy L. (2006): The cultural contradictions of managing change: Using horizon scanning in an evidence-based policy context. *Foresight*, 8 (4), (2006), 5.

'scan of scans' and covers trends across the full public policy agenda. It draws its information from think-tanks, corporate foresight, governments, academia, NGOs, blogs, mainstream media, or music, which indicate the diversity of potential information sources.[67]

The second main element of the UK Foresight Programme[68] is the rolling programme of three or four futures projects to create high-quality overviews of a given issue and to develop a vision of how the UK can meet the associated future challenges. All futures projects should have a longer term impact by raising awareness, offering policy recommendations, and establishing networks among professionals within and outside of government who can translate the recommendations into policy. The projects last between 18 and 24 months, and they must also either deal with some important current issue that science, technology, the social sciences, and economics can help address, or with a current aspect of science or technology that is likely to have wider potential in the future.

Each of the projects needs a sponsoring minister to ensure high-level political backing, and is thus chaired by the minister of the lead department, and led by senior decision-makers from relevant departments, research bodies, and other organizations. Projects are only started when support from all relevant stakeholders is guaranteed, and thus a high-level stakeholder group oversees each project. A steering group invites between 90 and 120 scientists from different disciplines to join the project in order to review the scientific literature extensively and to participate in workshops or seminars. The ultimate objective is to produce a set of clear, comprehensive, and comprehensible project reports, often rewritten by specialized science writers to make them accessible to all the interdisciplinary team members.[69]

The third pillar of the Foresight Programme is a broad public outreach that builds networks of futures thinkers and practitioners in the public, private, academic, and other sectors. The HSC established the Futures Analysts' Network (FAN Club) as a forum where those who have an interest in horizon scanning and futures analysis can meet to exchange new ideas, innovative thinking, and good practice.

---

67 Habegger (2010, 53).
68 Miles, Ian (2005): UK foresight: Three cycles on a highway. *International Journal of Foresight and Innovation Policy*, 2 (1), 17; Habegger (2010, 53).
69 Ibid.

9

Strategic Foresight in the European Union's Ten New Member State's Public Policy Making

> *Fools say they learn from experience – I prefer to profit from the experience of others.*
>
> *Otto von Bismarck*

In May 2004, ten new member states, Poland, the Czech Republic, Hungary, Slovakia, Lithuania, Latvia, Slovenia, Estonia, Cyprus and Malta, joined the European Union. According to Colson and Corm, although these ten new member states have experienced very different historical and political systems, they have all begun to develop competencies in analysing the future, and they all do foresight or futures studies *sensu lato*, often according to the same institutional outline: a public player (a department under the aegis of the Prime Minister or a main ministry), an academic player (research institute within an academy or one of the country's major universities) and, where appropriate, a private player (regional or independent organizations). In particular, several countries (Poland, the Czech Republic, Hungary, Estonia and Lithuania) have each drawn up an overall futures study, with the time horizon being 2015 or 2020, in the socio-economic, strategic or demographic fields. Lastly, it is worth noting that technology forecasts are increasingly common in the new member countries.[1]

The following short summaries of the foresight systems of the ten new member states of the EU are based on Colson and Corm's study[2] and a few

---

1   Colson, Aurelien and Corm, Mounir (2006): Futures studies in the European Union's new member states. *Foresight*, 8 (3), 55–64.
2   Ibid.

external links. Within these ten countries, the whole system and all its key players are not listed. Instead, it has been attempted with the new member states cases to identify the key public foresight agents from each country, and to say something about the level of foresight in each country. The systems of the ten new member states are presented in size order of the country's population.

Cases from Cyprus

According to Colson and Corm,[3] Cyprus' economic policy has been based on flexible planning for more than 40 years. In Cyprus economic activity is taken care of by private players and is based on market systems, when the government uses indicative planning its purpose is twofold: to secure a favourable economic and social environment (infra-structures) and to direct the private sector towards strategic and priority sectors.

The most senior authority for planning in Cyprus is the Central Planning Commission (Nicosia), which is responsible for formulating the development strategy, defining the objectives for each development plan, coordinating the decisions and measures needed to fulfill the plans, and making sure they are carried out properly. It is chaired by the President of the Republic and includes all the ministers whilst the governor of the Central Bank plays an advisory role.

Cases from the Czech Republic

The Czech Republic[4] has several agencies and projects related to public foresight. The key public foresight agent of the country was the Council of the Czech Republic for Social and Economic Strategy[5] (Rady vlady Ceske republiky pro socialni a ekonomikou strategii – CCRSES, Prague). The CCRSES was set up in 1999 by the government which it advises on matters of long-term economic and social strategy. The Deputy Prime Minister was in charge of economic policy and social affairs. Council members came from ministries, other federal authorities, local authorities and social partners. Its main lines of study were, inter alia, the strategic impact of globalization on Czech society, sustainable development, and long-term economic development. The council was dissolved by the government on 31 July 2003.

---

3   Ibid.
4   Ibid.
5   The CCRSES. Available at: http://wtd.vlada.cz/scripts/detail.php?id ¼ 4801

Cases from Estonia

The most well-known futures research and foresight agency in Estonia is The Estonian Institute for Futures Studies[6] (Eesti tulevikuuuringute instituut – ETI, under the University of Tallinn). The ETI is directed by a quite well-known futurist Dr Erik Terk who has had a long and remarkable experience in working in the Estonian government during the Soviet time.

The ETI is a not-for-profit organization, which was established and government-approved in 1991. The ETI has done many foresight studies for public policy makers, such as 'Estonia 2010' (1995–98), which have probably had a direct influence on national politics. The ETI has been active in doing large regional scenario works related, for example, to developments of the Baltic Sea area, the Tallsinki twin city plan and Russia-EU futures relationship situations. Most recently the ETI has been working on a project on the evolution of service design,[7] a mutual project with the Lahti University of Applied Sciences and the Dynamic Futures from Finland.

Another noticeable Estonian foresight agency is the Institute of Baltic Studies,[8] Tartu, which is an independent, non-profit organization as well. It was established in 1995, and it works in partnership with universities. It has developed futures or strategy studies on the information society and sustainable development. Otherwise, there seems to be few public foresight agencies in Estonia

Cases from Hungary

Hungary is one of the countries in which organizations dedicated to futures research are the most plentiful and the most active even on a world scale.[9] The key public foresight agent of the country is the Strategic Analyst Center[10] (Strategiai elemzoko zpont – STRATEK, Budapest). The STRATEK is a think tank attached to the Prime Minister's office and under the management of the Secretary of State responsible for government strategy. Its mission is to provide forecasts for, and assessments of, public policy. This centre produces information to help define the government's economic, social and European integration policies. It

---

6   See www.eti.ee/english
7   See www.servicedesign.tv
8   The Institute of Baltic Studies. Available at: www.ibs.ee/ibs/index.html.en
9   Colson and Corm (2006).
10 The STRATEK. Available at: www.stratek.hu/index.php?L ¼ 2

uses its studies to put forward proposals with the aim of improving the public management of long-term challenges: demography, migration, etc. At the government's request, it also publishes targeted research work.

Cases from Lithania

Lithuania has several agencies and projects related to public foresight. The key public foresight agent of the country is the Division of Strategic Planning, in the Office of the Prime Minister[11] (Strateginio planavimo skyrius, Ministro Pirmininko, Vilnius). The Division of Strategic Planning plays the classic part of preparing the executive's decisions, combining duties equivalent in France to those of the former government's General Secretariat and of the Prime Minister's Office.

In 2002, the Lithuanian Parliament approved and published a particularly important study: 'Long-term development strategy of the state'.[12] This presented a strategic analysis of state institutions and market trends by the year 2015. It also assessed strategies and programmes that had already been implemented.

Cases from Latvia

According to the study of Colson and Corm,[13] Latvia seems to be the country that is least concerned about futures studies among the group. However, Latvian institutions carry out a whole host of spatial planning activities via the preparation of national programmes in various areas, each one taken care of by a different organization. One such agent which does some spatial development planning is the Center of Spatial Development Planning, which prepares the National Plan of Latvia under the authority of the Ministry of Environmental Protection and Regional Development.

Cases from Malta

As a very small country, Malta has few public foresight initiatives. One of the most notorious is the NDP Drafting Group,[14] under the Economic Policy

---

11 See www.lrvk.lt/main_en.php?cat¼ 36&d ¼ 2007
12 See www.lrs.lt/cgi-bin/preps2?ConditionI ¼ 219184&Condition2 ¼
13 Colson and Corm (2006, 55–64).
14 See www.ndp.gov.mt/index.html

Division of the Ministry for Economic Services, Floriana. The NDP was tasked with coordinating and preparing the 'Malta national development plan for economic and social cohesion 2003–2006'. This programme had to set the development framework for Malta in all aspects of both social and economic areas, defining objectives supported by multi-annual investment in infrastructures, education and training, the productive sector, and the promotion of social inclusion.[15]

Cases from Poland

There are several agencies and projects related to public foresight in Poland. The key public foresight agent in the country is the Government Center for Strategic Studies (Rzadowe centrum studiow strategicznych – RCSS, Warsaw)[16] which was set up in 1997. It is a state-run organization under the aegis of the Prime Minister, tasked with developing 'strategic programming' and forecasting. The RCSS takes part in defining strategic programmes and forecasts for economic and social development at both national and regional levels. It prepares and presents town and country planning policy and regional action plans to the cabinet as well as assessing state organizations and public policies. Lastly, using studies it conducts on Poland's strategic international environment, it develops the long-term mainspring concepts for the country's foreign policy.[17]

Cases from Slovakia

There are several agencies and projects related to public foresight in Slovakia. The key public foresight agent of the country is the Institute for Forecasting[18] (Prognostickyustav Slovenskej akademie vied, Bratislava). The Institute for Forecasting is dependent on the Slovak Academy of Sciences. It recently carried out a foresight study, *'Technology foresight Slovakia 2015'*[19] which aimed at identifying future trends in science and technology under the conditions of sustainable development and globalization, in order to help the implementation of a technology and research and development policy within the framework of Slovakia in the European Union.

---

15 Colson and Corm (2006, 62).
16 See www.rcss.gov.pl
17 Colson and Corm (2006, 57).
18 See http://progeko.savba.sk/pu/pueng.htm
19 2003–2004, see www.foresight.sav.sk

Cases from Slovenia

There are several agencies and projects related to public foresight in Slovenia. The key public foresight agent in the country is the Institute of Macroeconomic Analysis and Development[20] (Urad republike slovenije za Makroekonomske analize in razvoj, Ljubljana). The Institute of Macroeconomic Analysis and Development was set up after World War II and carried out economic, social and spatial planning activities. It was a constituent body of the Ministry of Economic Relations and Development, but since 2000, it has become an independent government agency and its director is directly responsible to the Prime Minister. Its work covers three main areas of activity:

1. Monitoring, analysing, and forecasting economic development;

2. Participating in the preparation of the main strategic documents and in the formulation of government policies (performing strategic or futures studies about Slovenia); and

3. Research and international cooperation.

---

20 Slovenia's most remarkable foresight studies are: 'The strategy for the economic development of Slovenia 2001–2006' (1999–2001, available at: www.gov.si/zmar/aprojekt/seds/document. html); 'The factors and the impacts of the information society: A prospective analysis in candidate countries' (2003, available at: www.gov.si/zmar/aprojekt/ainfdruz.php); and 'Strategy of the Republic of Slovenia for accession (available at: www.gov.si/zmar/aindex. php).

10

Strategic Foresight in the Public Policy Making of other Countries and Transnational Organizations

This chapter discusses the public strategic foresight systems of two countries, Singapore and the US, which have put considerable effort into strengthening their national security through various intelligence practices. This discussion is continued with examples of three transnational organizations, OECD, UNIDO and IIASA, and strategic foresight systems. These examples have not been selected because they have put more effort into strategic foresight than the others, but because they are genuinely transnational and open for information distribution.

Cases from Singapore

The evolution of Singaporean strategic foresight began in 1991 from the establishment of the Risk Detection and Scenario Planning Office at the Ministry of Defence in 1991. In 1995 it was moved to the Prime Minister's Office's Public Service Division (PSD). In 2003 it acquired new objectives and a new name: the Strategic Policy Office. The next big steps in the evolution of Singaporean strategic foresight were establishing the Risk Assessment and Horizons Scanning Programme (RAHS) in 2004, and the Horizon Scanning Centre (HSC) in 2008 (as can be seen in Figure 10.1). After that the pace of distributing foresight units, functions or capabilities across the government of Singapore speeded up significantly leading to the need to establish the Strategic Futures Network (SFN) for coordination and collaboration between all the new foresight units.

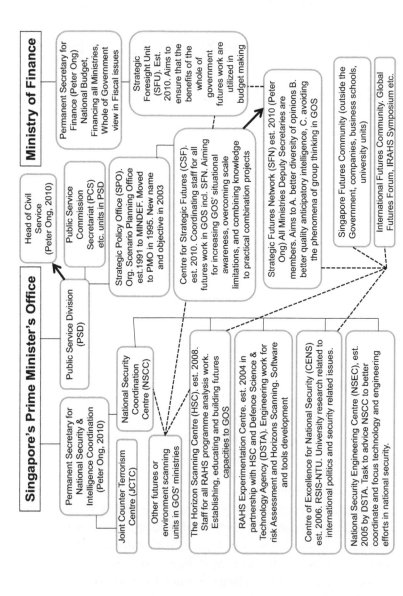

Figure 10.1 Singaporean public strategic foresight system

Note: The arrows in Figure 10.1 mark the directions of mandatory reporting relationships. Solid lines mark hierarchical or other direct relationships or permanent duties, the dotted line describes unofficial linkage between the units, such as quite frequent information sharing or ad hoc collaboration.

Most of the Singapore government's foresight functions are located under the Prime Minister's Office. These functions are mainly under two Permanent Secretaries for National Security & Intelligence Coordination (NSIC) and the Public Service Division (PSD) which has the role of supporting the whole of government policy making coordination. Under the NSIC and its National Security Coordination Centre (NSCC)[1] the main foresight coordinating body is the Horizon Scanning Centre (HSC) which was established in 2008. Under the Public Service Division (PSD) and its Strategic Policy Office (SPO), the main coordinating agent for foresight functions is the Centre for Strategic Futures (CSF) which was established in 2010. Besides the CSF, the Strategic Futures Network (SFN) was established at the SPO at the same time. The CSF functions as a high level network for futures thinking within the whole the public sector. The SFN is coordinated by the head of civil service who has the overall responsibility of supporting all aspects of government approach.

At the time of writing, the SFN has been in place for a short time, but has already reported the following practical benefits. First, raising situational awareness within the whole of the government for what each futures unit is doing. Second, by encouraging futures units to come together it helps achieve a critical mass for training and learning activities. Third, it allows for a greater scope for combining projects where ministries recognize through situational awareness their common interests even if they come from different perspectives, and then work together to achieve better outcomes than they would have done by attacking the problem alone.

Along with the PM's Office's NSIC and PSD, the Ministry of Finance is known in the government as a 'central agency' as it has a role in supporting the overall governmental approach in financial matters. In 2010, the Ministry of Finance established a Strategic Foresight Unit[2] or SFU to ensure that the benefits of the whole of government futures thinking, namely improved situational awareness, diversity of thinking and avoiding the phenomena of group thinking, are utilized in the Ministry of Finance's long term budget considerations.

As is the case in most countries, there are two spheres in the futures community in Singapore. First, is the futures community within the

1   NSCC and its supporting centres. Available at: http://app.nscs.gov.sg/public/content.aspx?sid=28
2   Strategic Foresight Unit in Ministry of Finance. Available at: http://app.sgdi.gov.sg/listing_expand.asp?agency_subtype=dept&agency_id=0000001005

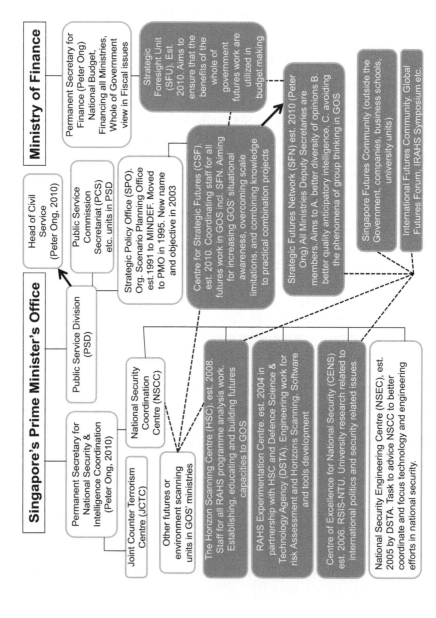

Figure 10.2 Foresight knowledge production parts in Singaporean public strategic foresight system

government which is well developed and which has distributed capabilities across the whole of government. Second, is the futures community outside the government which is far less developed as Singapore does not have any dedicated private futures entities. However, there are institutions such as the RSIS[3] which collaborate with government futures units to study particular issues such as regional security from a futures perspective. There are also several notable individuals in academia and in private companies who are in leading positions and who have to make decisions regarding the future. The CSF is part of the government's attempt to incorporate them into the forum of free flowing dialogue so that both private and public sectors can share their thoughts regarding mutual interests.

What is really significant about the Singaporean strategic foresight system is its strong centrally steered orientation that is designed to pursue, distribute, and contextually differentiate foresight functions across all ministries, as can be seen in Figure 10.3. Practically all Singaporean public foresight functions are linked directly to the Singapore government's leading official, the Head of Civil Services, Mr Peter Ong, who succeeded Peter Ho in this post on 1 September 2010. As the key node of Singapore's strategic foresight system, Mr Ong is also the Permanent Secretary of Finance, and the Permanent Secretary of National Security and Intelligence Coordination,[4] and he chairs both the Strategic Futures Network (SFN), and the Committee of Permanent Secretaries, to which all Ministries Permanent Secretaries belong. This practice enables good knowledge sharing and collaboration between the growing number of public foresight units in Singapore, and it verifies that foresight work can influence the whole of government decision making.

Cases from the United States

We have good reason to believe that modern foresight and futures studies were initiated by the US military's think tanks and research and planning units during the 1940s and 1950s. The most famous of these units was RAND

---

3   RSIS (S. Rajaratnam School of International Studies of Nanyang Technological University, Singapore) is an internationally recognized think tank and a university faculty or school for international politics and social risks assessment.

4   On 1 September 2010, Mr Peter Ong, the standing Permanent secretary of Finance, was appointed the Singapore Government's Head of the Civil Service (Permanent secretary, special duties), and also Permanent secretary of National Security and Intelligence Coordination. In these duties he is following his predecessor Peter Ho. See http://app.psd.gov.sg/data/Press%20 release%20-%20Appointment%20of%20HCS%20and%20PS.pdf

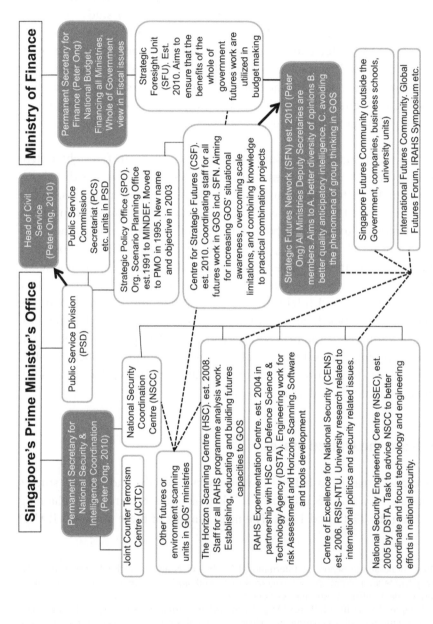

Figure 10.3 Strong node in the Singaporean public strategic foresight system

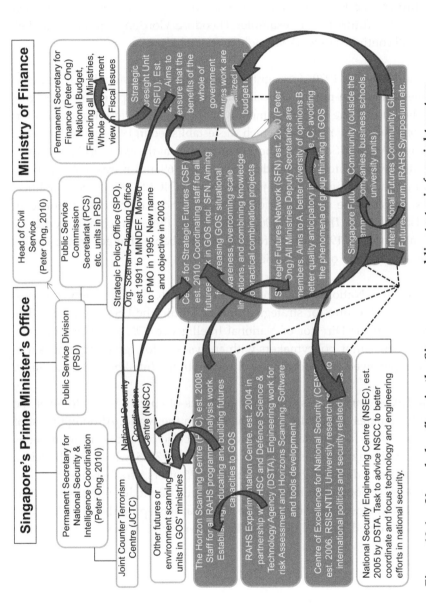

Figure 10.4   Knowledge flow in the Singaporean public strategic foresight system

(Research and Development), a mutual project of the US Army Air Corps and the Douglas Aircraft Company, established by General H.H. Arnold. The project employed researchers such as Olaf Helmer, Norman C. Dalkey, Bernie Brown, and Herman Kahn who worked in close co-operation with their contemporary futurists, for example, Theodore Gordon and Wendell Bell. RAND still continues to work strongly in the field.[5]

In the 1960s and 1970s foresight started to spread outside the US military, and several new non-military foresight and public policy planning units were established under the US government. One of the most significant units was the *Commission on the Year 2000*, which was established in 1965 by the American Academy of Arts and Sciences.[6] Another such unit was the *National Goals Research Staff*, which was created by President Nixon in 1969, but it was disbanded the following year, having produced just one report (NGRS 1970), due to political reasons. Possibly the most notorious foresight and public policy report ever in the US has been *The Global 2000 Report to the President*, commissioned by President Carter in 1977, which forecast the probable changes in the earth's climate until the end of the twentieth century.[7]

Today, the National Intelligence Council (NIC)[8] is probably the best known research centre for strategic thinking within the US government. The NIC reports to the Director of National Intelligence (DNI) and provides the President and senior policymakers with analyses of foreign policy issues that have been reviewed and coordinated throughout the Intelligence Community.

The NIC's work ranges from brief analyses of current issues to 'over the horizon' estimates of broader trends at work in the world. Although most of the NIC's work is for internal government use, it also produces or commissions some unclassified reports,[9] such as *The Global Trends 2025*, which was the NIC's fourth unclassified report. *The Global Trends 2025* offers a fresh, long-term view of the future, by looking at how key global trends might develop over the next 15 years to influence world events. The NIC's earlier report *Mapping The Global Future 2020* aimed to provide US policymakers with a view of how world

---

5   Bell (2005, 29).
6   Ibid.
7   Leigh (2003).
8   See http://www.dni.gov/nic/NIC_home.html
9   National Intelligence Council (2008): *Global Trends 2025: A Transformed World*. National Intelligence Council's 2025 Project. Available at: http://www.dni.gov/nic/PDF_2025/2025_ Global_Trends_Final_Report.pdf; National Intelligence Council (2004): *Mapping the Global Futures*. The National Intelligence Council's 2020 Project. Available at: http://www.foia.cia. gov/2020/2020.pdf

developments could evolve, identifying opportunities and potentially negative developments that might warrant policy action.

Despite the fact that the US is probably the country which has the biggest total number of strategic foresight and long-range planning professionals working inside its borders, there has not been that many notorious public foresight reports published as one could expect. The most successful public foresight reports that have come from the US are, among many others, the Maxwell Air Force Base's The *Air Force 2025 Study*,[10] of which around a million paid copies have by now been distributedtogether with its well distributed *The Blue Horizons*.[11] Studies published among other Occasional Paper Series publications include *Spacecast 2020*, the four NIC's reports, the *Global 2000*, and the *Global Future: Time to Act* report, which was published in 1981. Despite the success of many US government foresight publications, Andrew Leigh[12] has described the quantity by bluntly stating that the public foresight of the US is less advanced compared, for example, to the public foresight of the UK, and he implies that there can only be political reasons for such fragmentation.

However, strategic foresight and intelligence live strongly[13] in the US military, namely in the Pentagon and Air Force, the US private sector, and the national intelligence agencies, namely in the CIA and FBI, but this work is quite often secret by nature as discussed in earlier chapters. Furthermore, there are various foresight or long-range planning orientated transnational organizations which are mainly located, funded or headed by the US, such as the Millennium Project under the UNU/World Federation of United Nations Associations, or the World Bank, IMF, WTO or NATO. It may be that strategic foresight is well developed in the US and affects government work and its public policies at all levels all of the time, but due to the federal secret policy, the rest of the world is not aware.

Cases from OECD

The Organisation for Economic Co-operation and Development (OECD) was established in 1961, and it has gradually grown to an organization of 32 member states which share its expertise and accumulated experience

---

10 Englebrecht, et al. (1996): *Alternate Futures for Air Force 2025*. Maxwell Air Force Base.
11 Geis, John et al. (2009): *Blue Horizons II: Future Capabilities and Technologies for 2030*.
12 Leigh, Andrew (2003); C.f. Slaughter (2008).
13 C.f. Slaughter (2008).

with more than 100 developing and emerging market economies around the world. The OECD is funded by its member states, and its objective is to bring together the governments of countries committed to democracy and the market economy from around the world to support sustainable economic growth, boost employment, raise living standards, maintain financial stability, assist other countries' economic development, and contribute to growth in world trade. The organization provides a setting where governments compare policy experiences, seek answers to common problems, identify good practice and coordinate domestic and international policies. For more than 40 years, the OECD has been one of the world's largest sources of comparable statistics and economic and social data. As well as collecting data, the OECD monitors trends, analyses and forecasts of economic developments and researches social changes or evolving patterns[14] concentrating on issues of economy, migration, infrastructure to 2030, and risk management.

The OECD has had several strongly futures-oriented programmes such as its CERI units Long-term Schooling for Tomorrow, but probably the most significant futures programme of the OECD is The International Futures Programme (IFP).[15] It is designed to help policy makers in government and business better grasp the challenges of today's complex and uncertain world, where any sort of valid assessment of future trends is said to be a formidable challenge, as economic, social and technological forces are combining to drive change along at great speed, and bewildering torrents of ideas and information compete for attention. The IFP is a small core team of professionals acting as a Secretariat within the OECD. The team works with over 500 seniors in-house and outside professionals and experts worldwide.

One of the aims[16] of the IFP is to offer a platform where policy makers can freely confront their visions and concerns about the future, seek the views of others, and engage in a stimulating dialogue. In this way they are believed to gain a better understanding of the issues at stake. Here, the key features of the IFP are: improved monitoring of the long-term economic and social horizon, with early warnings for emerging domestic and international issues; more accurate pinpointing of major developments and possible trend breaks; greater analytical appreciation of key long-term issues; and better dialogue and information sharing to help set policy agendas and map strategy.

---

14 See http://www.oecd.org/home/0,3305,en_2649_201185_1_1_1_1_1,00.html
15 OECD International Futures Programme. Available at: www.oecd.org/department/0,2688, en_2649_33707_1_1_1_1_1,00.html
16 See http://www.oecd.org/dataoecd/37/54/42332642.pdf

The tool box of the IFP covers the use of horizon scanning and trend analysis, scenario construction, focus groups and policy analysis. Its methods involve a variety of tools including multi-year projects, high-level conferences, expert workshops, and consultations; a futures-oriented online information system and a network of contacts from government, industry, academia and civil society. IFP activities are especially underpinned by a continual process of horizon scanning to keep abreast of global and regional developments and events, review longer-term challenges for OECD economies and societies, and identify new key issues as they emerge. Once an issue has been selected for further consideration, the scoping process begins. This involves, inter alia, a systematic assessment of a topic's suitability as a future project in terms of its policy relevance, the risk of duplication with other work within or outside the organization, potential value added for the OECD and member countries, and potential sponsors.

Another futures-oriented function of the IFP is the risk management reviews which are an example of the 'hands-on' advice it offers member governments on implementing results from previous projects. One such example is the OECD's 'Emerging Systemic Risks' project.

Future Global Shocks project (FGS)[17] is a third key futures-oriented function of the IFP. The FGS brings together experts from the public and private sectors in order to review the changing risks landscape; analyse the increasing complexity of systems and the lessons learned from past and recent small- and large-scale disasters; identify gaps in knowledge and requirements for cooperation between actors; and finally, propose a set of policy options to OECD governments that aim to anticipate future global shocks and enhance the shock-resilience of the global economy and society in the years to come.

Cases from IIASA

The International Institute for Applied Systems Analysis (IIASA)[18] is an international research organization that conducts policy-oriented research into problems that are too large or too complex to be solved by a single country or academic discipline, such as climate change, that have a global reach and can be resolved only by international cooperative action; and problems of common

---

17 Ibid.
18 The International Institute for Applied Systems Analysis (IIASA). Available at: www.iiasa. ac.at/docs/IIASA_Info.html

concern to many countries that need to be addressed at a national level, such as energy security, population aging, and sustainable development.

IIASA was founded in 1972, and is sponsored by its national member organizations in Africa, Asia, Europe, and North America, and it is located in Austria near Vienna. Its research investigates the critical issues of global environmental, economic, technological, and social change that we face in the twenty-first century. The researchers, some 200 mathematicians, social scientists, natural scientists, economists, and engineers, develop assessment and decision-support methodologies, global databases, and analytical tools to study the issues. IIASA is an independent and completely unconstrained by political or national self-interest.

Cases from UNIDO

The United Nations Industrial Development Organization (UNIDO)[19] is one of the units of the UN which provides foresight and foresight education for public policy making. The UNIDO Technology Foresight Programme is intended to assist the transition of former eastern bloc states to a market economy. One of the tools used has been a technology foresight manual that includes guidance on the use of foresight methods, because technology foresight is regarded in the UNIDO as the most upstream element of the technology development process. It provides inputs for the formulation of technology policies and strategies that guide the development of the technological infrastructure. In addition, technology foresight provides support to innovation, and incentives and assistance to enterprises in the domain of technology management and technology transfer, leading to enhanced competitiveness and growth. Alongside the manual, the UNIDO is implementing a global and regional initiative on technology foresight as well. The aim is to build the capability of using foresight as a practical tool in designing policies and strategies that exploit emerging and critical technologies for the benefit of developing countries and countries with economies in transition. The technology foresight initiative also provides suitable methodologies to promote sustainable and innovative development, fostering economic, environmental and social benefits at national and regional levels. Its outcomes are policies and programmes that deal with innovation, industrial growth and competitiveness.

---

19 UNIDO Technology Foresight Programme. Available at: www.unido.org/doc/5216

PART III

Process

One must have chaos in oneself in order to give birth to a dancing star.

Friedrich Nietzsche

Introduction

This part of the book presents the views and suggestions of nine strategic foresight producers and users from countries around the world. The experts have been selected based on their specific experience and knowledge of different sides of strategic foresight. Several of the experts have been responsible for big branches of their country's national security, particularly from counter-terrorism and international risks' detection points of view. One is a professor of futures studies who has made a career in the transnational bank and insurance sector as the head of foresight, one is an international early warning systems establishment consultant for state actors, one is intelligence officer, professor, and the head of armed forces technological development centre, one is lead foresight strategist in the Ministry of Finance, one is a long-term futurist and a senior adviser of national parliament's committee for the future, one is coordinating and directing all public foresight functions in a country, and one is a member of parliament and the long-term vice-chair of the national parliament's committee for the future.

The name of this part of the book is 'Process' as it describes the practice and practical suggestions for public strategic foresight. It begins with questions such as, 'how could strategic foresight better facilitate national decision making?' and 'how would you measure the success of foresight work?', which are discussed in Chapters 11 and 12, and then continues to ask questions such as 'how could we improve our public strategic foresight systems?', which is discussed in Chapters 13 and 14. The answers to both questions are discussed in different chapters because I have wanted to separate the outcomes based on the backgrounds of the interviewees. In other words, the four chapters present the opinions of the two groups, 'policy makers and high government officials', and 'foresight knowledge producers' to both of the main questions.

11

How Could the Strategic Foresight Process Better Facilitate National Decision Making? – Views of Policy Makers and High Government Officials

Dr Jyrki Kasvi
Member of the Finnish Parliament and the Vice-Chair of the Parliament's Committee for the Future

'How could strategic foresight better facilitate national decision making?'

As a public policy maker, the only thing I really want from the Finnish universities and the other research and futurists communities is that they start to practise the universities' official third task which is participating and facilitating the societal discussion on issues which have great significance to society. At the moment they are failing in that third task. And the reason for this is the fact that scholars are not rewarded for practising it. Not in official research points, in direct money compensations or any wage increase, or in any other way. Further those who try to contribute the public discussion may be 'punished' for doing so by the questioning of their scholarly ethics. What needs to be done on this matter is to change the university sector's quite twisted reward principles which now favour only the production of new graduates and publications on closed scientific forums. The new discoveries, breakthroughs, and new science-based initiatives made by the scholars should be simplified and popularized into understandable forms, and they should be published broadly in the national media. If scholars would start actively facilitating societal discussion through the media, all the obvious problems that there are in parliamentary work due to a lack of knowledge would be solved.

Author's comment: See the third level of the three levels in which strategic foresight can contribute to national decision making from Chapter 7.

Mr Patrick Nathan
Deputy Director of National Security Coordination Centre (NSCC) in Singapore's Prime Minister's Office[1]

'How could strategic foresight better facilitate national decision making?'

The best contribution that strategic foresight work under the government could do for national decision making is to produce accurate, on-time knowledge of the top emerging issues in well selected packages. There should not be too many emerging issues with broad descriptions handed to the decision makers, but a manageable amount of valid and well augmented issues which may require further action.

Mr Devadas Krishnadas
Deputy Director of Strategic Planning and Lead Foresight Strategist at Singapore's Ministry of Finance

'How could strategic foresight better facilitate national decision making?'

The objective of futures thinking within the Singaporean government is not prediction, but to make sure that our decision makers have the following advantages. First, a robust diversity of opinions and thinking. Second, the provision of good anticipatory intelligence. Third, that we avoid group thinking. Diversity of opinions and thinking means that we enhance our ability to come to the same question from various perspectives – this is a fairly recent

---

1   Mr Patrick Nathan was interviewed twice, on 27 August 2009 and in 12 November 2010. Two persons (Jeanette Kwek, Senior Strategist, Strategic Policy Office, Public Service Division, Prime Minister's Office and Bernard Toh, Strategist, Strategic Policy Office, Public Service Division, Prime Minister's Office) participated in Nathan's interview on 27 August 2009. Jeremy Tan, Assistant Director, Horizon Scanning Centre, National Security Coordination Centre (NSCC) participated in Nathan's interview on 12 November 2010.

understanding that we have. It means that you could have a fundamental national challenge, but you could have the answers coming to it from energy, social or security points of view. So it is more than having a difference in thinking within each of those 'chunks' of thinking, but having different 'chunks' of thinking to begin with.

Group thinking is a dangerous quality to which all government and private organizations are vulnerable. This can result in strategic surprise. Strategic surprise is defined as an unforeseen situation that can disrupt and dislocate one's decision making paradigm. The way we try to avoid strategic surprises is to enhance anticipatory intelligence which means identifying and interpreting weak signals so that we can experiment with potentially different pathways for the future before these pathways become more consolidated and concrete. This allows us to undertake policy innovation and experimentation and both of these enable us to be better prepared. Policy innovation is a more active form through which you can change your policy according to what you anticipate could happen. Policy experimentation is a form where you think through what your responses could be without necessarily implementing them. This permits decision makers to be mentally better prepared. In an emerging crisis, this mental preparation means that we could rapidly scale up our ability to respond, because we have thought through some of the steps. This is important for preparing the government for decision making in the context of the twenty-first century, which has two determinative characteristics. One, it is increasingly uncertain, and two, it is highly complex. These two characteristics are now the two permanent dimensional parameters of public policy.

'How would you measure the success of strategic foresight?'

Conventional success/failure measurements don't work with strategic foresight work because it is inherently long-term, which doesn't pay out in short term. Second, foresight is meant to provide a policy intervention, which changes the landscape of decision making. Therefore we have a 'quantum mechanics problem' as the actors of the observation are changing the nature/field of observation. Therefore estimating whether we have successfully influenced the decision making landscape cannot be done using the conventional success/failure scale. Rather we should estimate if the quality of decision making work has benefited from foresight work. And this evaluation should be made both subjectively and objectively. Subjectively refers to the decision makers' feeling of confidence – do they feel more confident in making decisions when they have foresight knowledge, and objectively refers to the retrospective study of the quality of decisions that had been made based on foresight knowledge.

Dr Osmo Kuusi
Senior Adviser, Committee for the Future of Finnish Parliament, Senior Researcher in Government Institute for Economic Research (VATT)

'How could strategic foresight better facilitate national decision making?'

First of all, the foresight practitioners should show the politicians how foresight actually can help them in decision making. Foresight experts should organize, together with the Parliamentary Committees, a really good seminar for parliamentary members where they would demonstrate why it is so important to understand the principles of science, to know the foresight methods, and what is a plausible scientific argument. This should be a thorough discussion of why a politician should be 'more scientific in his arguments than the science itself' in order to be taken seriously, and not be considered as just an opinion factory. That way the trust and demand for foresight could be built.

In the case of the Finnish Parliament's Committee for the Future, which directly facilitates parliamentary decision making, I would recommend that the whole fields of science and technology politics, including the preparation of the laws regarding these fields, should be put under its domain. For foresight, that would open the space of a real contribution to national decision making.

Ms Riitta Kirjavainen
Counsellor, Finland's Prime Minister's Office, Deputy Head of the Policy-analysis Unit

'How could strategic foresight better facilitate national decision making?'

First of all, there is no need for a large unified foresight unit in government. In the 1960s and 1970s the Finnish government used to have a State Planning Office with various experts from different fields working together on the state's long-range planning projects. That was a time when we still believed that the society could be planned. Nowadays, our model is based on flexibility and networking which allows us to establish and end projects, and to cross ministerial teams according to the fast changing needs of political decision making and according societal development. What is needed next, and what is already being discussed in government, is the development of state sector research centres. The idea is that in the future, these research centres, which are directly or indirectly funded by the government's ministries, work together better in producing knowledge according the fast changing needs of political decision making. So far we have not reached that level yet, as paradoxically, the Finnish government is at the same time both very flexible, and very strictly sectored to silos. In the PM's Office we want to break that habit in order to better facilitate national decision making.

12

How Could the Strategic Foresight Process Better Facilitate National Decision Making? – Views of Strategic Foresight Knowledge Producers

Mr Ilan Mizrahi
Former Deputy Head of Mossad, and Former Head of Israel's National Security Council (NSC)

'How could strategic foresight better facilitate national decision making?'

In intelligence work we can foresee processes not events. Sometimes we may get good and direct information so that we know of an event in advance, but we still would not know its implications. No one can know how the masses will react or what the motives of the decision makers are. And it is still an undecided issue: which affects more things that happen – decision makers or masses of people?

The history of the world is full of examples of intelligence failures such as Pearl Harbour or Port Arthur. Despite the fact that we have always tried to improve all parts of intelligence work and to establish a theory of non-failing intelligence, new failures keep coming. Why? The answer is because it is impossible to prevent failures in intelligence. It is still quite easy to work with natural disasters such as tsunamis or earthquakes, but when it comes to systems of people it is completely different. If we do not have direct knowledge and we usually do not, we can only establish scenarios and give probabilities at best. This helps our decision makers to do pre-emptive strategies or alternative counter-strategies, which again can only mitigate the failures of intelligence.

Dr Markku Wilenius

Ex-Senior Vice President of German International Allianz Corporation, Professor, Chief Strategic Officer (Insurance and Finance)

'How could strategic foresight better facilitate national decision making?'

Let's take an example. How could we have avoided the financial crisis in Finland? First of all, we should have had a system in which the Prime Minister's Office of the Economic Council is heavily involved. They should have woken up to the crisis right after we got the first signs of it in the summer of 2008. And that was much before Lehman Brothers went bankrupt. The system should also have contained expert nodes that would have analysed in real time the impacts and effects of such a crisis on the banks and financial institutions' multilateral lending. There should have been several research institutes outside the government involved such as VATT and the Finland Futures Research Centre.

What else should the system have contained? The Finnish Innovation Fund (SITRA) should have been heavily involved in the system, as it is the main engine and financer of the national innovation initiatives and policy. As soon as we had got analysis results of the possible development of the financial crisis, that knowledge would have been brought to societal discussions, including participatory elements, the results of these would then have been brought to parliamentary discussions. Then the Finnish Parliament's Committee for the Future would have asked the Economic Council about its thoughts on the evolving crisis. Could it have been possible to do in advance some descriptive scenarios for the finance crisis too? That is something we had hardly done before the crisis. Only a few specific research institutes had completed types of assessment of the possible depth of the crisis before it broke out.

After we had obtained a good mutual understanding of the nature of the crisis, both the government and parliament should have started discussions with the Federation of Finnish Financial Services (FK) and with the biggest banks and insurance institutes, in order to locate the space of potential actions, and each viable actions' probable influences on lending, solvency and deposits in the markets. That way the result would have been much better than the result which we ended up with.

Therefore, the role of societal foresight is to anticipate potential problems in public discussions before they occur. Then, based on that knowledge, different stakeholder organizations' decision makers and their key experts should be able to make sense of their own roles in the broader picture and change their actions accordingly.

'How would you measure the success of strategic foresight?'

First we need to select a list of Key Performance Indicators that check its success. Then we need to study three levels of success.

1.   How the strategic foresight process has affected the day-to-day practice of different stakeholders?

2.   Are the strategic foresight knowledge producers satisfied with the process and the results?

3.   How has the strategic foresight process affected society in the long-run?

Have there been decisions related to the issues that have arisen in the foresight process, and have these decisions been implemented in practice? If strategic foresight has made an impact on the practice, has that impact been mostly positive or negative based on the long-term results? The third assessment can only be done from a historical perspective. All assessments should be made regularly.

13

How Could We Improve Our Public Strategic Foresight Systems? – Views of Strategic Foresight Knowledge Producers

Mr Ilan Mizrahi
Former Deputy Head of Mossad, and Former Head of Israel's National
Security Council (NSC)

'How could we improve our strategic foresight systems?'

I will tell what my ideal strategic intelligence system would be like if I could
design it from the beginning. First, we should use as authentic observations
and data as possible, not estimations or interpretations. When a relevant piece
of information is detected in intelligence, one analyst should be required to do
a basic blueprint and analysis of it. Then this presentation should be discussed
within specialist analyst team A, which contains devil's advocates as well.
Team A gives several alternative explanations, views and scenarios of the
detected information. Then all these alternative explanations and scenarios of
team A are analysed and tested by analysts. If they are able to identify any
piece of information which speaks against any of those that have been created,
it becomes falsified according the Popperian falsification process. After this
evaluation phase we may have 2–3 explanations or scenarios left which will
be processed into presentations by an analyst. Now the presentations of these
remaining issues or theories are given to another team, team B, which is
gathered from non-specialists on the issue. Team B, evaluates the importance of
each of the given issues or theories, and creates their alternative explanations,

views and scenarios to the issues. Team A is then challenged with the outcomes from team B and as a result team A prepares the final 2–3 scenarios which are given to the decision makers. Decision makers need to decide what to do in each of the possible cases.

'What are the requirements for the success of the system's methodology?'

First, this methodology works only if the head of the department is an open minded person, who listens to all views, respects opinions that are different to his own, who is able to lead and make the discursive process function, who doesn't dictate the outcomes, who is able to select the best people for the right positions, knows the natural bias of all people and values, and who is able to adopt the methodology for different types of contexts.

Second, the specialists in the teams must be talented and real experts on their issues. They all should be aware of their own biases, that they always interpret observations and issues in a subjective way, and that they have a unique personal history and scars that have formed their values and worldview. Hence, they should be humble with their knowledge and estimation.

Third, the information that is gathered must be first class – not interpretations of intentions, but direct reliable knowledge. Information sources should be versatile and they should cover as large an area around the issue as possible, leaving no gaps or shadows. If we have a very good knowledge, we can know directly. If we end up needing to make estimates, the data gathering part has failed.

'Why would you establish two teams?'

First, you will never gather a really good team of analysts. There are always members in a team who are too self-confident, over conservative, more biased than the others, or not as good experts on the matter. Therefore, it is crucial to get the best possible heads in each department who make the teams accomplish their objectives. One way to reduce the conservatism and bias in a team is to train the newcomers outside the unit so that they have fresh ideas. If the newcomers were trained inside the unit by having them sit next to senior workers, they would just learn the old ways of thinking, and that would increase conservatism in the group.

Second, experts are always prisoners of their own theories and expertise. *Reginald Victor Jones* who headed scientific intelligence for the Air Staff during World War II and subsequently for the British Intelligence Service, once said that if you would go to your own organization's technology unit with a new product, they would oppose it because they hadn't come up with it. That is why you need to benchmark the product first with another team, and then challenge the technology unit's team with the ideas, not the other way around.

Due to this human bias, it is not enough to know only the history, for example, of how North-Korea will act in a certain situation. You have to understand its leaders' personalities and profiles, their culture's characteristics, values and mindsets. You have to know what affected or scared their values and world views, and you need to understand how they evaluate you. And in estimating that, you are always biased and half blind.

In the National Security Council (NSC) I used three teams to benchmark the ideas related to possible risks in order to reduce the bias. First there was my own team of 8–10 people. Then an intelligence team that was gathered from nominated experts on the issue, and third there was a versatile group of people who I esteemed for their intelligence and experience, but who were laypersons in the issue. That way we were able to reach a better and more pure intelligence of the issues.

Dr Rauno Kuusisto
Professor, Head of Electronics and Information Technology Division, Finnish Defence Forces Technical Research Centre, Adjunct Professor (Network Enabled Defence), Finnish National Defence University, LTCOL (ret.)

'How could we improve our strategic foresight systems?'

If I could establish a national foresight system all the way from the beginning, I would do it in the following way. First of all, I would not establish any new foresight units in government. In government, however, there could be one new position for strategic foresight coordination. That person would be responsible for gathering the best experts from each of the Ministries sector to participate in the foresight system as informants. What we need is a system that produces high quality synthesizing knowledge and methodological capabilities. As the government's duty is to make strategic and operational decisions for the country, not to develop methodologies, we need to establish a public private partnership for the system. The system itself would have three levels: contents, process, and structure.

In the first one, content is produced by people who do preparatory work in the organization that is doing preparatory work for public decision making. Those people in ministries are the best possible subject experts in the matters of their domain. If that is not the case, then they would have been wrongfully recruited. The information preparatory board of foresight issues would be gathered from these people. They would be the foresight process's informants who participate in workshops and surveys, and they would not participate in its method development work.

The second level, process, would be outsourced to an impartial private consultant who would be located outside the public preparatory work and the public decision making apparatus of the system. The knowledge/content however would of course come from the public preparatory agents of the government, as already explained.

As there are many different traditions and communication cultures inside the government units, which means that the economists in the Ministry of the Treasury do not use the same concepts as the people who work with social and health issues elsewhere, the first objective of the process would be to commit these different government's preparatory units to the process. The fact that we have these different traditions and communication cultures only enriches our government culture because it guarantees that the steered change proceeds in all levels and embraces all value aspects.

The second objective of the process would be to systematically and impartially filter persons and their ambitions, and other invalid information away from the process, in order to mould pure real time knowledge into a form that policy makers could utilize on a daily basis. Regarding this second objective, it is crucial that the agent who steers the process is located outside the government, for if he was inside it, he would be located under just one ministry and he would get politicized in time, and would not produce impartial knowledge anymore. The process would stagnate and become a dinosaur with its own traditions and language, and soon there would be 12 such foresight units as each ministry eventually needs its own.

The third level, structure, includes all the actors and units of all of the levels the national foresight system, like the facilitating private agent, the various public preparatory agents, and the decision makers.

'How would the process function?'

Nowadays foresight knowledge production is fragmented and not as synchronized. Hence, national foresight does not have the process. The process is the key to good foresight knowledge. That is why the consulting agent, who steers the whole process, should follow the principles of the process strictly itself, and the principles of the process should be taught to the consultant agents' new recruits immediately.

Objective and fact based decision making and information interpreting is highly difficult, because all issues have many layers that make them complex, and all humans have different experiences and mindsets that determine their views of the issue. That is why I suggest that we establish a multidisciplinary senior synthesis pool of experts for the system that would be able to synthesize these different views into versatile and multi-value clusters of views on the issues. In each workshop, the existence of sufficient versatile and multi-value views is facilitated by gathering experts from different fields. The senior synthesis experts do the synthesis of expressed views and argument in each workshop. These synthesized pure knowledge products are then delivered to the decision makers.

'What is the role and organization of the private facilitator in the system?'

The consultant needs to be able to refine the influential information into any context of decision making. The consultant organizes the workshops, does required preparation works, and synthesizes the knowledge into a useful form.

My ideal consulting company for this task would have three parts.

The first part is an executive unit which coordinates the workshop sparring, knowledge gathering, analysis, management and information distribution, writes workshop reports, and does project management and the sales and account work.

The second part is the method development unit which constantly develops the foresight and analysis methods. This unit would contain both internationally experienced professor-level foresight or ICT experts, and young enthusiastic developers and researchers. This would be a combination of a university's research centre and an industrial development unit.

The third part would be the senior synthesis pool of experts. The members of this pool would be at professor level, well over 60-years-old, and they would have a really long experience of industry, business or administration. They would have versatile backgrounds, and they would have the ability to make fast syntheses of the results of horizon's scanning processes and specialist workshops discussions. They would work in pairs in the workshops, and they would be the kind of people who are able to stand up at the end of the workshop and say 'this is what this means'. They are the key persons who are able to detect the emerging issues to which the decision makers will have to react. That is the fundamental basis of all strategic foresight and decision making.

The division of labour in foresight workshops would end so that the executive unit would select the experts and run the workshop, the method development unit would run background research and analysis that would facilitate the workshop, and the senior synthesis experts would participate only in the workshop part where they would put their sense-making ability and their instinct to use. Finally the executive unit would collect, visualize and write the product into a useful form which could be delivered to the decision makers.

'What kind of knowledge would the system try to reach?'

The process would focus on detecting new and emerging issues, weak signals, changes in trends, and drivers that are hard to see. Scenarios are a good tool for environmental change analysis as they help to identify potentially emerging issues to which the decision makers may have to react. A 20-year-old or someone with little life experience cannot find any relevant weak signals. Only a senior expert is able to identify signals that have any significance for national decision making. They have enough experience from various contexts so that they can differentiate the relevant from irrelevant and the novel from existing.

Dr Markku Wilenius
Ex-Senior Vice President of German International Allianz Corporation, Professor, Chief Strategic Officer (Insurance and Finance)

'How could we improve our strategic foresight systems?'

The creation of forums where contradictory information can be processed is core to better strategic foresight. We need new sophisticated methods and constant risk mapping. When building such a system, we should first assess the risks according to their probability and their potential impacts. Then we should make a matrix where the risks are both timed, and arranged according to the first assessment. The idea would be to identify what risks seem to be most urgent in a certain timeframe. In creating this matrix we should have an expert pool which represents all interest groups. The matrix itself should contain seven circles which are namely:

1.   Economic indicators of macro economy.

2.   Globalization and trends that affect societal stability and economic development, such as income and democracy issues.

3.   Technological trends, how technological change brings new societal risks and how that change affects societies' ability to tackle risks.

4.   Natural environmental problems, such as climate change, pollution, chemicalization and so on.

5.   Demographic factors, such as population size, location, immigration and ageing.

6.   Health of the population which is one of the issues that directly determines societal development.

7.   Societal mode or zeitgeist, which refers to society's shared values, feelings and views, which can be indexed by its citizens' general societal confidence towards the future, and with different national happiness indexes.

How could the national foresight and decision making system utilize the matrix?[1] Let's say we detect that the income differences start to increase between societal groups. After receiving that knowledge, we should identify the actors who are best able to follow each of the seven circles. Then we should name the actors that are responsible for foresight knowledge gathering in each of the circles. That would be the foundation of the national foresight system. We should not build any new research units or systems. Instead, we should rely on existing systems and units and enhance the knowledge sharing and interaction among them. All the data gathering and analysis should be done impartially. However, as the decision making is always political, the produced

---

1   C.f. Wilenius (2005).

foresight knowledge should be brought to a political forum as soon as possible. To ensure this, the body which would coordinate this national foresight system should be located under the parliament. The role of the government within this system would be to nominate in its government programme[2] the research units that are responsible for the system's data gathering and analysis during its four year term. The government programme would also define ways and methods through which environmental scanning is done, and outline how the results are interpreted and put into action during the particular government's term. Without this connection to the government programme, the system would not work.

To take an example, how could we tackle the downsides of adult-onset diabetes? When the phenomenon is identified, I would put the resources for locating and gathering all the information we already have on that issue. What kinds of living and eating habits do people usually have etc. What kind of futures scenarios we could project from that knowledge? Then I would put the effort into an expert evaluation around which the societal implications of that knowledge is assessed from all societal angles such as medical, food science, economical, and insurance points of view. The societal solution could be something like increasing the general awareness of need to change eating habits. Finally, the government programme would determine the ways that all the produced knowledge should be dealt with in political decision making and how the decisions should be put into action.

Dr Helene Lavoix
Specialist in strategic foresight and warning (conventional and unconventional security issues) for state actors, France

'How could we improve our strategic foresight systems?'

I will describe the type of system that I would like to create for national purposes. This description is based on my state actors' consulting and on my article in the European Commission's book *From Early Warning to Early Action.*[3]

---

2   The role of the Government Programme in Finnish Political System is defined in the Finnish case.

3   Interview answers are supplemented with citations from Lavoix's article: Developing an early warning system for crises. In David Sauveur (ed.) From early warning to early action? European Commission, due to her recommendations. Available at: http://ec.europa.eu/external_relations/ifs/publications/articles/book2/book%20vol2_part4_chapter47_developing%20an%20early%20warning%20system%20for%20crises_helene%20lavoix%20and%20ifri.pdf

In my national strategic foresight and warning (SF&W) system, notably for intelligence, I would establish two inter-related offices. The first would be a strategic foresight office and the second would be a warning office. In the foresight office I would rely on methods such as graphs and networks analysis – concept maps (e.g. Parmenides EIDOS, Singapore RAHS) and social network analysis (e.g. Gephi, UCInet), Bayesian networks – scenarios, morphological analysis.[4] The warning office would have all the classical functions of a warning office (from monitoring of issues to delivery of warnings). Two functions would be jointly assumed by the two offices, each bringing in their know-how: a unit for the detection of emerging issues, and one that would identify warning indicators (e.g. timeline indicators) for the issues and problems analysed by the foresight unit. Furthermore, the indications obtained by the warning office would be used to permanently update the existing foresight scenarios. Warning analysts should be involved furthermore in brainstorming and scenarios development exercises done by the foresight office.

In general, the methods used in foresight and warning can be placed along an axis ranging from the purely qualitative to the purely quantitative.

In terms of models and indicators for warning, the traditional qualitative approach, for its part, requires the use of many experts, which makes systematization and comparison difficult, although they are vital for understanding issues. The quantitative approach is usually based on a statistical approach that seeks to correlate various variables and the result sought. While the quantitative approach permits the necessary comparison and systematization, its main problem is an inability to highlight chains of causation and dynamics.

Both qualitative and quantitative approaches are subjective, as even in statistical methods you have to select the variables you use. However, keeping that in mind, I would rely more on qualitative methods in SF&W. It will furthermore be crucial to always keep in mind the importance of falsification.

---

4   Parmenides Eidos is a proprietary software, see http://www.parmenides-foundation.org/application/parmenides-eidos/; RAHS has been developed by the government of the Republic of Singapore, Prime Minister's Office, National Security Coordination Center, see http://app.hsc.gov.sg/public/www/home.aspx; Gephi is an open source graph and visualisation software, see http://gephi.org/; UCINET is a social network analysis software developed by Analystic Technologies, see http://www.analytictech.com/ucinet/

'What kind of information sources would you rely on?'

It depends on the issue. Information may come from open or restricted access sources. It is not so much the availability of information as the selection of the relevant data in a huge and increasing load that poses a problem, that is, the information overload problem. With regard to a state, in fact, a lot of data is available because of the existence of information services and networks of diplomatic bodies and other agencies covering the various political, military, economic and social milieux. Comprehensive access to the media and the use of external experts' networks is usually added to this arrangement.

The problem of selecting relevant information is directly related to the identification of the foresight question and to the design of the warning system and should therefore be resolved during the related steps. In particular, the model created must make it possible to combat involuntary biases (from cognitive biases to emotional, cultural, normative and organizational biases). It must also ensure that information from local or sub-national sources, depending on the circumstances, can be included. Whatever the SF&W system, the main concern when it is being used will be to assess the quality of the information, then to overcome at best any bias linked to the perceptions of the analyst.

With regard to the quality of information the double assessment system evaluating the source, on the one hand, and vectored information, on the other hand, has proved itself within the intelligence and should be widely adopted. It should, however, be noted that rumours, partially true news and narration may be useful, in that they reveal the beliefs and aims, concerns and anxieties of the actors under consideration.

In addition to minimizing them through the use of a systematic model and other specifically designed methods such as Red Teaming or alternative hypothesis, the perceptual bias of the analyst will be easier to correct by comparing analyses over time and across space, as well as through a check on the internal consistency and logic of the argument set out.

'What would you primarily try to focus on in your system?'

You cannot select just one thing to focus on because the threats and dangers are numerous and tend to be versatile. You need to understand human intentions, issues, underlying processes and variables and to look at them historically to grasp dynamics.

The aim of a SF&W system is to obtain sufficient details on the world situation sufficiently early to enable the authority in place either to establish a policy or to take actions related to existing policies, whether this is in terms of total prevention or mitigation of potential adverse consequences or taking advantage of opportunities.

Depending on the objectives defined, a SF&W warning system will attempt to identify the main elements and dynamics leading to the risk or situation being prevented, or to the opportunity that could be seized. For example, the delivered warning itself may relate to instability in a country X or Y, if instability in foreign countries has been identified as a security issue – which is most of the time the case, with varying global to regional foci. It may also relate to conflicts, if identifying and preventing them makes it possible to achieve the objectives already defined.

'What would your ideal team be like for a strategic foresight and warning system?'

I would select intelligent people with at least a M.Sc. degree, who can think outside-of-the-box. My team would be multidisciplinary, multicultural and a mix of different characters and cognitive make-ups. Each individual would be focusing on his or her area and responsible for a related set of issues, before all the work/issues are brought to a weekly team meeting where the knowledge is shared and brainstormed. One individual could be a member of several teams, clusters or units.

Regular outreach would be done, notably through intensive workshops with an array of diverse people from different walks of life, from scholars and specialists to gamers, chess players or writers.

'How would your strategic foresight and warning system function and how would it be part of an overall risk management system?'

My system would have five plus one stages:

1. Foresight;

2. Warning and delivery of the warning;

3. Diagnosis and optionally evaluation of policy or response options; plus1 – decision, which belongs to policy makers;

4.   Planning of the response;

5.   Response implementation.

The SF&W system covers steps 1 to 3, and then maybe involved or not in stage 4. Stage 5 will alter the world and thus feeds back in this way in the SF&W system.

The whole SF&W process would contain analysis of multiple issues and countries. In real life, for example, when it is about instability in countries, some systems revise their final product that produces a list of unstable countries according to different timelines once or twice a year. We also find systems where all countries can be monitored on an ongoing basis.

As far as the warning function is concerned, we shall first identify the indicators that will be grounded in the model underlying our understanding of the issue. Actually, this model should already have been made explicit during the strategic foresight analysis. During this phase a broad range of experts, scientists and other relevant actors may be involved. Notably for the foresight part, it would be useful to involve stakeholders to start working on their specific biases.

For each crucial variable that influences the dynamics of the system, corresponding indicators will be created. According to the resources available, the monitoring and surveillance of those indicators can be either done by one or many external centres or in-house by warning analysts or by both. Requirements for information, as demanded by each indicator, will then be sent to the relevant collectors. The system used traditionally by defence personnel is very efficient and should be used. The person in charge of a specific indicator will then be responsible for receiving the information and analysing it thus transforming it in indication. The various indications received will then be interpreted so as to make the judgement on the future for the issue at hand. Warnings will be delivered – or not, accordingly – as a result of the process.

When monitoring indicators over time, if indications suddenly appear to be very different from those obtained previously, the analyst must verify with the collector, if possible the reasons for this change in order to reduce the likelihood of disparities that might come from bias in perception.

It is important to combine two ingredients: the use of human analysis and the most systematic, comparative, and objective methods that exist. The aim is to obtain correction or minimization of any bias linked to human perception or, in the case of meetings, to group dynamics but without destroying intuition, synthetic capacities, emotional elements and complexity of thought.

It should be noted here that it is necessary for the organization to strive towards permanent update to include the results of new research as well as the result of self-assessment and lessons learned. Self-assessment allows learning from any errors that may be made. Each error detected must be the subject of a diagnosis to identify its origin and correct the system appropriately.

Finally, as a warning in itself may not be enough to attract the attention of policy makers, they may also need to see the warnings accompanied by potential policy options and their assessment.

'How would the system transmit its products to decision making?'

There are various ways to deliver products, which cannot be described in detail in such a short framework. The rule that needs to be followed is that the way to deliver the product should be adapted to the recipient of the product.

It is thus imperative first to map the clients or customers for the products, be it a foresight product or a delivered warning. The clients will depend upon the issue at hand, and the institutional framework of the country or organization (its administrative tradition and culture, the structure and agency of its organization, its history, the normative beliefs of the country, etc.). Once clients are identified, then it will be necessary to know the clients, their function and their institutional and professional surrounding (including in terms of individuals) as well as possible – feedback from them would be ideal. Considering this understanding, second best channels of communication, if they do not yet exist, must be created and mutually endorsed.

Finally, best forms of communication for the delivery of the product must be found. Biases will be kept in mind for those three stages (mapping, channels of communication and forms of the product delivered). Any change to the client nexus, from the individual to the agency of the function to evolution of channels of communications will imply a need to reassess the delivery system and eventually to adapt it to the new conditions.

14

How Could We Improve Our Public Strategic Foresight Systems? – Views of Policy Makers and High Government Officials

Dr Jyrki Kasvi
Member of the Parliament and the Vice-Chair of the Finnish
Parliament Committee for the Future

'How could we improve our strategic foresight systems?'

I would not create any monolithic foresight units in the Finnish government, because they would just focus on given themes and the possibility to produce or follow emerging 'runners' would be neglected. In foresight the 'runners' and wanderings are the most important things. It is only good that foresight is being done in many different places from their own specific perspectives. What is needed is more networking, collaboration and the transfer of knowledge between foresight experts. But how this could be done, as all sectors of the government are so far apart and highly fenced both mentally and by juridical and budgetary points? I would create a matrix organization for the strategic foresight of the government. This means that the foresight functions would still be distributed across the government, but each of them would be given a responsibility to report both vertically inside their own sector, and horizontally to the Prime Minister's Office which should coordinate this matrix organization. In order to establish this coordination body, I would move the State management unit from the Ministry of Finance to the Prime Minister's Office where it would be merged with this new strategic foresight matrix organization coordination body. A new very high official's position should be established for directing this new coordination body, so that this head of State strategic foresight would have the power to order things to happen in ministries.

Mr Patrick Nathan
Deputy Director of National Security Coordination Centre (NSCC) in Singapore's Prime Minister's Office, Colonel[1]

'How could we improve our strategic foresight systems?'

First of all we need to establish as many good quality futures units in all of Singapore's government ministries as possible. At the moment there are 4–5 futures or environmental scanning units across the Singapore Government's 15 ministries. As ministries are divided into semi-autonomous statutory boards, there are in theory over 60 governmental units in total to which we could establish futures units that function as the best experts on that particular domain's futures issues and analysis methods. By achieving such a large number of futures units across the Singapore Government's sectors and levels we would enhance its overall futures studies capability significantly in the long run, because the very existence of the units would affect the work and thinking in other units that collaborate with them. Second, by sharing knowledge between these expert units, which would have developed new specific methods to be used in their field, we could end up with a large pool of good foresight knowledge.

Along with increasing the number of the government's futures units, I would enhance the national strategic foresight capability by merging the three foresight functions that have always been very far from each other in all governments. These are: i) Scenario/Analysis work, ii) Emerging issues scanning/horizons scanning/early warning, and iii) Risks evaluation work. The new system that merges these three foresight functions would start from detecting and evaluating risks. Then it would build alternative scenarios for risk manifestations, and finally it would carry out an emerging issues detection

---

1   Mr Patrick Nathan was interviewed twice, on 27 August 2009 and on 12 November 2010. Two persons (Jeanette Kwek, Senior Strategist, Strategic Policy Office, Public Service Division, Prime Minister's Office and Bernard Toh, Strategist, Strategic Policy Office, Public Service Division, Prime Minister's Office) participated in Nathan's interview on 27 August 2009. Jeremy Tan, Assistant Director, Horizon Scanning Centre, National Security Coordination Centre (NSCC) participated in Nathan's interview on 12 November 2010.

phase to locate the space of issues that indicate potential realization of one of the scenarios.

Dr Osmo Kuusi

Senior Adviser, Committee for the Future of Finnish Parliament. Senior Researcher in Government Institute for Economic Research (VATT)

'How could we improve our strategic foresight systems?'

It is crucial to strengthen the science in foresight. The good thing in Finnish public foresight is the fact that we really have made considerable efforts. The risk here however is that, if the foresight could not reach its promise, then it could end up being put aside. This is a real risk now as Finland is in crisis due to the fact that two of its foundations are cracking. Forest industry is on its way out, and Nokia has not been as successful as it used to be, and it may leave the country as well, despite all the foresight that we have done. If after all, it is discovered that the foresight has been sloppy somehow, that would jeopardize the whole idea of foresight. It is a good thing that this risk is acknowledged and there is know-how for it. We cannot ride with fuzzy images anymore. What we need now is to establish strict science based rules for all foresight.

Mr Devadas Krishnadas

Deputy Director of Strategic Planning and Lead Foresight Strategist at the Singapore Ministry of Finance

'How could we improve our strategic foresight systems?'

I will start my answer from the background and evolution of the Singaporean foresight system. Singapore is a small and vulnerable country, which constantly challenges the government to analyse various risks. The evolution of foresight in the government of Singapore began from risk detection and scenario planning in the Ministry of Defence in 1991, but it was moved to the Public Service Division (PSD) in 1995, where it got a new name and objectives in 2003. The government of Singapore has always been willing to do experimentation on foresight work. One experiment is the Risk Assessment and Horizons Scanning Programme (RAHS), which was established in 2004. Overall the evolution is going from one centralized foresight thinking to many distributed foresight thinking and units across the government of Singapore's ministries. The increased distribution of foresight units across the government will mean that over time the policy analysis will more often come packaged together with the foresight types of thinking in order to give the decision makers the benefit of 'outside-of-the-box' thinking. This distribution is still an emerging process, but having come to this point of distribution in Singapore, we already recognize that we need to establish a network for coordination and collaboration in knowledge sharing between the foresight units. For this purpose we established the Strategic Futures Network (SFN) in 2010.

In the coming 4–5 years we will improve the Singaporean foresight system by stabilizing these units and networks. It is also necessary to build institutional norms and principles for how we use and develop these new units with a larger pool of practitioners.

After 4–5 years we will probably see a stronger role for the Centre for Strategic Futures (CSF) in building better networks between Strategic Futures units in ministries and outside the government futures community, including selected corporate officers or academics who are key figures or experts in their domain.

Ms Riitta Kirjavainen
Counsellor, Finland's Prime Minister's Office. Deputy Head of the Policy-analysis Unit

'How could we improve our strategic foresight systems?'

There is much to do with the methods. Nowadays the methods and practices are too expert oriented. When there are just few people involved in foresight who share information just among themselves, the limits of effectiveness are narrow. According to the EU's definition for foresight,[2] it is a systematic, participatory, future intelligence gathering and medium- to long-term vision building process aimed at present-day decisions and mobilizing joint actions. It has three dimensions in it: structured anticipation research, decision making and visioning, and participation. The last one is at the cutting edge, and should be present in order to be able to speak about good foresight. Hence, what we really need are tools for enhancing that dimension in foresight. We

---

2   See the definition in: European Commission Research Directorate General (2001): A Practical Guide to Regional Foresight (FOREN). Available at: http://foresight.jrc.ec.europa.eu/documents/eur20128en.pdf

should not only add citizens' participation rounds to public foresight as a sugar coating, but get real tools for participation and collaborative working between all key stakeholders, such as officials, politicians, researchers, and citizens. This is crucial as a big risk in Finland is consensus thinking. It helps decision making, but it can leave blind spots at crucial points too. In closed circles the understanding does not get renewed.

We also need new tools for the first dimension of foresight in order to detect weak signals, especially from so-called grey areas (areas between administrative sectors). And what we really need to get done under the PM's Office is the strengthening of political analysis. Traditionally PMO has been an office which delivers things from ministries to the national policy makers without deep analysis. We aim to carry out as relevant an analysis on horizontal issues for the policy makers as possible, but we need new tools too. We must be able to better combine the history knowledge with the foreknowledge regarding the issues that we are preparing. And finally, we need new tools for both fast reacting and creating futures visions. Otherwise we are lost in this complex world.

PART IV
Discussion

> *If the soul wants to recognize itself, it will have to look at the soul of the other.*
>
> Plato

Introduction

This 'Discussion' part contains two autonomous sections, which are Chapters 15 and 16. The first discussion chapter is written by Henry Kwok, a long-term strategic management consultant from Singapore, whom I asked to write about his understanding of the theme from a strategic management point of view. That chapter can stand alone as a solid article in response to the question, how can we produce a better strategic understanding for strategic decision making? It is also an important summarizing part of the book, which merges its three focal themes, systems thinking and evolutionary thinking, foresight thinking, and strategic management into a new type of management approach called 'Spaces'.

The second discussion chapter is my summary of the themes of the book. It begins with a comparison between the public strategic foresight systems in international country cases, and it continues with a summary of the views of the interviewed strategic foresight experts. Then it presents a possible organization of a large centrally steered public strategic foresight system, and finally it synthesizes the book's systemic themes, inferring and methodology themes, and foresight themes, into a table which summarizes the suitability of the various futures domain methods in different types of systems.

Trilogy of Systems Thinking, Foresight and Strategic Management[1]

Life, just a few short decades ago, was relatively simple and stable. The conditions were so benign that we could get away with reactivity and even passivity. However, globalization, scientific advancements and technological innovations, among other advancements, have reduced the physical distance to connect socially with others to no further than our computer screen. This connectivity is thrusting extreme pace of change in the way we live, communicate, socialize and work. We can beam almost instantaneously through the social media networks – YouTube, Facebook, Twitter, etc. – our pleasurable or nasty experiences at leisure, shopping and work and what we are observing and experiencing such as the floods in Queensland, Australia and the political protests in Egypt. Such changes have a great impact and alter our socio-cultural, environmental, economical, geopolitical landscape.

Life nowadays has become so complex and volatile. The world conditions have become more tumultuous, chaotic and unpredictable. The accelerating pace of change into the future will make the world even more complex and volatile. There is no way we can escape from the impact of the fast pace of change. Loathing the changes and remaining passive is no longer a viable and sustainable option. We will have to learn to love them and to be more proactive in the changing conditions. Then the future will become exciting.

---

1 This chapter is written by Henry Kwok.

A New Perspective Needed

It is not entirely our fault if we hate change, we have grown comfortable with the traditional methods of thinking. They have proven their worth albeit in a simple and stable environment. It is always unsettling to see the inability of such proven approaches when coping with the challenges posed by a complex and unstable world. However, we cannot march forward into the twenty-first century with a twentieth century mentality. We need a new paradigm shift.

One way is to re-discover the art of systems thinking by looking at all forms of human and natural activities as a multitude of systems in motion, each seeking to gain some sort of equilibrium or harmony. We have to learn to capture the quintessence of these systems in motion.

Flood (1999) made a poignant explanation on the nature of systems thinking:

> Systems thinking is not something that can be explained easily and understood comprehensively ... Very quickly we will lose touch with the notion of wholeness in a trivialised account of its so-called properties. Many textbooks ... make this mistake ... [and] explain the world in terms of systems and subsystems, what a system is and how it behaves. An account in these terms ... strips it (systemic thinking) of all essential meaning. Systemic thinking begins with an intuitive grasp of existence.

The extravagant claim on what systems thinking can achieve has unfortunately not met with expectation. Systems thinking fell in popularity. However, the problem does not lie with systems thinking but with the lingering influence of traditional thinking. The latter tends to favour a formal approach to each system.

Systems thinking is not by any measure a hard science, it is more an art! We have moved away from a formal form-centric appreciation of a system to something which is less formal and more open and free-flowing to discover the 'big picture' as to why the system exists. We must recognize that the form is an expression of the substance. Thus we must first grasp the substance of the system and its purpose before we can see how its component parts are structured to define the process through the activities and organization of the system. This process will determine the web of relationships and pattern of behaviour that will emerge. Such an approach will allow systems thinking to bring out the essence of the system in terms of its depth and complexity.

Singularity in time also implies that each system will evolve to be singular and unique. Thus two systems may look similar but they are never identical. Their surrounding environment would have changed. Their make-up would have changed over time too. Thus it is not surprising that even identical twins brought up in the same environment can have different behavioural characteristics.

If each system is unique, then we must approach each as openly. To approach it with some systematic pre-conceived ideas or with archetype models will rob it of its essence!

Systems Thinking 101

Flood's comment that 'systemic thinking begins with an intuitive grasp of existence' is a useful reminder. Nonetheless we still need to recognize some key concepts of systems thinking to help us put the pieces of the system together.

First, everything is part of a system or systems. The universe is one mega-system that contains an infinite number of systems and sub-systems in complex interactions. At one end, the cosmic world is made up of huge stellar systems stretching across the universe. At the other extreme is the sub-atomic world of quantum particles as already discussed in this book. These systems are in a dynamic state of flux, responding to external changes and changes from within. They are adapting and evolving all the time. This phenomenon provides an insight into the characteristics of complex evolving systems as follows:

- A 'system' is a dynamic complex whole – with parts interacting and functioning – as a self-organized unit. The whole system is primary while the parts are secondary to the system;

- A system has a structure within which the various parts are organized. The parts in a system are hierarchically tiered. It is in turn part of a bigger environment;

- The structure will influence the process in which energy-material-information are exchanged via semi-permeable membranes or boundaries – among the various parts within the system, and between the system and its surrounding environment. Once this process is disrupted, the system will malfunction or even perish; and

• This process will initiate a series of activities through which the system will seek equilibrium or harmony by behaving in rational, irrational, oscillating, chaotic, or exponential fashion. There can be more than one set of resultant behaviours that can emerge.

Thus a system is a group of interacting, interrelated, and interdependent components that work together as a unified and complex whole. A system can be mechanistic, living or a combination involving both.[2] A mechanistic system tends to be more deterministic in fulfilling the purpose it is designed for. A living system is open and self-organizing. It is capable of learning, adapting, changing and evolving.

A system is defined primarily by the interactions of the parts – not by the sum of its parts. We have seen often enough how all-star teams can lose league games to teams in the farm league or relegation zone. Thus the fact that individual parts can be performing efficiently, does not mean that the system is performing effectively. When a part is taken out of the system, the part will lose its properties, and so does the system. A heart taken out of a person will not beat nor can that person survive.

Systems exist in a three dimensional matrix of time-space-domain. There is a hierarchical structure in the way the parts and sub-parts are arranged within the system. Cells form the organs in our body. Some parts are tiered laterally and are supposed to function in harmony like partners in a tennis match; some parts in the diverse ecology of a pond or a forest can compete and co-operate at different times.

The relationships among the parts are dynamically interdependent. These relationships can be altered by both external and internal changes. As the system seeks to gain a new equilibrium, it can cause a rippling effect of reactions among various parts within the system. In the process, new connections can be established and existing connections can change and evolve. Some interrelations will be strengthened, some weakened and others broken over a physical-space-time domain. Though the processes and structures within the system can influence how the various parts will interact to a certain extent,

---

2   See the axis of systemic self-renewal in Figure 4.1 and the U-curve of complexity in Figure 4.2.

these interactions can be largely complex, chaotic, random and unpredictable as well.

Some relationships can be distinct and overt. Such visible relationships can be impervious to change. A culture or an ingrained habit can be highly resistant to change. Other relationships can be subtle or hardly noticeable – even remote – but they can gather strength over time to reach a tipping point on the system. 'Black swan' relationships may possess very low probability of incidence, but Hussein Taleb has highlighted their potential impacts. Thus the parts are not necessarily bound by singular dimensional cause-effect relationships among one another. They interact in the multi-dimensional space, time and domains – all within the confine or space of the system. 'Connecting the dots' is all about seeing these multi-dimensional relationships in the system holistically. Hence, clearly a much broader and deeper peripheral vision is needed to anticipate emerging trends and their potential implications.

The Age of Surprise

The moment we become engaged with a system, we become part of it as well. This relationship will prevent us from neither gaining full understanding of what is happening in any system nor gaining perfect knowledge of that system. Thus facing the unknown, uncertainties and unpredictability has to be an essential feature in the system. This further implies that we can never fully solve the complex issues in any system. Complex issues are not problems that can be mathematically proven or solved. Every now and again we are reminded that there can be more than one outcome in whatever we do. Some outcomes are intended; some are not. Complex issues have the propensity to evolve and to re-surface under different guises.

Humanity may be enjoying the benefits of economic wealth and well-being but this endeavour has led to pollution in the air, earth and water! These pollutions are not only threatening environmental sustainability but also affecting climatic conditions on a global basis. This deadly combination is now threatening the very existence of mankind.

While the controversy of natural causes or anthropological causes on climate change continues, we cannot deny that human activities are harming the environment at a pace much faster and at a scale much bigger than the earth can absorb – let alone repair. These activities are adding impetus to the process of climate change. As we move into the future, the hyper-rate of change will propel us into a new norm of greater systemic uncertainties. Such uncertainties and the accompanying risks will grow exponential correspondingly. Strategically the traditional approach towards control with absolute certainty will be a futile attempt. It will not only drain us of our precious time and resources. Worse still, it also can cause us to miss picking up opportunities, which are there for the picking.

Changes Can Make Us or Break Us!

Many solutions – no matter how well intended – to the problems of yesterday have come back to haunt us today with their unintended consequences. This underlines the need to approach problematic issues with a very different mindset. It can no longer be one of trying to solve them. Rather it should be one of trying to address or manage them. This implies that the issues are not put aside once the decisions or actions have been taken. The situations remain monitored for telling signs of unintended consequences so that timely corrective measures, whenever necessary, can be taken. The more significant the issue, the greater the need to keep regular and close tabs on the situation for any deviations from the desired results. There are more than subtle differences between this mindset and the traditional approaches. The new mindset recognizes that, no matter how well considered our decisions or actions may be, there can more than one set of outcomes. It also recognizes that some of these outcomes can be time delayed. At times, some solutions can appear to work initially but things can break down later in the future. At other times, the solutions may not appear to work initially but the situation can improve over time when critical changes fall into place to put things together.

Embracing uncertainty and risks as the new reality opens the way to more proactive and positive approaches. Such approaches incentivize us to think and find opportunities in the face of challenges not only for the here and now but more importantly into the future as well. It is like driving a car. The road condition is not only dictated by the car ahead of us; it is also dictated by the cars on the road in front, beside and behind. Keeping behind the car ahead and avoiding knocking into it may not be the best option. The drive could be faster and more pleasant by navigating safely and smoothly by anticipating the flow of traffic. Therefore we will need to develop our foresight competencies to anticipate emerging trends and how the future can possibly unfold.

Future Foresight

As discussed in the second chapter of this book, futuring, futurism, foresight, futurology or futures studies emerges as a discipline to help us peep into the wildly unpredictable future and to provide foresight on future trends. It transforms foresight from an intuitive skill into a coherent body of techniques and knowledge, with systems thinking providing the cognitive skill to envision dynamic interplay of the factors that will shape the future.

Futuring has developed hundreds of techniques as presented in Chapter 6, 'Inferring in foresight'. These techniques can be as confusing as the variety of labels they come with. Fortunately, The Office of Science and Innovation[3] provides a succinct description on how these techniques complement one another.

> Let us assume you are standing on the bridge of a ship. You scan the horizon (**horizon scanning**) and see an iceberg and your supply ship. You work out the likely speeds and directions of the iceberg and supply ship (**trend analysis**) and put the information into the ship's computer (**modelling**) and then plot a course (**roadmapping**) so that you meet with the supply ship and not the iceberg. While you are doing this you dream of eating some nice chocolate that you hope is on the supply ship (**visioning**). You realise that the speeds and directions of the iceberg and supply ship might change, so you work out a range of possible options to make sure you have the greatest chance of meeting the supply ship (**scenarios**). Even with all of this planning, you know there is a chance of the unexpected and hitting the iceberg so you get the crew to do an evacuation drill (**gaming**). While they are doing it, you work back from the most likely future position of the supply ship to work out the steps you need to get there (**backcasting**).

Each of these techniques does not only vary in the terms of the quantitative analysis and qualitative intuition involved. They also operate on a different set of underlying assumptions:

- *The past extends into the present and continues into the future.* The change will continue its momentum predictably into the future.

3   House of Commons Public Administration Select Committee, Governing the Future, Second Report of Session 2006–07. HC 123-I. Published on 6 March 2007 by authority of the House of Commons. London: The Stationery Office Limited.

The future is extrapolated using statistical trend analysis based on information gathered from past and current events, blog sites, patent registrations, web portals, etc.

- *History is repeated in identifiable cycles and predictable patterns.* Individual factors do not determine the probable future but their interactions do. The future is projected by tracing patterns of past events by using source analysis, signal strength, timeline analysis, narrative analysis, backcasting etc.

- *The future can be modified and changed by the beliefs and actions of key change makers.* The future is projected using the stated and implied goals of key decision-makers and trend setters in leaderships, organizations, and institutions. Techniques include visioning, cross-impact analysis, stakeholders' assessments, Delphi surveys and scenario planning.

- *The future is the result of a series of unpredictable, random and at times remote-looking activities.* Horizontal scanning, roadmapping, modelling, simulation and gaming provide views on possible change over time, novel situations and landscape.

- *The future can only be seen intuitively.* Rigid structured approaches restrict thinking within the confines of a box. A combination of insights and personal intuition is needed to capture unlikely possibilities beyond the information gathered from surveys, interviews, brainstorming, forums, etc.

Each technique has its own merits but each on their own may not be sufficient in providing the required rigidity of future foresight. We will have to use a combination of these methods. One systemic approach of integrating them holistically is to use a 5-step filtering approach adapted from the Eltville Model of Pero Micic:[4]

1. The possible future is explored by collecting as much information on the future as possible. We can research on what experts, futurists, periodicals and even opinion polls are saying. The emphasis is to

---

4   Micic, Pero (2010). The 'Eltville Model' of Future Management Group. See http://english. futuremanagementgroup.com/en/eltvillemodel/index.php and compare to Figure 2.7, 'Futures cone and wild cards', as well.

keep an open mind for weak signals – just like an AWAC system, which captures whatever appears on the radar screen.

2. The plausible future is refined by using projections, Delphi surveys, scenarios, roadmapping etc., to examine underlying assumptions critically and objectively.

3. The probable future is further refined with a creative and visionary mind with the intention to identify the opportunities and risks revealed by matrix and meta-opportunities etc.

4. The preferred future is determined, using a critical and visionary mind to evaluate morphologies and vision pictures.

5. The unlikely future is anticipated using assumption reversal, surprise scenario, gaming etc., as a cautious pessimistic but imaginative mind tries to find wild cards.

This will bring us right back to the present in which we have to plan on bridging the gap between where we are now and the preferred future we want to create.

Reacting to the Possible Future

Conflict and terrorism, fundamentalism, pluralism, differing ideologies, regional interest groupings, multi-polarity, economic dominance, highly volatile financial and commodities markets, food security, energy security, climate change, globalization, new technology, regulatory change, changing demographics and new societal values are a few of the ever increasing number of change drivers re-shaping our geopolitical landscape. The future may be uncertain but we can shape our own future by making reasoned decisions, guided by the emerging trends and weak signals we have identified and assessing their likely impact in the future as time unfolds. The risks of tomorrow can pose threats but they can offer opportunities with greater prospects for collaborations and disruptions.

The purpose of futuring is not to predict the future but to make it better. Futuring, futurism, futurology or futures studies was developed to provide foresight on future trends, and to decide what is desirable, and what to change in order to cope with the swirling current of the complex, accelerative and uncertain forces of changes ahead. It needs strategic management to provide longer term solutions.

Several strategic concepts must be considered when deciding the future we want to create. First, our decisions are based on our (intuitive) assumption – not probability. Possibility is based on assumptions whereas prediction is based on probability. Futuring makes assumptions – not prediction. We seldom plan our next car trip with a flat tyre in mind as the chances of a flat tyre is low but we nonetheless put a spare tyre in the boot because a flat tyre is possible. Moreover, it will be impossible to complete the journey without a spare tyre, in the event of a flat tyre.

Second we can manage uncertainty in two mutual but complementary ways. Initially we must plan with the end in mind, failing to plan means planning to fail. We can plan with as long a list of exhaustive possibilities as possible but it is still impossible to predict all the unexpected 'black swans'. Next and of equal importance is that we must also develop the ability to respond effectively to contingencies by being prepared to change the plan.

China has an insatiable appetite for fossil fuels to keep its economy going.[5] China is continuously challenged to secure a steady supply of fossil fuels without pushing oil prices to dizzy heights. Unfortunately the oil supply is prone to sudden disruption arising from numerous causes – extreme weather, labour unrest, political events, conflicts, field blow-ups, blockage of oil shipping lanes. The global demand of oil is fairly stable over the near future as it is difficult for power plants to make the switch to alternative fuels. This makes the global demand for oil fairly price inelastic in the short term. This volatility in supply and prices can make the Chinese economy extremely vulnerable. China can diversify its supply sources as much as possible to minimize the impact of any disruption in supplies but it cannot prevent the volatility in oil prices in the world market. It can increase the level of its strategic stock, it can hedge its purchases with futures contract, or it can buy oil fields overseas thus locking in the price with the oil in the ground as a hedge. These are more proactive steps in building resilience in securing oil supply than the futile exercise of predicting the next oil crunch. The critical difference between a crisis and an opportunity is in the state of preparedness.

---

5   C.f. Geis, et al. (2011): *Discord or 'Harmonious Society'? China in 2030.*

Putting Systems Thinking, Future Foresight and Strategic Management Together

We may put the key concepts of systems thinking into a simple framework. This frame should be considered as something conceptual, something more to organize our thinking process and something to help place various ideas in the right place in the big picture.

Let us consider 3 key concepts:

1.   Hierarchical level of engagement.

2.   Singularity of event.

3.   Complex evolving systems 'Black Box' Model.

Hierarchical Level of Engagement

Parts in a system are structurally hierarchical-tiered. The level at which the system is engaged will determine the level of control a given component in the system has in bringing about the changes it desires. When the system is engaged at the level at which a given component is positioned or lowered, that component will have greater control over the changes it needs to make. China has control over when, where and how it wants to allocate the fossil fuels it has in its inventory. However, China has less control over oils that are out of its inventory. It has less control over when, where and how it can secure the fossil fuel supplies, especially in a tight oil market. It may have to use its political and economic influence to secure the oil. It can also collaborate with other oil producers through the sharing of production technologies and the financing and construction of supporting infrastructures to secure the needed oil supplies.

Strategically, China's intention is not to achieve control over the causes of the problems or changes but to control the effects. It can never remove the causes for the disruption in oil supplies but the Chinese can take steps to minimize the effects of a sudden drop in oil supplies. We may not be able to prevent an earthquake but we can build houses that can withstand the shocks. Framing the issue we are studying within the context of the level of engagement with the overall system will help define the level of control the particular unit can exercise over the actions it can take to effect the changes that it wants.

The Singularity of Event

The environment changes as time changes. Just as time is singular, each event similarly has a singular nature. As no two events can be identical, we need to assess every situation from this point of uniqueness with an open mind.[6]

Back to Basics – Co-evolution, Complex Evolving Systems and a 'Black Box' Model

A basic universal conceptual 'black box' model must be based on how the world naturally works. All systems have a set of inputs. These inputs are subjected to a conversion process to produce a set of outputs. The efficiency of conversion not only depends on the quality of the input components but it is also affected by the operating environment. We can sow high-yielding seeds on the ground but the yield will depend on the fertility of the soil and favourability of the weather from the time of planting to harvesting. There is also a mechanism to provide feedback on whether the process is producing the right set of outputs so that corrective actions can be made.

There are five basic phases in this model – inputs, conversion, outputs, feedbacks and environment. At first glance this 'black box' model appears more appropriate for the mechanistic world. This is indeed correct. However, on closer examination, living systems undergo the same phases as well.

Mechanistic systems operate in closed loops. In contrast, living systems can learn, adapt and evolve and thus operate in open loops. A living system has more spontaneity in which its collection of agents (which may represent cells, individuals, species, communities, organizations, military units, and nations) can interact dynamically in a network – which can be called a co-evolutionary system.[7] In such a system, each agent will be constantly acting and reacting in parallel to what the other agents are doing. Each agent can decide on the rules of engagement with others – they will choose who they want to ignore, compete or co-operate with. The system as a whole unit will also decide on the

---

6   See the description of a strange attractor, which gives the scientific explanation to the idea that you can never cross the same river twice, as the river is constantly changing in local level, but on the bigger scale we can still call it the same river. Description in 'What is Chaos Theory' in the fourth chapter.

7   The co-evolution is the system type in the middle of the axis of systemic self-renewal as presented in Figure 4.1. See also the U-curve of complexity in Figure 4.2 for comparison.

interactions to respond, tolerate or ignore. A pattern of behaviours will emerge to define the part played by each agent within the system and the part played by the system at a given point in time.

In other words, while all systems exist within their own environment, they are also co-evolutionary actors of that environment. When the agents detect changes in the environment, they may find it necessary to respond to these changes in the 'new' environment. As they change, they will also be changing the environment of which they are part. As the environment responds to these changes, the agents may find it necessary to change once again – and the vicious cycle continues.

Complex Adaptive Systems and *Complex Evolving Systems* are very similar in many ways. They are both co-evolutionary systems that are collections of multiple interconnected diverse elements. A complex adaptive system may adapt to the changes around them but they may not necessarily learn from the process. Whereas, a complex evolving system is distinguished by its ability to learn and change from each experience enabling them to influence their environment, to better predict likely changes in the future, and to prepare for them accordingly. Ambiguity and paradox can abound in complex adaptive systems but complex evolving systems can use these contradictions to create new possibilities to co-evolve with their environment.

Figure 15.1 shows how the essence of complex evolving systems can be captured in the five basic phases – the operating environment, outputs, feedback, inputs and throughput – in an 'open loop' Black Box model.

'Spaces' – Future of Foresight, Systems Thinking and Strategy

For each of the five phases in Figure 15.1, there is a strategic question.

SURROUNDING

How will emerging trends in the environment change the way we are doing things now? These external environmental changes are beyond our control. They can greatly change the way we do things in the future. Each trend can present both opportunities and threats. How must we act to capitalize on the opportunities and to minimize or reduce the threats?

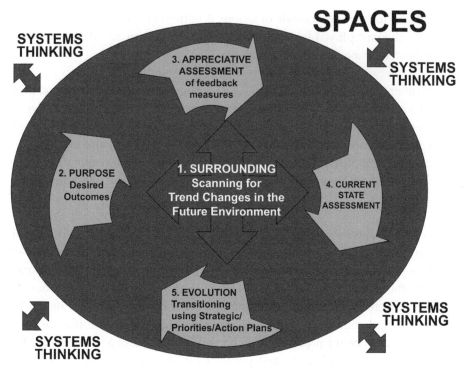

Figure 15.1   'Spaces', the black box model to strategic thinking

PURPOSE

What do we want to be? We must start with the future we want create in mind to bind and inspire the heart of others towards achieving the shared vision, mission, values and goals.

APPRECIATIVE ASSESSMENT

What does achieving 'what we want to be' mean? What are the key performance indicators? The shared dream or desired future can be abstract. However we need to articulate the desired future in measureable milestones to be achieved over time. The deviation between actual result and desired milestones will define the corrective actions needed to rectify the situation.

This assessment should embody a dynamic cross-impact analysis of the measures under consideration – possibly with some predictive measures. This is very different from some static 'score card' that measures the effectiveness of the strategic implementation. Logically a strategy should be modified in response to environmental changes. A constantly changing scorecard is of limited utility as it can create more confusion. Whereas, measuring milestones to be achieved in the context of a vision, mission and values, makes more sense of consistency as these milestones measure the progression made towards achieving the desired future!

CURRENT STATE ASSESSMENT

What are we now? What are our current strengths and weaknesses in the context of the future we want create? How do we position ourselves with the required competitive edge? Most SWOT assessments focus on the current time frame. Strategically it does not make sense to assess strengths and weaknesses in a present time frame. As the saying goes – come tomorrow, today will become yesterday – any measurement based on a SWOT in the present time frame will soon become out of date. We thus need to provide more stable focal points by selecting a forward time frame to assess our SWOT.[8]

EVOLUTION

How do we transition from what we are to what we want to be? What strategies or action plans will help us bridge this gap? How do we maximize our strength to seize the opportunities? What must we do with our weaknesses to lessen the threats? How do we align and integrate the citizens of the state or employees of the corporation to work together to realize the future? What are the strategies to adopt? How do we cascade the action plan and action plans we must plan, implement and sustain to transition towards the desired future?

Most causes of organizational failure in their strategic change management can be traced to misalignments in three areas:

- the body, which involves the conflict of stakeholders' interest;

- the spirit, which involves the clash of culture, values and issues of the heart;

- the mind, which involves the clash of mindsets and world views.

---

8   Compare to the Strategic SWOT method that was introduced in 'Strategic Management' of Chapter 6.

At this stage, we must take note of the subtle differences between strategic aims and strategies. Strategic aims have more to do with the future we want to create and thus should remain fairly stable over a period of time.

Strategies have more to do with how we transition the state or organization from what they are now to the future of what they want to be by aligning its body, spirit and mind. Strategies are the means for achieving an end or the strategic aim(s). Just as generals change their strategy in the battlefront depending on how their force is gaining or losing ground, strategies and supporting action plans too must change in response to a changing environment. When an organization treats strategies as ends unto themselves, their strategies will lack the flexibility to respond to any critical environmental change in a timely fashion, as discussed by Sun Tzu in Chapter 3, 'What is Strategic?'.

SYSTEMS THINKING

How do we dot the various ideas and join them coherently? Foresight, systems thinking and strategic thinking can be integrated into a workable and understandable framework so that the various ideas and concepts can be integrated and connected seamlessly. This calls for a departure from systems thinking being considered as the fifth discipline. Perhaps it is better to consider it as the discipline which is embedded in everything we think and do.

'Spaces' is an open loop model which is scalable. It can be used for critical analysis for both simple and complex evolving systems. A complex system will simply need more parameters.

The circular framework reflects the dynamic nature of the world. The sequential order of the various phases will help in putting the various strategic considerations in the right places. We cannot talk of our dream of what we want to be out of the context in what the future will be like. We cannot talk about strategies without defining the purposes or the ends we have in mind. If a strategy is a mean to an end, then there is no point measuring the effectiveness of that strategy. Instead, we will have to put the horse where it should be – before the cart! We should be measuring our performance against the progression we should be making towards what we want to be.

The world does not stand still! The environment changes and thus we must constantly monitor these changes to make the appropriate responses. Sometimes, the changing environment can alter our dream of what we want to be and the key performance indicators. The changing environment will alter our strategies.

What? So What? Now What? What Can We Learn?

As we go through each cycle of the five phases, the 'Spaces' model must also provide us with a framework to appreciate the situation, to anticipate what will come next and to better learn from our experience in a constantly changing landscape.

- We can use the model to appreciate 'what' our experience is telling by gathering information to gain knowledge and understanding.

- We can use the model to anticipate the 'so what' implications of current and impeding changes by analysing and evaluating major trends and drivers of change and discontinuity.

- We can use the model to learn from 'now what' of our engagement. In a time of exponential change and increasing volatility, the challenge is how to 'remake' ourselves xenomorphically or die.

16

Adjusting Foresight, Intelligence and Inferring for Different Types of Systems

We don't get any wisdom as a gift. We must find it in a jungle adventure,
which none can do for us, and from which none can spare us.

Marcel Proust

This concluding chapter begins with a comparison between the public strategic foresight systems that were presented in the structure part of this book. Then it summarizes the views of the nine strategic foresight experts who were interviewed. It continues presenting a possible model for a centrally steered strategic foresight system, based on some of the views from the interviews, and it ends with my methodological conclusion, which synthesizes the book's systemic themes, with the inferring and foresight themes of the book. The purpose of this synthesis is to conclude the usability of each of the futures domain's methods from the point of view of different types of systems that exist. But before this I make some conclusions on the characteristics of the national strategic foresight systems that were presented in the structure part.

As already discussed, there are various types of foresight systems around the world. In some countries, like Singapore, France and the Netherlands, the foresight capabilities are funded by the state and they are centrally coordinated and located under dedicated government units. In some other countries, like Finland and Germany, the foresight system is based on much more informal public–private cooperation where foresight capabilities are fragmented across various ministries, state research centres, universities, private businesses and other non-governmental organizations. Then there are countries, which have a strong representation of both features, the centrally steered approach and the public–private partnership approach, like the UK, and finally there are several countries which seem to have almost no dedicated strategic foresight functions, neither inside the government nor outside it, such as Latvia. Nevertheless, the purpose of strategic foresight in all countries is much the same, to enhance the decision makers' abilities to make better decisions. Some countries just have a more organized approach or a longer view to the future than others.

The interviewees from Singapore emphasized the need to establish as many specialized foresight units to the government as possible, and reorganizing the existing national strategic foresight capabilities into a new type of efficient system that produces cumulative foresight and a deeper understanding of emerging risks.

The interviewees of Finland saw the need for a strategic foresight system development in a different way. They did not see any need to establish new or strongly centralized monolithic foresight units to the government, because according to the interviewees, such units would focus on given themes and therefore the possibility to produce or follow emerging 'runners' would be neglected and the unit would become a silo itself. As one of the interviewees said, 'in foresight the "runners" and wandering are the most important thing'. However, one of the Finnish interviewees argued that there is a need for a national foresight system coordinating body because there is currently no process in foresight, but he emphasized that such body should not be located under the government in any circumstances. Another interviewee emphasized the need to strengthen the scientific base of foresight in Finland in order to increase its credibility in the eyes of both decision makers and citizens.

To sum up, all Finnish interviewees agreed that there are enough foresight producers in Finland but what is needed is a process or set of methods that would enhance the gathering, distributing, networking and genuine participation between all stakeholders and that would allow for the processing of contradictory information. Basically Finnish interviewees were hoping to see the creation of a new type of matrix organization for the purposes of national foresight. This would mean more flexible and efficient use of existing research capabilities, based on the decision makers changing needs, and the establishment of a new vacancy for foresight matrix coordination. It was highly emphasized by the Finnish interviewees that the holder of such role should be in a very high position in administration, otherwise the matrix would not function well and its outcomes would not be transferred to the policy makers. Actually what is interesting here is to see how the Finnish interviewees were calling for a similar power structure that already exists in Singapore, where Mr Peter Ong is the head of all government civil services and foresight functions

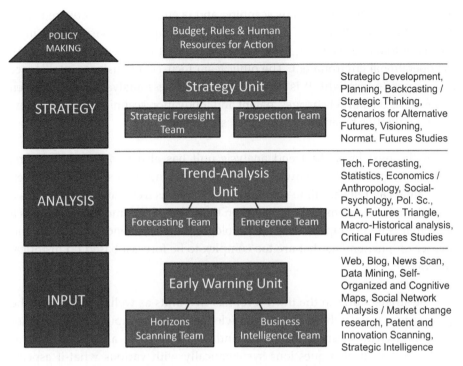

Figure 16.1   Possible organization of a large public strategic foresight system

at the same time but, on the other hand, they opposed the idea of having permanent foresight units with fixed duties under the government.

If I concentrate on those interviewees who were in favour of establishing a centrally steered strategic foresight system, or who suggested ways for developing national intelligence towards a system where knowledge cumulates and gets refined for the use in policy making, and if I combine a few of my own ideas, I can describe the following kind of organization for public strategic foresight, which would be interesting to see. The phases in the left side of Figure 16.1 are the same as in all strategic foresight, except that the prospection (scenarios and what-if) team is located under the strategic unit. The methods in the right side come quite directly from the ten futures domain methodologies that were discussed in inferring and methodologies chapters, but the units and teams in the middle are a new type of organizational suggestion. There the first level's 'early warning unit' has two very different teams that gather and cluster as much knowledge on a selected theme as possible. The first team is working with general horizons scanning and is engineer and software expert driven. It utilizes all types of data sources, ICT and quantitative methods in its mostly automated scanning in order to get the best knowledge of changes in the operational environment. The other team focuses on business intelligence and corporate foresight. It is economist and business analysis experts driven and focuses on market changes, patent and innovation scanning, and interview based qualitative business environment scanning.

In the next level the trend analysis unit has also two teams. The first focuses on quantitative knowledge based forecasting. It is statistician driven and gathers all relevant time-series and does various trend analysis and cross-impact-analysis and modelling based on that. The other 'emergence team' is a team that is ethnography, social-psychology, political science etc. driven and focuses on phenomena that are too complex to be forecast based on historical knowledge.

The strategy unit in the third level has two units as well. First there is the 'prospection team' which gathers knowledge from the input of all the other teams and creates various scenarios and descriptions of alternative futures based on that. It also questions systematically with various what-if aspects the conclusions that have been made by other teams and it suggests new wild cards that could jeopardize the forecast trends. Then there is the other team 'strategic foresight', which gathers knowledge from the input of all other teams and creates systematically well-structured strategic options for each of the scenarios that have been developed by the prospection team. Finally, these strategic options are brought to the decision makers.

I conclude the book with a table, which synthesizes the presented systemic and evolutionary themes, to the book's inferring and methodology themes. The purpose of this synthesis is to conclude the usability of each of the futures domain's methods from the point of view of the seven types of systems that exist. Namely the systems are the same that were presented in the axis of self-renewal in the third chapter: 'the systems that are in conservative self-organization, systems in autocatalysis, systems in autopoiesis, systems in co-evolution which also cover the complex adaptive systems and complex evolving systems that were discussed in the 'spaces model' in the fifteenth chapter, dynamical systems, systems in dissipative self-organization, and systems in chaos'. In other words the table answers the question, 'which of the futures domain methods are best suited for forecasting, understanding and affecting in each of the seven types of systems?'

Table 16.1   **Suitability of futures domain methods for different types of systems**

Types of systems	Methods of futures domain that suit especially well for that system type
System in conservative self-organisation =	Linear approaches, trend extrapolation and analysis, environmental scanning and data mining, FSSF.
System in autocatalysis =	Environmental scanning and data mining, pattern management, systems thinking, modelling, trend impact analysis, S-curve analysis, linear approaches, FSSF, forecasting radar, explorative forecasting, roadmapping.
System in autopoiesis =	Driver, forecasting radar, ICT modelling, FSSF, explorative forecasting, strategic SWOT, backcasting, relevance tree, pattern management, SOM, futures wheel, critical futures studies (CLA, FQM, macro-historical analysis).
System in co-evolution =	Integrated foresight, drivers analysis, PVT-method, participatory foresight, strategic management, strategic SWOT, backcasting, scenarios, FSSF, forecasting radar, SIF-model, futures wheel, critical futures studies (CLA, FQM, macro-historical analysis), ICT modelling, early warning and emerging issues, forecasting radar.
Dynamical system =	Drivers analysis, weak signals analysis, wild cards analysis, critical futures studies (CLA, FQM, macro-historical analysis), scenarios, integrated foresight, non-linear methods, normative forecasting, creative visioning.
System in dissipative self-organisation =	Scenarios, ATF-lenses, visionary management, creative visioning.
System in in chaos =	Visionary management, creative visioning, scenarios, ATF-lenses.

Conclusion

The main objective of this book has been to introduce the extension and boundaries of contemporary strategic foresight and discuss the evolution of its theory and practice. Because I have wanted to go deep to the roots of strategic foresight, I have dedicated many chapters to discussing our contemporary understanding of the 'game situation' that a strategic foresight project must deal with, and the present usability of scientific method and different epistemological principles for understanding such situations. All that deeper knowledge of the laws and inter-linkages beneath the surface level is needed in order to obtain good situational awareness, necessary in contemporary strategic foresight.

Second, I have wanted to discuss the state-of-the-art and the future of strategic foresight methods. For this reason I have presented a list of ten fully-fledged methodologies of futures domain, many popular research strategies and principles, and many new foresight methods that I think deserve more publicity.

I also wanted to provide some useful insight into the state-of-art of the public authorities' practices of strategic foresight, and especially to present various expert interviewees' views on questions such as 'How could strategic foresight better facilitate national decision making' and 'How could we improve our strategic foresight systems'?

As the book has been about the evolution of strategic foresight, I also wanted to give you, as a reader, an overview of the foundations from which the new discipline 'strategic foresight' is emerging. Everything in it is about helping a decision maker to obtain better situational awareness on complex, contextual, non-linear and co-evolutive 'game situations' that cannot be reached by using only one narrow disciplinary approach or principle.

Finally we can end the conclusion of the book with quotes from Sun Tzu and Bertrand de Jouvenel.

> *Foreknowledge enables the wise general to achieve things beyond the reach of ordinary men.*
>
> *Sun Tzu*

> *If we do not know the consequences of our choices, our freedom to choose is an illusion – hence, no freedom exists without forecasting.*
>
> *Bertrand de Jouvenel*

These old statements are still valid and they will stay that way. We can follow these wise words by stating that foresight, whether it is strategic or participatory by its nature, is necessary for steering the future. Decisions can be made without any foresight, but that lacks the steering part. Hence, without any foresight we are like logs adrift in a river.

Bibliography

Abell, Derek F. and Hammond, John S. (1979): *Strategic Market Planning: Problems and Analytical Approach*. Englewood Cliffs, CA, Prentice-Hall.

Alsan, Alper and Oner, Atilla M. (2004): Comparison of national foresight studies by integrated foresight management model. *Futures*, 36 (8), 889–902.

Amara, Roy (1984): New directions for futures research: Setting the stage. *Futures*, 36 (1–2), 43–7. ISSN 0016–3287.

Amara, Roy (1981): The futures field: Searching for definitions and boundaries. *The Futurist*, 15, Feb., 25–9.

Ansoff, Igor H. (1975): Managing strategic surprise by response to weak signals. *California Management Review*, XVIII (2), 21–33.

Aristotle (1999): *Metaphysics* (written orig. 350 BC, tr. Joe Sachs). Santa Fe, NM, Green Lion Press.

Aristotle (1995): *Nicomachean Ethics* (written orig. 325 BC, tr. W.D. Ross). Oxford, Clarendon Press.

Aristotle (2007): *On Rhetoric: A Theory of Civic Discourse* (written orig. 350 BC, tr. George A. Kennedy) 2nd edition. New York, Oxford University Press.

Armstrong, J. Scott (2001): *Principles of Forecasting: A Handbook for Researchers and Practitioners*. New York, Springer.

Arthur, Brian W. (1990): Positive feedbacks in economy. *Scientific American*, February 1990.

Ball, Phillip (2004): *Critical Mass: How One Thing Leads to Another*. New York, Farrar, Straus and Giroux.

Bak, Per and Chen, Kan (1991): Self-organized criticality. *Scientific American*, January, 26–33.

Bak, Per; Chao, Tang and Wiesenfeld, Kurt (1987): Self-organized criticality: An explanation of 1/f noise. *Physical Review Letters*, 59, 381–4.

Barabasi, Albert-Laszlo (2003): *Linked: How Everything is Connected to Everything Else and What it Means for Business, Science, and Everything*. New York, Plume.

Bell, Wendell (2005): *Foundations of Futures Studies: Human Science for a New Era*. Vol. 2: Values, objectivity, and good society. New Brunswick, NJ, Transaction Publishers.

Bezold, Clem (2010): Lessons from using scenarios for strategic foresight. *Technological Forecasting & Social Change*, 77, 1513–18.

Biloslavo, Roberto and Dolinšek, Slavko (2009): Scenario planning for climate strategies development by integrating group Delphi, AHP and dynamic fuzzy cognitive maps. *Foresight*, 12 (2), (2010), 38–48.

Boggs, Danny J. (1985): When governments forecast. *Futures*, 17 (5), 435–9.

Botterhuis, Lineke, Duin, Patrick van der, Ruijter, Paul de and Wijck, Peter van (2010): Monitoring the future: Building an early warning system for the Dutch Ministry of Justice. *Futures*, 42, 454–65.

Brown, D. (2007): Horizon scanning and the business environment: The implications for risk management. *BT Technology Journal*, 25 (1), 208–14.

Buchanan, Mark (2002): *Nexus: Small Worlds and the Groundbreaking Theory of Networks*. New York, Norton & Company.

Casti, John L. (2004): *5 Golden Rules: Great Theories of 20th-century Mathematics and Why They Matter*. New York, MJF Books.

Checkland, Peter (1981): *Systems Thinking, Systems Practice*. Bath, Avon, John Wiley & Sons, Pitman Press.

Chuberre, Nicolas and Liolis, Konstantinos (2010): ISI contribution to grand societal challenges. European Technology Platform. 30 April 2010.

CIA (2006): *Factbook on Intelligence*. [The George Bush Center for Intelligence, Washington, DC, Office of Public Affairs CIA]. Available at: http://www.cia. gov/cia/publications/facttell/index.html

CIA (2000): International crime threat assessment. *Office of Public Affairs CIA*. January, 130.

Cilliers, Paul (1998): *Complexity and Postmodernism: Understanding Complex Systems*. New York, Routledge.

Clausewitz, Carl von (1989): *On War* (written orig. 1832, tr. M. Howard and P. Paret). Princeton, Princeton University Press.

Coates, Joseph F. (2009): Normative forecasting. In: *Futures Research Methodology – Version 3.0*. (eds) Jerome C. Glenn and Theodore J. Gordon. CD-rom. World Federation of United Nations Associations.

Coates, Joseph F. and Glenn, Jerome C. (2009): Normative forecasting. In: *Futures Research Methodology – Version 3.0*. (eds) Jerome C. Glenn and Theodore J. Gordon. CD-rom. World Federation of United Nations Associations.

Coates, Joseph F., Mahaffie, John and Hines, Andy (1997): *2025 Scenarios of US and Global Society Reshaped by Science and Technology*. Greensboro, Oakhill Press.

Colson, Aurelien and Corm, Mounir (2006): Futures studies in the European Union's new member states. *Foresight*, 8 (3), 55–64.

Commission for Consultation of Sector Councils (2008): *Horizon Scan Report 2007: Towards a Future Oriented Policy and Knowledge Agenda*. The Hague.

Concise Oxford English Dictionary (2002): 10th Edition, Judy Pearsall (ed.). New York, Oxford University Press.

Costanzo, Laura A. (2004): Strategic foresight in a high-speed environment. *Futures*, 36, 219–35.

Council of the Five Wise Men (2003): *Twenty Proposals for Employment and Growth. Annual Report 2002–2003*, Chapter 1, Council of the Five Wise Men, Reutlingen.

Dawkins, Richard (2006): *The God Delusion*. London, Bantam Press.

Dawkins, Richard (1989): *The Selfish Gene*. London, Oxford University Press.

Dijk, J.W. Asje van (1991): Foresight studies: A new approach in anticipatory policy making in the Netherlands. *Technological Forecasting and Social Change*, 40, 223–34.

Earle, Edward M. (1962): *Makers of Modern Strategy*. Princeton, NJ, Princeton University Press.

Durkheim, Emil (1912): *Les formes elementaires de la vie religieuse: Le systeme tetemique en Australie*. Paris, Presses Universitaires de France.

Englebrecht, Joseph A. Jr, Bivins, Robert L., Condray, Patrick M., Fecteau, Merrily D., Geis, John P. and Smith, Kevin C. (1996): *Alternate Futures for Air Force 2025*. A research paper presented to Air Force 2025. Maxwell Air Force Base, Air University Press.

European Commission Research Directorate General (2001): *A Practical Guide to Regional Foresight (FOREN)*. European Commission – Joint Research Centre – Institute for Prospective Technological Studies (IPTS) (eds). European Communities, STRATA Programme.

Fairclough, Norman (1992): *Discourse and Social Change*. Cambridge, Polity Press.

Flechtheim, Ossip K. (1972): Futurologie. In: *Historisches wörterbuch der philosophie*. Basel, Schwabe & Co Verlag, 1150–52.

Flood, Robert L. (1999): *Rethinking the Fifth Discipline*. New York, Routledge.

Finnish Ministry of Defence (2006): Securely into the future – Ministry of Defence strategy 2025. Helsinki. Available at: http://www.defmin.fi/index.phtml?l=en&s=318

Freedman, Lawrence (2008): Strategic studies and the problem of power. In: *Strategic Studies: A Reader* (eds) Thomas G. Mahnken and Joseph A. Maiolo. New York, Routledge.

Fuller, William C. Jr. (2008): What is a military lesson? In: *Strategic Studies: A Reader* (eds) Thomas G. Mahnken and Joseph A. Maiolo. New York, Routledge.

Futures Group International (2009): Relevance tree. In: *Futures Research Methodology – Version 3.0.* (eds) Jerome C. Glenn and Theodore J. Gordon. CD-rom. World Federation of United Nations Associations.

Galtung, Johan and Inayatullah, Sohail (1997): *Macrohistory and Macrohistorians.* Westport, CT, Praeger.

Geis, John P., Caine, Scott E., Donaldson, Edwin F., Holt, Blaine D. and Sandfry, Ralph A. (2011): *Discord or 'Harmonious Society'? China in 2030.* Occasional Paper No. 68. Air War.

College. Maxwell Air Force Base, Center for Strategy and Technology, Alabama 36112, Air University Press.

Geis, John P., Kinnan, Christopher J., Hailes, Ted, Foster, Harry A. and Blanks, David (2009): *Blue Horizons II: Future Capabilities and Technologies for 2030.* Occasional Paper No. 65, Maxwell Air Force Base, Center for Strategy and Technology, Alabama 36112, Air University Press.

Georghiou, Luke; Keenan, Michael and Miles, Ian (2010): Assessing the impact of the UK's evolving national foresight programme. *International Journal of Foresight and Innovation Policy (IJFIP),* 6 (1/2/3), (2010), 131–50.

Gladwell, Malcolm (2000): *The Tipping Point: How Little Things Can Make a Big Difference.* New York, Little Brown.

Glenn, Jerome C. (2009a): Introduction. In: *Futures Research Methodology – Version 3.0.* (eds) Jerome C. Glenn and Theodore J. Gordon. CD-rom. World Federation of United Nations Associations.

Glenn, Jerome C. (2009b): Genius forecasting, intuition, and vision. In: *Futures Research Methodology – Version 3.0.* (eds) Jerome C. Glenn and Theodore J. Gordon. CD-rom. World Federation of United Nations Associations.

Glenn, Jerome C. and The Futures Group International (2009): Scenarios. In: *Futures Research Methodology – Version 3.0.* (eds) Jerome C. Glenn and Theodore J. Gordon. CD-rom. World Federation of United Nations Associations.

Global Trends 2025: The National Intelligence Council's 2025 Project.

Godet, Michel, Monti, Régine, Meunier, Franci and Robelat, Fabrice (2000): *Scenarios and Strategies: A Toolbox for Scenario Planning.* Paris, Cahiers du LIPS, LIPS Working Papers.

Godet, Michel (1993): *From Anticipation to Action: A Handbook of Strategic Prospective.* Paris, Unesco Publishing.

Gordon, Theodore (2009a): Trend impact analysis. In: *Futures Research Methodology – Version 3.0.* (eds) Jerome C. Glenn and Theodore J. Gordon. CD-rom. World Federation of United Nations Associations.

Gordon, Theodore (2009b): Science and technology roadmapping. In: *Futures Research Methodology – Version 3.0.* (eds) Jerome C. Glenn and Theodore J. Gordon. CD-rom. World Federation of United Nations Associations.

Gordon, Theodore (2009c): Cross-impact analysis. In: *Futures Research Methodology – Version 3.0.* (eds) Jerome C. Glenn and Theodore J. Gordon. CD-rom. World Federation of United Nations Associations.

Habegger, Beat (2010): Strategic foresight in public policy: Reviewing the experiences of the UK, Singapore, and the Netherlands. *Futures*, 42, 49–58.

Habermas, Jürgen (1986): *Knowledge and Human Interests* (orig. 1972). London, Polity Press.

Habermas, Jürgen (1984): The Theory of Communicative Action. Vol. 1: *Reason and the Rationalization of Society.* Boston, MA, Beacon Press.

Hamcock, T. and Bexold, C. (1994): Possible futures, preferable futures. *Healthcare Forum Journal*, 37 (2), 23–9.

Hamel, Gary (1994): The concept of core competence. In: *Competence Based Competition* (eds) Gary Hamel and Aimé Heene. Chichester, Wiley.

Hamel, Gary and Prahalad, C.K. (1994): *Competing for the Future.* Boston, Harvard Business School Press.

Handel, Michael I. (2000): *Masters of War: Classical Strategic Thought.* 3rd edition. London, Frank Cass.

Hasselblatt, Boris and Anatole Katok (2003): *A First Course in Dynamics: With a Panorama of Recent Developments.* Cambridge, Cambridge University Press.

Heinonen, Sirkka (1999): *Prometheus Revisited: Human Interaction with Nature Through Technology in Seneca.* Helsinki, Yliopistopaino.

Heinonen, Sirkka (1990): *Time and Future in the Production of Seneca* [*Aika ja tulevaisuus Sencan tuotannossa* in Finnish]. Helsinki, Acta Futura Fennica No. 1. Vapk-kustannus.

Herault, Bruno (2006a): Public forecasting and futures studies in Germany. *Foresight*, 8 (6), 71–7.

Herault, Bruno (2006b): Public futures studies: Themes and variations. *Foresight*, 8 (2), 57–69.

Hideg, Eva (1997): Theory and practice in the field of foresight. *Foresight*, 9 (6), 36–46.

Hines, Andy and Bishop, Peter (2006): *Thinking About the Future: Guidelines for the Strategic Foresight.* Washington, DC, Social Technologies LLC.

Hintikka, Jaakko (1998): What is abduction? The fundamental problem of contemporary epistemology. *Transactions of the Charles S. Peirce Society*, 34 (3), 503–33.

Hirsjarvi, Sirkka, Remes, Pirkko and Sajavaara, Paula (1997): *Tutki ja kirjoita* [*Study and Write*]. Helsinki, Kirjayhtyma.

Holm, Richard L. (2003): *The American Agent: My Life in the CIA.* London, St. Ermins Press.

Horton, Averil. (1999): 'Forefront' a simple guide to successful foresight. *Foresight*, 1 (1), 5–9.

IBM (2006): Public Image Monitoring, OmniFind. Available at: http://www-306.ibm.com/software/data/integration/db2ii/editions_womnifind.html

Inayatullah, Sohail (2008): Six pillars: Futures thinking for transforming. *Foresight*, 10 (1), 4–12.

Inayatullah, Sohail (1998a): Macrohistory and the futures studies. *Futures*, 30, ISSN 0016–3287, 381–94.

Inayatullah, Sohail (1998b): Causal layered analysis: Poststructuralism as method. *Futures*, 30 (8), ISSN 0016–3287, 815–29.

Inayatullah, Sohail (1990): Deconstructing and reconstructing the future: Predictive, cultural and critical epistemologies. *Futures*, 22 (2), ISSN 0016–3287115–41.

Johansson, Frans (2004): *The Medici Effect: Breakthrough Insights at the Intersections of Ideas, Concepts and Cultures*. Boston, MA, Harvard Business School Press.

Johnson, Loch K. (2007): *Handbook of Intelligence Studies*. London, Routledge.

Jouvenel, Hugues de (2004): Invitation á la prospective/An Invitation to Foresight. *Futuribles Perspectives Series*. Paris, Futuribles, July 2004.

Jouvenel, Bertrand de (1967): *The Art of Conjecture*. New York, Basic Books.

Kahn, Herman, Brown, William and Martel, Leon (1976): *The Next 200 Years: A Scenario for America and the World*. New York, Morrow.

Kahn, Herman and Wiener, Anthony J. (1967): *The Year 2000: The Framework for Speculation on the Next Thirty-three Years*. New York, Macmillan.

Kaivo-oja, Jari, Katko, Tapio and Osmo Seppälä (2004): Seeking convergence between history and futures research. *Futures*, 36, 527–47.

Kaufmann, Stuart (2007): *Beyond Reductionism: Reinventing the Sacred*, 42 (4), 903–14.

Kauffman, Stuart (2003): *The Adjacent Possible*. www.edge.org (ed.) John Brockman, 11.3.03. Available at: http://www.edge.org/3rd_culture/kauffman03/kauffman_index.html

Kauffman, Stuart (2000): *Investigations*. New York, Oxford University Press.

Kauffman, Stuart (1995): *At Home in the Universe: The Search for the Laws of Self-organization and Complexity*. New York, Oxford University Press.

Kauffman, Stuart (1993): *The Origins of Order: Self-organization and Selection in Evolution*. Oxford, Oxford University Press.

Kirwin, Christopher (1995): Reasoning. In: *The Oxford Companion to Philosophy* (ed.) Ted Honderich. Oxford, Oxford University Press.

Klein, Naomi (2001): *No Logo*. London, Flamingo.

Krawczyk, Ela and Slaughter, Richard (2010): New generations of futures methods. *Futures*, 42, 75–82.

Kuosa, Tuomo (2011a): Practicing strategic foresight in government: The cases of Finland, Singapore and European Union. *RSIS Monograph No. 19*. S. Rajaratnam School of International Studies of Nanyang Technological University, Singapore, Booksmith.

Kuosa, Tuomo (2011b): Different approaches of pattern management and strategic intelligence. *Technological Forecasting and Social Change*, 78, 458–67.

Kuosa, Tuomo (2011c): Evolution of futures studies. *Futures*, 43 (3), 327–36.

Kuosa, Tuomo (2010a): Futures signals sense-making framework (FSSF): A startup with tool for analysing and categorising weak signals, wild cards, drivers, trends and any other types of information. *Futures*, 42 (1), 42–8.

Kuosa, Tuomo (2010b): Future of U.S. power: Is China going to eclipse the United States? Two possible scenarios to 2040. *RSIS Working Paper No. 203*. Nanyang Technological University, Singapore, 45. Available at: http://www.rsis.edu.sg/publications/WorkingPapers/WP203.pdf

Kuosa, Tuomo (2009): Towards the dynamic paradigm of futures research: How to grasp a complex futures problem with multiple phases and multiple methods. *Turku School of Economics, Series A–8: 2009*, 232. Available at: http://info.tse.fi/julkaisut/vk/Ae8_2009.pdf

Kuosa, Tuomo (2007): A few extensions to path-dependence and emergence in complex social systems. *Emergence: Complexity & Organisations*, (E:CO), 9 (4), 3–16.

Kuosa, Tuomo (2005): Study on logics on society's macro-level transformation: A macrohistorical comparison of Pentti Malaska's theory of societal change compared to other theories of transformation. *Journal of Futures Studies*, 10 (1), 15–30.

Kuusi, Osmo (1999): Expertise in the future use of generic technologies: Epistemic and methodological considerations concerning Delphi studies. *Acta Universitatis Oeconomicae Helsingiensis A–159*, Helsinki School of Economics and Business Administration, HeSe Print, 268.

Kuusisto, Rauno (2008): *'Shift' Theoretically-practically Motivated Framework: Information Exchange Viewpoint on Developing Collaboration Support Systems*. Finnish Defence University, Department of Tactics and Operations Art, Series 3, No 1. Helsinki, Edita Prima Oy.

Lane, D.A. and Maxfield, R. (1997) Foresight, complexity and strategy. In: *The Economy as an Evolving Complex System II*: Proceedings, Brian W. Arthur, S. Durlauf and D.A. Lane (eds), vol. 27, Sante Fe Institute Studies in Sciences of Complexity.

Laszlo, Ervin (2003): Introduction. *World Futures – The Journal of General Evolution*, 59 (3–4), 125–6.

Lavoix, Helene (2006): Developing an early warning system for crises. In: *From Early Warning to Early Action?* (ed.) Andrea Ricci. European Commission. Available at: http://ec.europa.eu/external_relations/ifs/publications/articles/book2/book%20vol2_part4_chapter47_developing%20an%20early%20warning%20system%20for%20crises_helene%20lavoix%20and%20ifri.pdf

Leigh, Andrew (2003): Thinking ahead: Strategic foresight and government. *Australian Journal of Public Administration*, 62 (2), 3–10.

Liebl, Franz and Schwarz, Jan Oliver (2010): Normality of the future: Trend diagnosis for strategic foresight. *Futures*, 42, 313–27.

Lindeman-Viitasalo, Marjaana (1995): *Toden näköiset harhat [Delusions that look real]*. Helsinki, Duodecim.

Linstone, Harold A. (2010): On terminology. *Technological Forecasting & Social Change*, 77, 1426–7.

Linstone, Harold A. (2009): The multiple perspective concept. In: *Futures Research Methodology – Version 3.0.* (eds) Jerome C. Glenn and Theodore J. Gordon. CD-rom. World Federation of United Nations Associations.

Linstone, Harold A. (2007): Science and technology: Questions of control. *Technological Forecasting and Social Change*, 74 (2), 230–37.

Linstone, Harold A. and Turoff Murray (1975): *The Delphi Method – Techniques and Applications*. Boston, Massachusetts, Addison-Wesley Publishing Company.

Lorenz, Edward N. (1963) Deterministic non-periodic flow. *Journal of the Atmospheric Sciences*, 20, 130–41

Luhmann, Niklas (1990a): *Ökologische Kommukation [Ecological Communication]*. Westdeutscher Verlag, Oplanden/Wiesbaden.

Luhmann, Niklas (1990b): *Essays of Self Reference*. New York, Columbia University Press.

Machiavelli, Niccolò (2004): *The Prince* (orig. Il Principe, published 1532). London, Penguin.

Mahnken, Thomas G. and Maiolo, Joseph A. (2008): *Strategic Studies: A Reader*. New York, Routledge.

Mainzer, Klaus (1997): *Thinking in Complexity: The Complex Dynamics of Matter, Mind and Mankind*. 4th edition. New York, Springer, 361.

Major, Edward, Asch, David and Cordey-Hayes, Martyn (2001): Foresight as a core competence. *Futures*, 33 (2), 91–107.

Malaska, Pentti (2003a): Futures knowledge and penetration to the futures. In: *Kuinka tutkimme tulevaisuutta? [How We Research the Futures]* (eds) Matti Vapaavuori and Santtu von Bruun. Acta Futura Fennica No 5. Helsinki, Vapk-kustannus, 9–23.

Malaska, Pentti (2003b): Synchronic – diachronic system analysis. In: *Statistics, Econometrics and Society: Essays in Honour of Leif Nordberg* (eds) Rune Höglund, Markus Jäntti and Gunnar Rosenqvist. Statistics Finland Research Report 238, Helsinki.

Malaska, Pentti and Holstius, Karin (1999): Visionary management. *Foresight*, 1 (4), 353–61.

Malaska, Pentti (1991): Economic and social evolution: The transformational dynamics approach. In: *The New Evolutionary Paradigm: The World Futures General Evolution Studies* (ed.) Ervin Laszlo, vol. 2. New York, Gordon and Breach Science Publishers.

Malaska, Pentti (1989): A conceptual framework for the self-reliant transformation of Africa. In: Africa Beyond Famine: A Report to the Club of Rome (eds) Akilu Lemma and Pentti Malaska, *African Studies Review*, 34 (2), 158–9, ISSN 00020206.

Mandelbrot, Benoit (1977): *The Fractal Geometry of Nature*. New York, Freeman.

Mareuge, Celine (2006): Futures studies and public advisory work in Ireland. *Foresight*, 8 (4), 55–61.

Masini, Eleonora B. (1993): *Why Futures Studies?* London, Grey Seal.

Masini, Eleonora B. (1989): The future of future studies. *Futures*, 21 (2), 152–60.

Masse, Pierre (1965): *Le plan ou l'anti-hasard*. Paris, Idées Gallimard.

Maturana, Humberto R. and Varela, Francisco J. (1992): *The Tree of Knowledge: The Biological Roots of Human Understanding*. London, Shambhala.

May, Graham H. (2009): Foresight and futures in Europe: An overview. *Foresight*, 11 (5), 57–67.

May, Timothy (2007): *The Mongol Art of War: Chinggis Khan and the Mongol Military System*. Barnsley, Pen & Sword Military.

Merriden, Trevor (2001): *Business the Nokia Way: Secrets of the World's Fastest Moving Company*. Oxford, Capstone Publishing.

Meulen, Barend van der (1999): The impact of foresight on environmental science and technology policy in the Netherlands. *Futures*, 31 (1), 7–23.

Micic, Pero (2010): *The Five Futures Glasses: How to See and Understand More of the Future with the Eltville Model*. London, Palgrave Macmillan.

Miles, Ian (2010): The development of technology foresight: A review. *Technological Forecasting & Social Change*, 77, 1448–56.

Miles, Ian (2005): UK foresight: Three cycles on a highway. *International Journal of Foresight and Innovation Policy*, 2 (1), 1–34.

Miles, Ian, Keenan, Michael and Kaivo-oja, Jari (2002): *Handbook of Knowledge Society Foresight*. Prepared by PREST and FFCR for the European Foundation for the improvement of living and working conditions.

Mintzberg, Henry, Ahlstrand, Bruce and Lampel, Joseph (1998): *Strategy Safari. A Guided Tour Through the Wilds of Strategic Management*. New York, The Free Press.

Mintzberg, Henry (1994): The fall and rise of strategic planning. *Harvard Business Review*, 72 (1), 107–14.

Mitleton-Kelly, Eve (2003): *Complex Systems and Evolutionary Perspectives on Organisations: The Application of Complexity Theory to Organisations* . Oxford, Pergamon.

Molitor, Graham T.T. (2003): The power to change the world: The Art of forecasting. *Public Policy Forecasting*, Potomac, MD.

Naisbitt, John and Aburdene, Patricia (1991): *Megatrends 2000: Ten New Directions for the 1990s*. New York, Morrow.

Nicolis, Grégoire and Prigogine, Ilya (1989): *Exploring Complexity: An Introduction*. New York, Freeman and Company.

National Intelligence Council (2008): *Global Trends 2025: A Transformed World*. National Intelligence Council's 2025 Project. Available at: http://www.dni.gov/nic/PDF_2025/2025_Global_Trends_Final_Report.pdf

National Intelligence Council (2004): *Mapping the Global Futures*. The National Intelligence Council's 2020 Project. Available at: http://www.foia.cia.gov/2020/2020.pdf

Niiniluoto, Ilkka (2002): *Critical Scientific Realism*. Oxford, Oxford University Press.

Omnes, Roland (1999): *Quantum Philosophy: Understanding and Interpreting Contemporary Science*. Princeton, NJ, Princeton University Press.

Paavola, Sami (2004a): Abduction as a logic and methodology of discovery: The importance of strategies. *Foundation of Science*, 9, 267–83.

Paavola, Sami (2004b): Abduction through grammar, critic, and methodeutic. *Transactions of the Charles S. Peirce Society*, 40 (2), 245–70.

Paavola, Sami, Hakkarainen, Kai and Sintonen, Matti (2006): Abduction with dialogical and trialogical means. *Logic Journal of IGPL*, 14 (2), 137.

Paillard, Sandrine (2006): Futures studies and public decision in Sweden. *Futures*, 38 (1), 67–73.

Parsaye, Kamran (1999): From data management to pattern management. *DM Review Magazine*, January issue, 1–8.

Paya, Ali and Shoraka Baradaran, Hamid-Reza (2010): Futures studies in Iran: Learning through trial and error. *Futures*, 42, 484–95.

Pearson, Ian and Lyons, Michael (2003): *Business 2010: Mapping the New Commercial Landscape*. Rollinsford, NH, Spiro Press.

Peirce, Charles S. (ed. Kenneth Ketner) (1992): *Reasoning and the Logic of Things: The Cambridge Conferences Lectures of 1898*. Cambridge, Harvard University Press.

Peirce, Charles S. (1905): 'What pragmatism is', *The Monist*, XV (2), 161–81, Chicago, IL, The Open Court Publishing Co., April 1905, for the Hegeler Institute. Reprinted in *Collected Papers*, vol. 5, paragraphs 411–37 and *Charles S. Peirce: Selected Writings*, 180–202. *Arisbe*.

Peirce, Charles S. (1903): Pragmatism – the logic of abduction. *Collected Papers*, 5, 195–205, especially 196.

Piercy, Nigel and Giles, William (1989): Making SWOT analysis work. *Marketing Intelligence & Planning*, 7 (5/6), 5–7.

Popper, Karl R. (1979): *Objective of Knowledge: An Evolutionary Approach*. Oxford, Oxford University Press.

Porter, Michael (1980): *Competitive Strategy*. New York, Free Press.

Potter, Jonathan (1996): *Representing Reality: Discourse, Rhetoric and Social Construction*. London, Sage.

Prahalad C.K and Hamel, Gary (1990): The core competence of the corporation. *Harvard Business Review*, May–June, 79–91.

Prigogine, Ilya (1967): *Dissapative Process, Quantum States and Feld Theory*. XIVe Conseil de Physique Solvay. October 1967. Bruxelles.

Prigogine, Ilya and Stengers, Isabelle (1984): *Order Out of Chaos: Man's New Dialogue with Nature*. New York, Bantam Books.

Prime Minister's Office (2010): *Finland 2020 – From Thought to Action: Final Report by the Growth Initiative Working Group*. Finnish Prime Minister's Office Publications 13/2010, 38.

Prime Minister's Office (2010): *Together and Independently – The World and Finland in the 2010s: Description of the Finnish Policy-making Environment for the Ministries' Future Reviews*. Finnish Prime Minister's Office Publications 3/2010, 150.

Prime Minister's Office (2009): *Government Foresight Report on Long-term Climate and Energy Policy: Towards a Low-carbon Finland*. Finnish Prime Minister's Office Publications 30/2009, 188.

Prime Minister's Office (2007): *Government Statement to Parliament on the Programme of Prime Minister Matti Vanhanen's Second Cabinet Appointed on 19 April 2007*.

Quiggin, Thomas (2007): *Seeing the Invisible: National Security Intelligence in an Uncertain Age*. Singapore, World Scientific Publishing.

Ramos, José M. (2003): From critique to cultural recovery: Critical futures studies and causal layered analysis. *Monograph Series*, No. 2, Australian Foresight Institute, Swinburne University.

Ratcliffe, John S. (2006): Challenges for corporate foresight: Towards strategic prospective through scenario thinking. *Foresight*, 8 (1), 39–54.

Raunio, Kyosti (1999): *Positivismi ja ihmistiede: Sosiaalitutkimuksen perustat ja kaytannot [Positivism and human sciences]*. Tampere, Gaudeamus.

Reinhardt, W.A. (1984): An early warning system for strategic planning. *Long Range Planning*, 17 (5), 25–34.

Russell, Richard L. (2007): *Sharpening Strategic Intelligence: Why the CIA Gets it Wrong and What Needs to be Done to Get it Right*. Cambridge, Cambridge University Press.

Schlossstein, Dominik and Park, Byeongwon (2006): Comparing recent technology foresight studies in Korea and China: Towards foresight-minded governments? *Foresight*, 8 (6), 48–70.

Schultz, Wendy L. (2008): The cultural contradictions of managing change: Using horizon scanning in an evidence-based policy context. *Foresight*, 8 (4), 3–12.

Schwarz, Jan O. (2006): *The Future of Futures Studies: A Delphi Study with a German Perspective*. Aachen, Shaker Verlag.

Schwarz, Peter (2003): *Inevitable Surprises: Thinking Ahead in a Time of Turbulence*. New York, Gotham.

Schwarz, Peter (1996): *The Art of the Long View: Planning for the Future in an Uncertain World*. New York, Currency Doubleday.

Silverman, David (2000): *Doing Qualitative Research: A Practical Handbook*. London, Sage.

Simmonds, W.W. Clive (1993): Monograph. *Insight Analysis*, 2–3.

Singapore National Security Coordination Centre (2007): Technical Paper on RAHS. RAHS Experimentation Centre, Singapore. Available at: http://www.rahs.org.sg/rahs%20publication/ICCRTSP/Technical_Paper_on_RAHS_(3_Jan_07).pdf

Singapore National Security Coordination Secretariat (2006): *1826 Days: A Diary of Resolve. Securing Singapore Since 9/11*. Singapore, SNP International Publishing.

Singapore National Security Coordination Centre (2004): *The Fight Against Terror: Singapore's National Security Strategy*, Singapore, Atlas Associates PTE Ltd. Available at: http://www.mindef.gov.sg/imindef/resources/e-books/ebklist.-imindefPars-0004-DownloadFile.tmp/FightAgainstTerror.pdf

Singapore National Security Coordination Secretariat (2007–2009): *International Risk Assessment and Horizon Scanning Symposium* (Symposium Report), Singapore, SNP International Publishing. Available at: http://rahs.org.sg/t2_irahss07_sr.html

Slaughter, Richard A. and Riedy, Chris (2009): Understanding and resolving the global problematique: Assessing the balance between progressive and socially conservative foresight. *Foresight*, 11 (5), 21–39.

Slaughter, Richard A. (2008): Is America the land of the future? A response. *Foresight*, 10 (5), 60–64.

Slaughter, Richard A. (2004): *Futures Beyond Dystopia: Creating Social Foresight*. London, Routledge.

Slaughter, Richard A. (1999): A new framework for environmental scanning. *Foresight*, 1 (5), 441–51.

Slaughter, Richard A. (1995): *The Foresight Principle: Cultural Recovery in the 21st Century*. Westport, Praeger.

Slaughter, Richard A. (1982): *Critical Futures Studies and Curriculum Renewal*. PhD dissertation, University of Lancaster, UK.

S. Rajaratnam School of International Studies, 2nd Asia-Pacific Programme for Senior National Security Officers (Conference Report), Singapore (2008–2010). Available at: http://www.rsis.edu.sg/publications/conference_reports/APPSNO_08.pdf [accessed January 31, 2009].

Strogatz, Steven H. (1994): *Nonlinear Dynamics and Chaos: With Application to Physics, Biology, Chemisty and Engineering*. Cambridge, Westview Press.

Ståhle, Pirjo and Kuosa, Tuomo (2009): *Systeemien itseuudistuminen: Menestymisen perusta ja päämäärä* [in Finnish, *Self-renewal of Systems: Basis of Success and Objective*]. *Aikuiskasvatus 2*.

Sun, Tzu (2004): *The Art of War* (written originally 6th Century BC) (ed.) Dallas Galvin. New York, Barnes & Noble Classics.

Tapio, Petri, Paloniemi, Riikka, Varjo, Vilja and Vinnari, Markus (2011): The unholy marriage? Integrating qualitative and quantitative information in Delphi process. *Technological Forecasting and Social Change*, doi:10.1016/j.techfore.2011.03.016.

Tapio, Petri (2003): Disaggregative policy Delphi – Using cluster analysis as a tool for systematic scenario formation. *Technological Forecasting and Social Change*, 70 (1), 83–101.

Teknologian arviointeja 17 (2004): Teknologian arviointitoiminta eduskunnassa [The practice of technology assessment in the Finnish Parliament]. Tulevaisuusvaliokunta. Osmo Kuusi. Eduskunnan kanslian julkaisu 4/2004.

Thornton, Stephen (2009): Karl Popper. In: *The Stanford Encyclopedia of Philosophy* (ed.) Edward N. Zalta. Stanford, CA.

Toffler, Alvin (1991): *The Big Turn* [Finnish edition, tr. Heikki Eskelinen]. Helsinki, Otava.

Toffler, Alvin (1981): *The Third Wave*. London, Collins.

United Kingdom Ministry of Defence (2007): *The DC Global Strategic Trends Programme 2007–2036*. 3rd edition. London. Available at: http://www.dcdc-strategictrends.org.uk/viewdoc.aspx?doc=1 [accessed January 31, 2009].

United Kingdom HM Treasury (2004): *Science and Innovation Investment Framework 2004–2014*. London. Available at: http://www.hm-treasury.gov.uk/spending_sr04_science.htm [accessed January 31, 2009].

United Kingdom (2005): *Guidelines on Scientific Analysis in Policy Making*. London. http://www.berr.gov.uk/files/file9767.pdf [accessed January 31, 2009].

United Kingdom Cabinet Office (2002): *Risk: Improving Government's Capability to Handle Risk and Uncertainty*. Strategy Unit Report, London, November 2002. Available at: http://www.cabinetoffice.gov.uk/strategy/work_areas/risk.aspx [accessed January 31, 2009].

Valtioneuvoston ennakointiverkoston raportti (2005): Valtioneuvoston ennakointiverkosto ja ennakointi ministerioissa [The Finnish Government's foresight network and foresight in ministries]. Valtioneuvoston ennakointiverkoston raportti 1/2005.

Vézina, Jeff (2009): *Necessary Chances: Syncronicity in the Encounters that Transform us*. Via Tozzi, Pari Publishing.

Vise, David A. (2002): *The Bureau and the Mole: The Unmasking of Robert Philip Hansse, the Most Dangerous Double Agent in FBI History*. New York, Grove Press.

Vliet, Mathijs van, Kok, Kasper and Veldkamp, Tom (2010): Linking stakeholders and modellers in scenario studies: The use of Fuzzy Cognitive Maps as a communication and learning tool. *Futures*, 42, 1–14.

Voros, Joseph (2003): A generic foresight process framework. *Foresight*, 5 (3), 10–21.

Voros, Joseph (2001): Re-Framing environmental scanning: An integral approach. *Foresight*, 3 (6), 533–51.

Waldrop, M. Mitchell (1992): *Complexity: The Emerging Science at the Edge of Order and Chaos*. New York, Simon & Schuster.

Watson, Richard (2010): *Future Files: A Brief History of the Next 50 Years*. London, Nicholas Brealey Publishing.

Webster's New International Dictionary of the English Language (1950): Second Edition, Unabridged (eds) W.A. Neilson, T.A. Knott and P.W. Carhart. Springfield, MA, G. and C. Merriam Company.

Webster's New Twentieth Century Dictionary of the English Language (1971): Second Edition, Unabridged. Cleveland and New York, The World Publishing Company, 1134.

Weick, E. Karl (2001): *Making Sense of the Organization*. Oxford, Blackwell Publishers Inc.

Wilber, Ken (2000): *Integral Psychology: Consciousness, Spirit, Psychology, Therapy*. Boston, MA, Shambala.

Wilber, Ken (1997): An integral theory of consciousness. *Journal of Consciousness Studies*, 4 (1), 71–92.

Wilenius, Markku (2005): Yhteiskunnallisen ennakoinnin rooli tulevaisuuden haasteiden tunnistamisessa [The role of public foresight in the detection of futures challenges]. Turku School of Economics. TUTU-julkaisuja 1/2005.

Willmott, Hugh (2003): Organization theory as a critical science? Forms of analysis and 'new organizational forms'. In: *The Oxford Handbook of Organization Theory* (eds) Haridimos Tsoukas and Chritian Knudsen. New York, Oxford University Press, 88–112.

Index

Printed by Printforce, the Netherlands

Printing: Lightning Source UK Ltd. Milton Keynes UK
UKHW... Kreuzbergstraße 24, 82515 Wolfratshausen Germany